Thought Leadership in Education

A Comprehensive Exploration of Transformative Educational Ideas

Luis R Valentino, Ed.D.

For information, address Valgar LLC, Indio, California 92201.

Although the author and publisher have made every effort to ensure that the information in this book was correct at press time, the author and publisher do not assume and hereby disclaim any liability to any party for any loss, damage, or disruption caused by errors or omissions, whether such errors or omissions result from negligence, accident, or any other cause.

This publication is designed to provide accurate and authoritative information with regard to the subject matter covered. It is sold with the understanding that the publisher does not render professional services. The fact that an organization or website is referred to in this work as a citation and/or a potential source of further information does not mean that the author or the publisher endorses the information the organization or website may provide or recommendations it may make. Please remember that Internet websites listed in this work may have changed or disappeared between its creation and its publication.

Valentino, Ed.D., Luis R.
Thought Leadership: A Comprehensive Exploration of Transformative Educational Ideas

ISBN-13: 978-0-9905660-6-9

1.   Education 2. Leadership 3. Philosophy

Table of Contents

Chapter 6: Content Creation and Thought Leadership in Education

Chapter 7: Building Networks and Communities of Practice 146

Chapter 10: Future Directions in Educational Thought Leadership 224

Introduction

Today, in education, ideas move fast, but not all of them stick, and even fewer truly change how we teach, learn, or think about learning itself. That's where educational thought leadership comes in. You don't need to have the loudest voice or the biggest following. What you need is the kind of thinking that reshapes how we understand education at its core—how we approach learning, design systems, and define success. Educational thought leaders challenge the status quo, introduce bold new perspectives, and give others the language and tools they need to imagine something better.

In this book, we'll look at how transformative ideas in education come to life—where they start, how they grow, and why some take root across classrooms, institutions, and even policy, while others fade despite their promise. Along the way, we'll explore real-world examples, both historical and current, to better understand what sets influential educational thinking apart.

But first, we must ask ourselves, "Why focus on this now?"

Because education, more than most sectors, runs on ideas. We're not building gadgets or measuring output—we're shaping how people learn, grow, and engage with the world.

When thought leadership is done well, its impact ripples far beyond the classroom. It influences how societies understand learning and human development and what kind of future we hope to build (*Thought Leadership in Education Strategies*, 2025). This matters more now than ever before, as the world of education is undergoing major shifts, driven by tech, policy changes, global challenges, and changing expectations about what education should do. Through this disruption, we need leaders who don't just react but rethink. Thought leadership can offer clarity, vision, and direction while keeping us grounded in education's deeper human purpose.

The pages ahead approach thought leadership using different perspectives. You'll find discussions about where thought leadership comes from, how it works in practice, and how it can drive real change in systems, institutions, and classrooms. Furthermore, we'll explore the conditions that help good ideas spread, the barriers they face, and the practical strategies that move ideas from theory to implementation.

Defining Educational Thought Leadership

More than a buzzword, education thought leadership is a powerful, idea-driven form of influence that reshapes the way people understand and practice education across a wide range of settings. While the term has been stretched thin in some corporate circles, in education, it points to something very real and worth studying: The development and spread of ideas that spark conversations, challenge assumptions, and lead to meaningful changes beyond any one classroom or institution (*Thought Leadership in Education Strategies*, 2025).

So, what sets thought leadership apart from other forms of influence in education?

- **Ideas Over Titles:** Thought leaders influence through the strength of their thinking, not by relying on formal roles or authority. Their ideas create change even in places where they hold no official power.

- **Original Thinking:** They move the field forward by generating new frameworks, making unexpected connections, or applying existing ideas to fresh challenges. Their contributions offer real intellectual value, not just repackaged concepts.

- **Broad Resonance:** Unlike local innovations, thought leadership travels. The most impactful ideas adapt across disciplines, cultures, and systems, sparking change on a wider scale.

- **Theory in Action:** Thought leadership bridges the gap between big-picture thinking and real-world application. It offers educators insights into teaching, leading, and learning more effectively.

- **Purposeful:** Genuine thought leadership is rooted in education's core mission: supporting growth, responsibility, and ethical reflection. Rather than simply follow trends, it serves learners and communities in meaningful ways.

These five elements—idea-based influence, originality, broad impact, practical relevance, and ethical purpose—help us recognize true educational thought leadership when we see it. They move us beyond vague labels toward a more precise understanding of how transformative educational thinking takes shape (*How to Create a Thought Leadership Strategy*, 2023).

We'll be looking at some people who have driven powerful ideas forward; however, our goal isn't to idolize them. We'll, instead, be digging into the ideas themselves: where they come from, how they spread, and what makes them stick. As such, we'll look beyond personality or branding to understand how real, lasting educational change happens.

The Significance of Educational Thought Leadership

Educational thought leadership matters, not just as an academic curiosity but also as a force that actively shapes the way millions of people experience education. The ideas that define how we think about learning, knowledge, and human development influence what happens in classrooms and shape the policies we write, the practices we adopt, and the values we pass on through education.

- **Makes sense of complexity:** In a world that's constantly changing, educators need more than helpful tips—they need actionable frameworks. Thought leadership helps them understand what's happening and respond with insight rather than reacting with quick fixes.

- **Shapes policy thinking:** Thought leaders influence how policymakers define problems and imagine solutions. Their ideas help set the agenda by shaping what's considered possible, not just by promoting specific reforms.

- **Connects research to practice:** Research alone isn't enough—someone has to make it usable. Thought leaders interpret findings, draw connections, and translate data into meaningful, actionable ideas without oversimplifications.

- **Encourages rethinking:** When old methods stop working, thought leaders help educators reflect, question, and reimagine. They offer grounded alternatives instead of trendy replacements or knee-jerk reactions.

- **Defends education's deeper purpose:** In addition to focusing on economic outcomes, thought leadership keeps education focused on growth, humanity, and democracy. It protects education's ethical core and reminds us of what it's really for.

All of the above functions prove why educational thought leadership is not just relevant but essential. Understanding how powerful educational ideas emerge, spread, and take hold isn't a theoretical exercise but a practical concern for anyone who cares about the future of education in a rapidly changing world.

We will explore educational thought leadership comprehensively to help us understand how transformative ideas in education are created, spread, and put into practice across different settings. Rather than focusing only on individual leaders, we will focus on the ideas themselves—their development, their influence, and the ways in which they shape educational experiences, policies, and systems. Each chapter in this book will elaborate on something new:

1. How big educational ideas are rooted in philosophical traditions and shaped by historical context.

2. What makes some ideas catch on and gain wide influence while others fade, even if they're promising?

3. The personal, intellectual, and professional journeys that push individuals to generate transformative ideas.

4. How ideas move through networks, communication, and institutions and across cultures and systems.

5. What it takes for new ideas to work within real-world educational systems without losing their core purpose.

6. How theory becomes practice, and how abstract concepts turn into changes that impact classrooms and communities.

7. The role of collaboration, professional networks, and community in expanding and sustaining new thinking.

8. How thought leadership shapes education policy by influencing the way problems and solutions are defined.

9. Why ethical reflection matters, and how values guide responsible educational leadership.

10. What the future holds—how educational thought leadership can respond to the major changes shaping the world today.

By the end of this book, you will have a holistic view of what educational thought leadership really is—how ideas take shape, how they spread, how they are applied, and how they survive institutional and ethical challenges. You'll find deep analyses of the past and present examples and practical insights into how transformative thinking can be nurtured in real time.

Regardless of your role in education—whether you're a teacher, administrator, policymaker, or researcher, you can engage more thoughtfully with the ideas shaping your field. By understanding how educational thought leadership works, you can contribute more effectively to the conversations and changes that matter most.

The journey that follows honors education's rich intellectual legacy while staying grounded in the urgent challenges of the present. If we want to lead, influence, or simply teach with greater intention, understanding how transformative ideas come to life—and how they grow—is a powerful place to start.

Chapter 1:
The Evolution of Thought Leadership
in Educational Contexts

Even before we had a name for it, educational thought leadership was already in motion. Across history, certain individuals have stood out—not because of their job titles, but because their ideas reshaped the way we thought about teaching, learning, and the purpose of education. They weren't just managing systems; they were changing the conversation.

This chapter traces how thought leadership in education has shifted over time, from top-down authority to a more idea-driven form of influence. It explores the key figures and moments that pushed the field forward, showing how visionary thinking has always been part of education's DNA, even if we're only now beginning to fully name and study it.

The roots of educational leadership go back centuries. Think Socrates—he taught through questions, not lectures; he didn't hold a title yet changed the way people thought. That's leadership (Philosophy Institute, 2023). Still, for much of history, education leadership was about position. Power came from roles: headmasters, superintendents, and university presidents. The influence was tied to a hierarchy, not necessarily to ideas.

In medieval universities, leadership meant scholarly authority. Professors at Bologna, Paris, and Oxford led by mastering the canon, interpreting established texts while not challenging them. The goal was to preserve and pass down knowledge. There was innovation, but only within narrow boundaries (*Nation | Student Guilds, Charters & Scholars*, n.d.).

Things began to shift in the 19th century. As public education systems expanded, new types of leaders emerged—people like Horace Mann in the US and Sir James Kay-Shuttleworth in England. Instead of simply managing schools, they were pushing for a bigger social vision. Mann's push for public education as a tool for equality was a powerful idea. When he called education "the great equalizer," he wasn't issuing an order but casting a vision that stuck (Encyclopaedia Britannica, 2023).

By the early 20th century, thought leadership took another step thanks to John Dewey. Dewey didn't need a big title to make a big impact. His ideas—like learning through doing and teaching for democracy—reshaped classrooms across the world. Yes, he taught at major universities, but his true influence came from the frameworks he offered, not the roles he held (*Great Pedagogical Thinkers: John Dewey*, 2019).

This was a key turning point: leadership moving from titles to ideas. What mattered wasn't where you sat in the system but whether your thinking could change it. This chapter explores that shift and sets the stage for what we now call educational thought leadership.

The Emergence of Thought Leadership as Distinct From Traditional Leadership

The term "thought leader" wasn't used in the education sector until relatively recently. It first gained traction in the business world in the 1990s (Kurtzman, 1994). However, the idea behind it—leading through influence and vision rather than just formal authority—has long been a part of the process of change in education.

Traditional leadership in schools tends to follow the organizational chart. Principals and superintendents have clear roles and responsibilities. Their impact often comes through policies, decisions, and institutional mandates. They may inspire and innovate, but their influence is tied to their position.

Thought leadership works differently. It focuses on shaping how people think about teaching, learning, and education systems and education as a whole. Thought leaders might hold formal roles, but their biggest influence usually lies beyond job descriptions. Their ideas spread because they were relevant, not because someone *had* to listen.

This distinction became clearer throughout the 20th century. As education research expanded and specialized, people began shaping the field through theory, critique, and vision. Benjamin Bloom, for example, changed how educators everywhere designed curriculum, not by exerting administrative power but by creating a framework that made sense and proved useful (Krathwohl, 2002).

In the 1960s and '70s, critical thinkers like Paulo Freire were challenging the very foundation of education. Freire's (1970) concept of "education as a practice of freedom" reshaped classrooms around the world. He didn't lead from a position of control but through bold, clear thinking that invited others to see education differently.

By the late 20th century, thought leadership had taken root in education, even if the term wasn't always used. As hierarchies flattened and ideas spread more easily, influence increasingly flowed through networks, publications, and movements. Education—always a space for ideas—was especially well suited for this shift.

Importantly, thought leadership didn't replace traditional leadership but expanded the idea of leadership. The most effective educational changemakers often blend both—using formal authority to support innovation and strong ideas to inspire others. Leadership through vision isn't just a nice bonus; in today's educational world, it's an essential factor.

Key Figures Who Shaped Educational Thought Leadership

The best way to understand how thought leadership has evolved is to look at the people who embodied it, those whose ideas changed how others taught, led, and learned.

Maria Montessori (2023) is one of the earliest and clearest thought leaders. She started as a physician in 19th-century Italy and went on to develop an educational approach centered on children's natural development. More than her methods, it was her philosophy behind them that spread. Her ideas transcended borders and generations because they offered a coherent, compelling alternative to traditional instruction.

In the US, William Edward Burghardt Du Bois brought a different kind of vision. He saw education not just as a tool for knowledge but as a path to justice. While others advocated for vocational training, Du Bois argued for a broad, liberal education that would prepare Black Americans for full citizenship. His leadership came through books, speeches, and a deep commitment to equity rather than any single institution he ran (TuSmith, 2010).

Other figures led from the intersection of research and classroom practice. Jean Piaget, a psychologist, wasn't primarily an educator, but his work on how children learn transformed educational theory. His stage model of cognitive development gave teachers a map for designing age-appropriate learning. The strength of his ideas—not his position—made the impact (Cherry, 2023).

Howard Gardner continued in this tradition. His theory of multiple intelligences challenged narrow definitions of ability. It offered teachers a new lens to see their students and new ways to engage them. Though based in academia, Gardner's influence came from his ability to translate complex theories into tools that could change classroom practices (Northern Illinois University, n.d.).

More recently, Linda Darling-Hammond has shown how thought leadership can move across research, policy, and implementation. Her work on teacher training and education equity has shaped national conversations. Through her writing, advocacy, and leadership at organizations like the Learning Policy Institute, she's shown how research can drive change at scale—when it's presented clearly and tied to real-world solutions (Learning Policy Institute, n.d.).

These figures didn't all come from the same background, follow the same path, or share the same style. But what they had in common was that they introduced ideas that stuck. They helped others see education differently and gave them the tools to act on their visions. That's what makes them thought leaders.

The Transition From Management to Visionary Leadership in Education

The evolution from management-driven to visionary leadership marks a turning point in how educational improvement is understood and pursued. While this shift didn't happen overnight, it gained momentum in the late 20th century, as schools and systems faced challenges that couldn't be solved by efficiency alone.

Early models of educational leadership, especially in the US, were heavily influenced by industrial management. Think of Frederick Taylor's "scientific management" applied to schools. Ellwood Cubberley's (1916) book, *Public School Administration*, laid out a vision of school systems as machines—standardized, hierarchical, and focused on output. In this model, educational leaders were expected to ensure compliance, track performance, and allocate resources efficiently. This approach helped organize rapidly growing school systems but offered little room for deeper thinking about teaching, learning, or purpose.

By the mid-20th century, this framework displayed cracks in its foundation. Scholars like Arthur Halpin (1955) and Don Griffiths began to push for a clearer distinction between administration and leadership. They argued that running a school well requires more than process management—it requires vision, direction, and the ability to lead change.

The 1980s and '90s brought more urgency. Reports like *A Nation at Risk* raised alarms about the state of education and demanded serious reform. Incremental improvements weren't enough; schools needed transformation. In this context, leaders focused solely on management found themselves unprepared for the depth and complexity of the changes being called for (National Commission on Excellence in Education, 1983).

Enter transformational leadership. First introduced by political theorist James MacGregor Burns (1978) and later adapted to education by Kenneth Leithwood (1992) and others, this model shifted focus from control to inspiration. Transformational leaders didn't just implement; they envisioned, motivated, and built capacity. They guided their schools and systems through logistics, meaning, and direction.

This shift overlapped with the rise of educational thought leadership. Both reflected a broader realization: meaningful change in education requires more than technical solutions, calling for people who can question assumptions, challenge norms, and imagine new possibilities. It also calls for leaders who influence through insight rather than authority.

While transformational leadership was introduced to education by thinkers like Burns and later Leithwood, the ground for this shift had been laid decades earlier. The educational philosophies of Maria Montessori (1967), Jean Piaget (1952), and Lev Vygotsky (1978)—emphasizing child-centered learning, cognitive development, and socially mediated knowledge—did not directly inform transformational leadership theory. However, their work created a pedagogical foundation that naturally aligned with the principles of inspiration, personal growth, and meaning-making later emphasized by leadership scholars.

That said, this shift hasn't been universal. In many systems, especially those driven by high-stakes accountability, the management mindset still dominates. Compliance, metrics, and control remain the norm. However, the most impactful educational leaders today blend both: They manage well and lead with vision, ensuring systems run smoothly while pushing them toward something better.

We needn't reject administrative skills but expand what leadership looks like. Vision without execution falters, and execution without vision leads nowhere. The best educational thought leaders understand this balance. As Michael Fullan (2006) puts it, real change requires both "pressure and support." It's not either/or. It's both/and.

Contemporary Understanding of Thought Leadership in Educational Settings

Today's understanding of thought leadership in education reflects both a long historical evolution and the pressing realities of a rapidly changing world marked by intense political complexity. Modern educational thought leaders navigate a landscape shaped by technological disruption, social complexity, and ongoing debates about what education should be and who it should serve. Their influence spans multiple levels—from classrooms to policy arenas—and speaks to a wide range of stakeholders.

Bridging Research, Practice, and Policy

Contemporary thought leaders move fluidly between research, classroom practice, and policy-making. While older models often treated these domains as distinct, today's leaders understand that meaningful change depends on building coherence across them.

Take Dylan Wiliam, for example. His work on formative assessment is used in academic journals and has been translated into tools and strategies for teachers. He's engaged in broader discussions about how systems can support effective assessment practices. Wiliam's (2014) leadership lies in his ability to connect the dots between what we know, what we do, and how we scale it.

Evidence-Informed, Not Evidence-Blinded

The rise of evidence-based practice has shaped educational decision-making, pushing educators to ground their strategies in research. However, contemporary thought leaders also recognize that evidence isn't a silver bullet but something that's shaped by context, values, and interpretation.

Thomas Guskey's (2014) work on professional development embodies this balance. While his recommendations are research-informed, he doesn't treat them as one-size-fits-all, rather encouraging educators to adapt evidence to local needs and understand that numbers alone can't answer every question. His leadership comes from helping schools use evidence wisely, not mechanically.

A Systems Lens Over Isolated Innovation

Earlier waves of thought leadership often championed specific innovations: a new curriculum, a novel teaching method, or a unique assessment tool. Today, there's a growing awareness that innovation without systems thinking doesn't stick.

Michael Fullan's (2006) work highlights this shift. Instead of promoting standalone solutions, he focuses on the conditions that allow good ideas to take root systemwide, from classrooms and school districts to national policies. His leadership is about changing how we think about change itself, going beyond piecemeal efforts to sustainable transformation.

Centering Equity and Inclusion

Where equity was once treated as an add-on, today's thought leaders see it as central to educational effectiveness. Who benefits from a policy or practice is no longer a secondary question but the primary one.

Gloria Ladson-Billings (1992) illustrates this approach through her work on culturally relevant pedagogy. She showed that centering students' cultural identities isn't just about fairness but about improving outcomes. Her leadership reframes equity not as a challenge to overcome but as a strategy to embrace for better teaching and learning.

Focused on Implementation, Not Just Ideas

A brilliant idea without an implementation plan often dies in the field. Contemporary thought leaders know that real change is as much about how ideas are adopted and sustained as it is about what those ideas are.

Ann Lieberman's work on teacher leadership and professional learning communities underscores this. She argued for collaboration and studied what makes it work in real schools, under real constraints. Her leadership is grounded in the practicalities of lasting change (Lieberman & Miller, 2004).

A New Profile of Educational Thought Leadership

These five factors—transcendence, context-aware use of evidence, systems thinking, equity-centeredness, and attention to implementation—define the profile of a modern educational thought leader.

This approach to thought leadership isn't confined to academia or top-down policy circles. It's a way of thinking, acting, and influencing that reflects the complexity of education today. Educational thought leadership now asks not only "What works?" but also "For whom? Under what conditions? And how do we make it last?" It's this layered, reflective, and action-oriented approach that sets today's thought leaders apart.

The Unique Challenges and Opportunities of Thought Leadership in Education

Education is grounded in moral purpose, shaped by political realities, carried out through human relationships, and dispersed across highly variable local contexts. These traits create both complex challenges and meaningful opportunities for those seeking to lead through ideas rather than authority.

Navigating Deep Value Conflicts

At its core, education isn't just about methods; it's also about values. What should we teach? How should we define success? What kind of citizens are we hoping to shape? What is the purpose of schooling, and for whose benefit? These aren't neutral questions, and they don't have easy answers.

Nel Noddings' (2005) work on care ethics speaks directly to this tension. She didn't frame care as another item on a list of best practices. She rooted it in the moral foundation of education itself. Her influence comes not from avoiding conflict but from engaging it, showing that leading in education often means asking uncomfortable but necessary questions.

Embracing Contextual Complexity

Educational environments vary widely across countries, districts, and even classrooms, influenced by student needs, available resources, community norms, and institutional histories. Ann Brown's (1992) design experiments highlighted the need for flexible, context-sensitive learning models—like communities of learners—that respond to this diversity.

Confronting Political Realities

Education is inherently political. Shifts in curriculum, funding, and policy are shaped by competing interests. Jeannie Oakes (1985) exemplified this in her research on tracking, exposing how educational structures can reinforce inequality and advocating for systemic reforms aligned with social justice.

Bridging Research Practices and Policies

Effective thought leadership in education requires communication across silos. Linda Darling-Hammond (2000) demonstrated this bridge-building in her work on teacher quality, translating rigorous scholarship into actionable recommendations for policymakers and practitioners alike.

Opportunities Unique to Education

While the challenges are real, education offers a level of moral and social influence that few other fields can match. These very complexities allow educational thought leaders to catalyze change at both intimate and global scales.

Moral Purpose as a Driver

Unlike industries that rely on profit as a measure of success, education is mission-driven. Its aim is human development—intellectual, emotional, and social. This shared moral foundation is both a compass and a source of resilience for thought leaders in the field (Noddings, 2005).

Emotional and Intellectual Influence

Educational leadership is personal. Teachers, students, and leaders are shaped by their experiences and identities. Parker Palmer (1998) argues that effective educators must explore the "inner landscape" of their lives—integrating self-knowledge into their work to foster authentic and meaningful learning relationships.

Networked, Not Hierarchical, Leadership

Education lacks a centralized structure, so change spreads laterally through relationships and shared practice rather than through mandates. Etienne Wenger (1998) explains how "communities of practice" foster innovation and learning by connecting people with shared goals across institutions and disciplines.

A Global Reach Through Connection

Digital networks and international policy collaborations have made it easier than ever for educators to influence systems globally. Andreas Schleicher's (n.d.) work with the Organization for Economic Co-operation and Development (OECD) and its Programme for International Student Assessment (PISA) exemplifies how comparative data and global dialogue can help countries learn from one another while refining their own approaches.

Leading in a Complex Field

What sets the most effective educational thought leaders apart is not just their ideas but their way of responding to education's unique terrain. They don't import leadership models from elsewhere. They design for complexity, engage value tensions, adapt to context, and build across boundaries.

In the chapters ahead, we'll explore how that kind of leadership takes shape: How powerful ideas emerge, spread, and ultimately transform what educators believe and do. We'll look at the tools, mindsets, and relationships that sustain influence in a field where authority is not centralized but its impact is profound.

In education, leadership isn't about being in charge but about sparking change that others want to carry forward, and this, more than anything, is the promise and challenge of educational thought leadership today.

Chapter 2:
Defining Educational Thought Leadership Beyond Administration and Management

The term *thought leader* gets tossed around so often that it risks losing its meaning. In education, especially, where influence can stem from many different places, policy, pedagogy, and practice, it's easy to confuse visibility with vision. However, genuine thought leadership in education is something distinct. It's not just another word for administrator, researcher, or popular speaker. It represents a powerful, idea-driven approach to shaping practice and policy that lives outside traditional roles or hierarchies. To understand its role in educational transformation, we have to unpack what it is, how it works, and why it matters.

At its core, educational thought leadership sits at the intersection of three essential elements:

1. Deep expertise

2. Innovative thinking

3. Influential communication.

It's not about popularity for its own sake, it's not about credentials alone, and it's certainly not about formal authority. True thought leadership emerges when someone

1. brings deep understanding to bear on a challenge.

2. offers a meaningful new way of looking at it.

3. communicates that perspective in a way that propels others to action.

This three-part structure—expertise, innovation, and influence—helps distinguish thought leadership from adjacent roles in education. None of these elements is sufficient on its own. Expertise without innovation tends to reinforce the status quo: Innovation without expertise risks shallow thinking or short-lived trends. Either one, without the capacity to communicate and connect, struggles to gain traction or inspire change.

Expertise, in this context, means more than knowing a lot about one thing. It involves both depth and breadth. Thought leaders in education typically have a command of a particular area, be it curriculum design, assessment, leadership, or learning science. However, they also understand how their work connects to larger educational questions. That broader view allows them to speak to real problems and possibilities in practice and theory.

Take Howard Gardner's (1983) work on multiple intelligences. His background in cognitive psychology provided the necessary foundation to propose a radically different model of human ability. But what made his ideas stick was how clearly they resonated with educators' lived experiences. He generated a framework, translated it into a language, and specified its implications such that teachers and school leaders could recognize and use it. That's the difference between academic contribution and thought leadership.

Innovation, too, is more than novelty. Thought leadership doesn't just dress old ideas in a new language. It offers a genuine shift in perspective. Sometimes, this means reframing existing problems in new ways. Other times, it means drawing on ideas from outside education and applying them to classroom or system challenges. In many cases, it involves synthesizing insights from research, practice, and lived experience into something new and actionable.

Carol Dweck's (2006) work on the growth mindset is a prime example. The core idea that intelligence is malleable, not fixed, wasn't entirely new. However, her ability to reframe this insight, ground it in research, and speak to its practical implications for motivation, instruction, and feedback gave it staying power. Her innovation wasn't just conceptual; it was strategic, connecting big ideas with everyday decisions in schools.

Influence is what sets thought leadership apart from private insight. You can have brilliant ideas and deep expertise, but if they don't travel or don't reach others in ways that stick, they don't become leaders. Educational thought leaders understand how to make their thinking visible, accessible, and relevant. They write, speak, present, and build relationships in ways that allow their ideas to spread and take hold.

John Hattie's (2009) work on visible learning illustrates this point clearly. His meta-analyses brought together a vast amount of research into a coherent, digestible framework. However, his influence comes not just from what he studied but also from how he shared it with educators, policymakers, and the broader public. His writing is clear. His presentations are engaging. His tools are practical. That's what allows his research to shape real-world decisions.

This tripartite model—expertise, innovation, and influence—provides a way for recognizing real thought leadership when we see it. It distinguishes thought leaders from accomplished practitioners who don't seek to reshape systems, creative thinkers whose ideas lack grounding, and popular figures whose influence outpaces the strength of their insights.

It also underscores something important: Thought leadership is dynamic. It's not a fixed identity or a one-time contribution but a process—ongoing, iterative, and responsive. Educational thought leaders evolve their thinking as new evidence emerges and as they engage with practitioners and policy realities. They learn from how their ideas are received, misinterpreted, implemented, or adapted. They don't just offer a solution; they stay in the conversation, adjusting and improving as they go.

In short, while educational thought leadership is about being smart, original, and well-spoken, it's also about combining those traits in service of ideas that matter, those that challenge assumptions, offer new possibilities, and move people toward better outcomes. Rather than commanding authority from a title, you earn influence through clarity, relevance, and impact.

Understanding the difference between administration and thought leadership recognizes that the most transformative change in education often comes not from policy mandates or managerial control but from the power of a well-timed, well-communicated idea.

This is the heart of thought leadership, and it's where we will turn next.

Distinguishing Characteristics of Thought Leaders vs. Managers or Administrators

Clarifying the distinctions between thought leaders and managers or administrators not only helps define what thought leadership uniquely offers but also reinforces why schools and systems need those who keep things running and those who imagine how they might run differently.

Primary Focus: Operational Stability vs. Transformational Possibility

Managers and administrators are chiefly concerned with operational effectiveness. Their focus is on making sure existing systems function smoothly, like allocating resources, managing personnel, ensuring compliance, and meeting policy expectations. In short, they keep the ship steady.

Thought leaders, by contrast, are oriented toward change. They're less concerned with keeping the system running as it is and more interested in how it could run better, more equitably, and more imaginatively. They ask the hard questions, challenge outdated assumptions, and offer alternative visions of what education might become.

Their success is measured not by consistency or control but by influence, resonance, and the spread of new thinking.

This isn't to say that managers don't have vision or that thought leaders don't care about execution. The difference lies in emphasis. Managers ensure the present holds together; thought leaders aim to reshape the future.

Relationship to Systems: Working Within vs. Challenging the Framework

Management typically happens within established structures. Administrators work to improve processes, optimize outcomes, and implement changes that align with existing rules or goals. The underlying architecture is rarely questioned.

Thought leaders, conversely, often question the very systems others are trying to refine. They ask whether those systems serve their intended purpose or whether new frameworks are needed.

Their work can be disruptive, but intentionally so. They don't settle for improvement within the lines; they redraw the lines.

Take assessment, for example. A managerial lens focuses on ensuring consistency, reliability, and compliance with policy mandates. A thought leadership lens steps back and asks: "Are we measuring what matters? What if the entire system of evaluation needs to change?"

Mechanism of Influence: Formal Authority vs. Idea-Driven Impact

Managers lead through position and structure. They influence outcomes via official channels—policy enforcement, resource control, and performance evaluation (Kotter, 1996).

Thought leaders operate differently. Their influence doesn't rely on organizational hierarchy. It comes from ideas that resonate, frameworks that clarify, and the ability to spark reflection and inspire action (Sinek, 2009). They build influence through communication, credibility, and relevance, not job titles.

That's why a teacher, researcher, or even a student can exert thought leadership. If their ideas change how others think, lead to shifts in practice, or expand what's possible, they're shaping the field— no formal title required.

Time Horizon: Present Operations vs. Long-Term Vision

Management tends to operate on short- and medium-term cycles. Goals are often tied to the academic calendar, strategic plans, or policy deadlines. The focus is immediate: What needs to get done now? What are the measurable outcomes this year?

Thought leaders play a longer game. They imagine possibilities that may take years—or even generations—to unfold. Their work may not yield quick wins, but it lays the groundwork for deeper change. They plant seeds that others may harvest later.

This difference in timeline can create tension but also synergy. Systems need people who can execute today and those who are already thinking about tomorrow.

Approach to Complexity: Reducing Uncertainty vs. Embracing It

Administrators often work to reduce ambiguity. They clarify expectations, standardize procedures, and seek predictable outcomes. In complex systems like schools, this kind of clarity can be stabilizing.

Thought leadership, however, often lives in the gray areas. It thrives on complexity, ambiguity, and difficult questions without simple answers. Rather than resolving uncertainty, thought leaders help others navigate it. They don't offer formulas but invite exploration.

This approach is especially vital in today's educational landscape, where one-size-fits-all solutions rarely work and rapid change demands adaptive, nuanced thinking.

Educational thought leadership and educational management are not opposites—they're interdependent. One maintains momentum, the other challenges direction. Systems that lean too heavily on management risk stagnation; systems that rely solely on vision can drift into chaos. The most effective leaders understand how to balance both: execute well and think beyond the present and optimize what works while daring to imagine what's next.

The Intersection of Scholarship, Practice, and Innovation

Educational thought leadership doesn't come from just one place. It shows up where three powerful forces overlap:

- Scholarship

- Practice

- Innovation

Each one is valuable on its own, but when they work together, real change starts to happen.

Scholarship: Solid Ground

Strong ideas need strong foundations. The most lasting educational frameworks aren't based on trends or personal opinions but are rooted in research. Thought leaders dig deep. They know the literature, understand the theories, and can back up their ideas with evidence. Their work holds up because it's built on something solid.

However, research can be a double-edged sword.

Too often, academic work is stuck behind paywalls or written in a language that feels like a world away from that used in actual classrooms. This is where thought leaders step in. They cite studies, translate them, and turn rigorous research into usable, relevant insights without watering it down.

Take Ann Lieberman, for example. Her work on teacher leadership didn't just live in academic journals. She brought those ideas to teachers in a way that felt both informed and usable. (Lieberman & Miller, 2001). Serious work made accessible.

Practice: Ground-Level Relevance

Theory matters, but if it doesn't land in the real world, it doesn't go far. Great thought leadership is grounded in practice. It reflects the messiness of schools, the constraints of policy, and the challenge of daily decision-making.

The best educational ideas aren't created in isolation. They come from people who've taught, coached, collaborated, or stayed in close touch with the actual work of education.

These leaders get context. Their thinking focuses on real students, real teachers, and the systems they move through rather than imaginary classrooms.

Ted Sizer (1984) is a strong example here. His work with the Coalition of Essential Schools was shaped by years of deep, firsthand engagement with educators. He didn't theorize from a distance or just lay out a philosophy. He listened, tested, and refined alongside schools.

Innovation: Not Just Change, But Rethinking

What sets thought leaders apart is their willingness to reimagine things rather than just improve what exists.

They don't simply ask, "How can we do this better?"

They ask, "Is this the right thing to do in the first place?"

They connect dots across disciplines. They challenge the rules everyone else works within. They take creative risks, not to be edgy but to move things forward with purpose.

Let's take the work of Sir Ken Robinson, a prime example of someone who didn't just propose small adjustments to the existing educational systems but fundamentally shifted the entire conversation. Robinson's work, particularly around creativity, challenged the traditional structures and assumptions about how education should function. One of his most significant contributions was his critique of how schools typically define intelligence.

In his groundbreaking TED Talk and later in his book, *The Element*, Robinson (2009) argued that our current education systems are overly focused on a narrow conception of intelligence—one that emphasizes standardized testing, rote memorization, and a rigid hierarchy of subjects. According to him, this model neglects the rich diversity of human talents, especially creative abilities, which often go unrecognized in traditional academic settings.

Robinson didn't just advocate for incremental change; he proposed a radical rethinking of what education should prioritize. He suggested that creativity is just as important as literacy and should be treated with the same level of importance in schools. His perspective wasn't about improving existing systems within the framework of how they already operate but about reimagining the very structure of schooling itself.

In this sense, Robinson's influence went beyond fine-tuning a well-oiled machine to questioning whether that machine was even the right tool for the job. His ideas encouraged educators, policymakers, and parents to reconsider long-held beliefs about intelligence and talent, urging them to embrace a more inclusive, flexible approach that celebrates diverse forms of thinking.

By shifting the conversation from "How do we fix what's broken?" to "What if we redefined success in education?" Robinson (2009) instigated a deeper, more transformational dialogue about how we prepare future generations for an ever-changing world. This beautifully encapsulates thought leadership—challenging the status quo not with incremental tweaks but with ideas that alter the very lens through which we view the purpose of education.

Where It All Comes Together

The most powerful educational ideas sit at the intersection of scholarship, practice, and innovation. They're research-backed, grounded in the realities of schools, and creatively bold. That combination is rare, but that's why it matters.

Look at *Understanding by Design* by Wiggins and McTighe (2011). It's grounded in cognitive science. It responds to practical needs in curriculum design. And it introduces a fresh way to think about planning instruction. Their work lasts because it bridges all three areas.

This kind of crossover thinking is the heart of thought leadership. You needn't be the smartest person in the room or the most radical. You need only know what's out there, understand what's happening on the ground, and imagine what could be. As such, you stand between what is and what could be and do something meaningful with that tension.

Core Competencies and Attributes of Educational Thought Leaders

Thought leadership transcends formal titles and hierarchical authority; it centers on the capacity to influence educational discourse and practice. This influence necessitates a unique blend of competencies and personal attributes—tools essential for leading through ideas rather than positions.

Conceptual Thinking: Making Sense of Complexity

Thought leaders excel in identifying patterns and constructing frameworks that render complex educational challenges more comprehensible. For instance, Robert Marzano synthesized extensive research to identify nine high-yield instructional strategies that enhance student achievement across various grade levels and subjects

(Marzano et al., 2001). This work exemplifies conceptual thinking by organizing empirical evidence into accessible and broadly applicable instructional models.

Contextual Understanding: Knowing the Terrain

Effective thought leaders possess a deep understanding of the multifaceted nature of educational environments, recognizing the interplay of values, politics, relationships, and local realities. Michael Fullan's (2006) work on educational change emphasizes the importance of addressing human and systemic factors that influence the success of reform efforts. His insights resonate because they reflect an acute awareness of the complexities inherent in educational systems.

Communication Skill: Making Ideas Stick

The ability to convey complex concepts clearly and persuasively is crucial for thought leaders. Carol Ann Tomlinson's (2004) approach to differentiated instruction demonstrates this skill; she translates intricate ideas into practical strategies that educators can implement to address diverse student needs. Her work underscores the importance of effective communication in making innovative ideas accessible and actionable.

Implementation Thinking: Bridging Vision and Reality

Thought leadership involves envisioning transformative ideas and considering their practical application. Richard Elmore's (2006) contributions to school improvement highlight the necessity of building organizational capacity to support effective instruction, emphasizing the importance of aligning visionary ideas with the realities of educational practice.

Personal Attributes That Support Thought Leadership

Beyond skills, thought leadership depends on ways of being. Qualities that shape how individuals engage with their work, ideas, and audiences.

- **Intellectual Curiosity:** Thought leaders are lifelong learners. They read widely, listen closely, and seek insight from diverse perspectives. Curiosity fuels their ability to connect ideas, ask new questions, and avoid intellectual stagnation.

- **Intellectual Courage:** They're willing to challenge assumptions—even popular ones—when evidence or experience points elsewhere. Courage allows them to convey uncomfortable truths and offer alternatives, even when those ideas go against the grain.

- **Intellectual Humility:** At the same time, they recognize the limits of their knowledge. They're open to feedback, willing to revise their views, and aware that good ideas evolve. This humility makes their work more collaborative and credible.

- **Empathic Understanding:** Great thought leaders don't speak *at* educators—they speak *with* them. They understand what it feels like to teach, to lead a school, and to navigate competing demands. That empathy allows them to craft ideas that feel relevant and respectful, not abstract or imposed.

- **Persistent Optimism:** Finally, they believe that change is possible, even when it's hard. Their optimism isn't naïve; it's grounded in experience. But it gives them the energy to keep pushing, keep refining, and keep engaging—even in the face of resistance or setbacks.

None of these competencies or attributes work in isolation. It's their *combination* that matters. The most impactful thought leaders pair conceptual depth with practical insight. They communicate clearly while understanding complexity. They challenge the status quo but stay rooted in empathy and humility.

That's what makes their ideas stick—and what gives those ideas the power to transform both how we think about education and how we approach it.

Importantly, these aren't fixed traits. They can be cultivated. Whether you're an educator, a policymaker, a researcher, or an advocate, building capacity in these areas can strengthen your potential to lead through ideas and help others do the same.

The Ethical Dimensions of Educational Thought Leadership

Being an educational thought leader doesn't just afford you influence; it also comes with responsibility. When your ideas shape classrooms, school systems, and public policy, the ethical stakes are high. Unlike traditional leadership roles, which often revolve around decision-making and accountability structures, thought leadership operates through persuasion, ideas, and public trust. As such, the ethics involved aren't only about professional conduct but also about purpose, representation, and impact.

Purpose Alignment: Ideas That Serve Education's Core Mission

The most important question any thought leader in education can ask is, "What is this idea really serving?"

It's easy for educational discourse to get hijacked by economic goals, institutional efficiency, or political agendas. Real thought leadership, however, remains grounded in what education is fundamentally about: helping people grow, participate in society, and live meaningful lives.

This means resisting the urge to reduce education to test scores, productivity metrics, or workforce preparation alone. It also means regularly stepping back and asking whose interests are being prioritized and whether those interests align with a vision of human development and equity.

Maxine Greene modeled this alignment beautifully in her work on aesthetic education. She championed the idea that the arts help us imagine new possibilities, which is at the heart of why we educate. Greene's (1995) contributions were technically sound and driven by a deep commitment to meaning, agency, and transformation.

Representation and Inclusion: Who's at the Table?

Educational ideas don't exist in a vacuum. They're shaped by perspective, lived experiences, and cultural context. If thought leadership only reflects dominant voices, it risks reinforcing systems that already marginalize students.

Inclusive thought leaders ask hard questions:

- Who's missing from the conversation?
- Whose experience isn't being considered?

They actively listen to others' voices and work to ensure their ideas support all learners, not just those who already feel seen in traditional systems.

Sonia Nieto's (2004) work on multicultural education is a powerful example. She didn't just bring visibility to diverse learners; no, she created frameworks that helped schools understand and value cultural differences. Her work challenged assumptions and pushed the field toward greater equity.

Evidence Integrity: Say What the Research Says

There's a lot of temptation to cherry-pick research, simplify complex findings, or stretch evidence to fit a catchy narrative. However, responsible thought leaders respect the nuance of the data and are upfront about what's known, what's promising, and what's still in question.

They're also honest about the difference between the following:

- Evidence

- Anecdote

- Correlation

- Causation

This kind of transparency builds trust and helps educators make informed choices, rather than follow trends that sound good but may not hold up under scrutiny.

Robert Slavin (2002) set the gold standard for this. His work on evidence-based education emphasized not only what works but also how we know it works. He helped build tools for evaluating research quality so educators could separate solid strategies from untested claims.

Implementation Responsibility: Ideas That Can Actually Work

Thought leadership can indeed bring about big changes. However, these leaders think beyond the idea itself and look at the implications of the idea. They consider the following:

- What happens when those ideas hit the ground?

- What does implementation look like in under-resourced schools?

35

- How do new strategies affect teachers' workload or students' sense of belonging?

Ethical thought leaders think about these practical realities from the start. They don't float idealized models disconnected from context. They work to ensure that their proposals are feasible and sustainable and don't unintentionally create new problems.

Hargreaves nailed this in his work on sustainable leadership. He paid attention to how reforms impact educators, not only in terms of student outcomes but also in terms of how they affect the everyday human experience of teaching. His frameworks respected the complexity of implementation without giving up on ambitious goals (Hargreaves & Fink, 2006).

Intellectual Honesty: Give Credit, Stay Humble, and Keep Learning

In a space where visibility and originality matter, it can be tempting to overstate the novelty of your ideas or to gloss over your intellectual influences. However, thought leadership built on shaky claims or borrowed concepts without credit doesn't last.

Ethical thought leaders are upfront about where their ideas come from, what inspired them, and what still needs to be figured out. They're okay with saying, "This builds on earlier work," or "I might be wrong." That kind of humility invites dialogue, fosters collaboration, and keeps the field moving forward (Brookfield, 2017).

Lee Shulman's (1987) articulation of pedagogical content knowledge didn't emerge out of nowhere. He acknowledged the scholarship he was building on and positioned his work as part of a larger conversation. That transparency didn't make his work less innovative—it made it more credible.

Putting It All Together: Ethics in Action

Purpose, inclusion, evidence, implementation, and honesty are not checkboxes but ongoing commitments. They show up in how you write, speak, respond to criticism, and engage with the communities affected by your work.

The thought leaders who make a lasting impact aren't the most charismatic or prolific. They're the ones whose ideas align with the deeper values of education. They understand that shaping minds and systems is ethical work, and they treat it that way.

Transformative Educational Thought Leaders

Examining specific cases of transformative educational thought leadership brings the previous conceptual framework to life. These profiles reveal how core characteristics, competencies, and ethical dimensions manifest in real-world contexts, demonstrating shared patterns alongside individual approaches to shaping educational thinking and practice.

John Dewey and Experiential Education

John Dewey is often considered the quintessential educational thought leader. His influence spans over a century, continuing to shape how educators think about learning, teaching, and the purposes of schooling. Dewey's thought leadership exemplified the integration of scholarship, practice, and innovation.

As a philosopher, Dewey explored foundational questions about knowledge and ethics. As a practitioner, his work at the University of Chicago Laboratory School grounded his ideas in classroom experience. As a reformer, he challenged prevailing assumptions, offering new frameworks that reshaped educational theory and practice.

His concept of education as the "reconstruction of experience" captured this synthesis, providing both a rigorous philosophical foundation and practical guidance for organizing learning environments (Dewey, 1916). Dewey didn't just theorize; he translated deep concepts into actionable approaches.

He also exemplified conceptual thinking at scale. Dewey's (1916) vision of democracy as "a mode of associated living" linked education to broader social ideals. This allowed him to argue persuasively that schools should cultivate collaborative inquiry, critical thinking, and shared responsibility, not just academic achievement.

Dewey's commitment to democratic ideals was more than abstract theory. He believed education should nurture the dispositions required for active citizenship, and he evaluated educational practices based on their capacity to foster participation in democratic life.

Equally important was his skill in communicating across audiences. Dewey authored dense philosophical texts like *Democracy and Education* but also wrote more accessible works, such as *The School and Society*, aimed at practitioners and the public. He understood that educational transformation requires the engagement of multiple stakeholders through varied forms of communication.

Taken together, Dewey's legacy illustrates how enduring thought leadership emerges from conceptual depth, ethical clarity, practical relevance, and communicative versatility. His impact endures not because of a singular insight but because of a holistic, integrated approach to reimagining education.

Lisa Delpit and Cultural Responsiveness

Lisa Delpit's thought leadership on cultural responsiveness reshaped how educators understand race, power, and communication in schools. Through her seminal work, *Other People's Children*, Delpit amplified marginalized voices and challenged dominant narratives in teacher education (Delpit, 2006).

Her ideas emerged from paying close attention to who was—and wasn't—being heard in educational discourse. Delpit exposed the hidden rules of power that shaped classroom interactions, particularly between white teachers and students of color. Her concept of "the culture of power" provided educators with a lens to examine the unspoken norms that perpetuate inequality.

What made Delpit's leadership transformative was not just what she said but how she said it. She brought clarity and nuance to complex issues, blending personal narrative, research, and practice in ways that resonated with a broad audience. Educators could see themselves and their students in her work, and they were better able to recognize how culture and power operated in their classrooms.

At the core of Delpit's work was an unwavering commitment to educational equity. She critiqued practices that claimed neutrality but produced unequal outcomes, insisting that good intentions are not enough. Her frameworks challenged educators to question their assumptions, listen deeply, and adjust their practices to truly support all learners.

Importantly, Delpit addressed not just ideals but also the messy realities of implementation. She acknowledged the discomfort and complexity of working across cultural differences and guided others without oversimplifying things. Her leadership bridged the gap between critical insight and practical application.

Delpit's legacy lies in her insistence that cultural responsiveness is not an optional add-on but a fundamental part of effective teaching. Her voice helped shift the conversation from a color-blind model of education to one that centers students' full identities.

Dylan Wiliam and Formative Assessment

Dylan Wiliam's work on formative assessment offers a compelling example of thought leadership grounded in rigorous research, refined through practice, and communicated for impact. His influence stems from how he has helped educators rethink assessment, not as a tool for ranking students but as a strategy for supporting learning.

Wiliam's ideas first gained wide attention through his collaboration with Paul Black on *Inside the Black Box*. That work synthesized research on assessment and made a strong, evidence-based case for formative practices (Black & Wiliam, 1998). However, Wiliam didn't stop at theory—he translated those findings into classroom strategies that teachers could adopt and adapt.

His five key strategies of formative assessment are practical yet anchored in research. What makes his work stand out is how effectively he communicates, taking complex educational psychology and turning it into usable insights for teachers worldwide (Wiliam, 2017).

Unlike some thought leaders who cling to a fixed model, Wiliam has consistently refined his ideas based on how they're used in practice. He has listened to educators' feedback, identified where misunderstandings emerge, and adjusted his frameworks accordingly. This iterative process reflects both humility and a deep respect for the realities of teaching.

Wiliam also demonstrates strong ethical grounding. He consistently emphasizes how formative assessment, when done well, can close opportunity gaps, providing the kinds of timely, targeted feedback that helps all students grow, especially those underserved by traditional systems.

Crucially, Wiliam has adapted his work across contexts. Whether working in the UK, the US, or internationally, he's shown how core principles can be maintained while flexibly responding to different educational settings. His balance of principled rigor and contextual sensitivity has made his ideas relevant across boundaries.

Wiliam's influence reflects a blend of scholarly depth, practical utility, communicative clarity, and moral focus. His leadership is a model of how educational ideas gain power through continuous dialogue with evidence and experience.

Shared Patterns, Distinctive Voices

Though Dewey, Delpit, and Wiliam worked in different eras and focused on different challenges, their stories share key throughlines.

- Each integrated scholarship with practice.
- Each developed a conceptual framework grounded in real-world challenges.
- Each communicated with clarity and purpose.
- Each maintained an ethical anchor tied to education's deeper mission.
- Each paid close attention to implementation, not just abstract vision.

What these leaders show is that educational thought leadership is not a fixed formula. It's a dynamic, evolving process. It blends the following elements:

- Theory
- Action
- Personal conviction
- Collaborative inquiry
- Big ideas
- Practical wisdom

The next chapters turn to the "how" of thought leadership: how these dynamics play out in specific domains, how aspiring leaders can cultivate the necessary skills and mindsets, and how ideas, rather than titles or roles, become the most powerful tools for educational change.

The framework developed here provides a foundation for that exploration. By studying these leaders and understanding the core dimensions of their work, we gain not just admiration but insight into how impactful educational thought leadership can be cultivated and sustained.

Chapter 3:
The Scholarship of Educational Thought Leadership

The relationship between scholarship and educational thought leadership is both powerful and complicated. Research provides the backbone for meaningful ideas, but much of that knowledge remains stuck behind paywalls or buried in language that feels out of reach for the people who need it most. Academic journals, conference presentations, and discipline-specific vocabulary often create more distance than connection.

Educational thought leaders help close that gap. They take what research tells us and translate it into frameworks, languages, and actions that practitioners can use, without watering down the substance. At their best, they hold the line on intellectual rigor and make ideas genuinely useful.

This chapter explores what that looks like in practice. We'll look at how strong scholarship fuels transformative ideas, how academic inquiry drives innovation, and how theory and practice can meet without one overpowering the other. We'll also dig into the challenge of building a scholarly voice that's both credible and accessible and explore how thought leaders contribute to the evolving body of knowledge while making a real difference on the ground.

Research Foundations for Effective Thought Leadership

Substantive educational thought leadership isn't just fueled by personal experience, intuition, or trending ideas. Its credibility and lasting influence come from a solid research foundation, one that separates meaningful leadership from passing opinions or fashionable buzzwords.

Conceptual Frameworks: Making Sense of Complexity

Educational research has developed sophisticated ways of framing how we think about learning, teaching, school systems, and change. These conceptual frameworks help thought leaders tackle complex issues with more depth and clarity than everyday language allows.

Take Lev Vygotsky's (Chaiklin, 2003) *zone of proximal development*, a concept that gives educators a precise way of understanding how scaffolding can help students grow beyond their current capabilities. When thought leaders tap into that framework, they're not just saying "meet students where they are," but offering a specific, research-backed explanation for how to move students forward.

Similarly, James Comer's (1980) School Development Program provides a framework that links child development with school improvement. Instead of centering reform efforts solely around test scores, thought leaders who draw from Comer's work are equipped to talk about developmental pathways, collaborative school culture, and holistic success.

These frameworks act as the architecture behind influential ideas. They help organize complex realities, expose hidden patterns, and provide tools for deeper analysis.

Empirical Evidence: Grounding Ideas in Reality

Beyond frameworks, research offers hard-earned evidence about what works, when it works, and for whom it works. It moves us from guesswork to informed action (Slavin, 2002; Bryk et al., 2015).

John Hattie's *Visible Learning* is a standout example. By synthesizing thousands of studies, Hattie (2009) ranks the impact of different teaching strategies based on effect sizes. This kind of research lets thought leaders shape ideas around proven effects, not just what sounds good or feels right.

In a similar vein, the work of Duke et al. (2021) and colleagues on evidence-based literacy practices gives thought leaders a more nuanced and context-sensitive understanding of what helps children learn to read. Their research highlights the importance of balancing foundational skills with knowledge-building, drawing on classroom-based studies and diverse student populations. These findings carry more weight than anecdotes or personal stories because they're based on patterns observed across varied educational contexts.

Empirical research acts as a reality check. It keeps thought leadership rooted in what's demonstrably effective, not just what's popular or comfortable (Wiliam, 2011).

Methodological Tools: Refining Ideas Through Inquiry

In addition to answers, research offers tools for asking better questions. Methodologies like design-based research and improvement science give thought leaders practical ways to develop, test, and improve ideas over time.

Design-based research, pioneered by Ann Brown (1992) and Collins et al. (2004), focuses on iterative testing and learning. It's especially useful when thought leaders are designing interventions in real-world settings and need to learn from each step along the way.

Improvement science, advanced in education by Bryk et al. (2015), does something similar—pairing disciplined inquiry with a focus on solving everyday problems. It's not about finding a one-time fix but building better systems through cycles of testing, learning, and refining.

By adopting these research methods, thought leaders can move beyond inspiration to innovation grounded in evidence and reflection.

Theoretical Perspectives: Seeing What's Often Overlooked

Finally, theory helps thought leaders see what's often missed. It shines a light on the social, cultural, or structural forces that shape educational outcomes.

Sociocultural learning theory, built on Vygotsky's findings and expanded by scholars like James Wertsch (1991) and Barbara Rogoff (2003), emphasizes how learning happens through participation in cultural practices. Thought leaders who understand this can develop approaches that move beyond the individual, addressing how communities, identities, and norms influence education.

Likewise, critical race theory—brought into education by Ladson-Billings and Tate (1995)—offers a lens for understanding how race and power operate in schools. It challenges thought leaders to move past superficial equity talk to confront the deeper systems that create and sustain inequality.

Theoretical perspectives give thought leaders language and insight to ask better questions, challenge conventional thinking, and create more just and inclusive visions of education.

The following are the four pillars we discussed in this section (Nutley et al., 2007; Van de Ven, 2007; Wenger, 1998):

- Frameworks

- Evidence

- Methods

- Theory

They form the intellectual backbone of effective thought leadership

and provide structure, credibility, and depth. Furthermore, they help leaders avoid the trap of reinventing the wheel so they can build upon the accumulated knowledge of the field.

Research alone, however, isn't enough. It must be translated, applied, and communicated clearly to truly make an impact. That's where the educational thought leader plays a vital role: as a scholar and a bridge between theory and practice, ensuring ideas stay both rigorous and relevant.

Evidence-Based Approaches to Educational Innovation

The relationship between evidence and innovation is both promising and complex. While research provides a vital foundation, clinging too tightly to what's already known can stall fresh thinking. The most impactful thought leaders understand this balance. They use research to guide and support innovation without letting it limit the creation of new ideas.

Methodological Pluralism: Matching Evidence to the Question

Thoughtful leaders don't treat all evidence as the same. They recognize that educational research employs diverse methods—randomized trials, design-based research, large-scale surveys, and ethnographies, each offering unique strengths suited to different kinds of questions.

Thomas Guskey's (2000) work on professional development exemplifies this approach. He integrates both experimental studies that explore cause-and-effect relationships and qualitative research that delves into the complexities of real-world school settings. This methodological range allows his work to be both rigorous and grounded in practical realities.

Ann Lieberman adopts a similar stance in her research on teacher leadership. Her insights are drawn from large-scale studies as well as personal narratives from educators, acknowledging that both quantitative data and qualitative experiences provide valuable knowledge. Rather than preferring one method over another, she allows the nature of the question to guide the choice of evidence (Lieberman & Miller, 2004).

This flexibility enables thought leaders to engage deeply with multifaceted challenges. They don't just ask what works in a general sense but also inquire for whom, in what setting, and how it works. Different types of evidence highlight different facets of these complex questions.

Context Matters: Avoiding One-Size-Fits-All Conclusions

Effective thought leaders understand that evidence doesn't travel well without context. What proves successful in one school or district might falter in another due to variations in students, communities, resources, or culture. Rather than offering universal prescriptions, they remain attuned to the specific realities of each educational setting.

Gloria Ladson-Billings' (1995) work on culturally relevant pedagogy embodies this sensitivity. She emphasizes not only the effectiveness of teaching strategies but also their interactions with students' cultural backgrounds. By doing so, she guides educators to adapt their practices in ways that are both meaningful and respectful.

Michael Fullan (2007) brings a similar perspective to educational change. He underscores that reforms don't yield identical results everywhere—not because the ideas are flawed but because schools differ. His leadership emphasizes attention to context, adaptation, and implementation, rather than the blind replication of strategies that succeeded elsewhere.

This kind of contextual awareness enables thought leaders to use research not as a rigid script but as a versatile toolkit—something to adapt and apply with care, not merely copy and paste.

Knowing When to Build Beyond the Evidence

While evidence is essential, it's not always enough, especially when existing strategies no longer work or fail to serve all students. The most effective thought leaders recognize when the current knowledge base is incomplete. They build on what's known and make room for new ideas and bold experimentation.

James Comer's (1980) *School Development Program* was one of the early examples of this kind of leadership. Seeing that conventional approaches were failing students in under-resourced urban schools, Comer drew on developmental psychology to create a new model centered on child development, collaboration, and whole-school change, well before those principles were widely accepted in mainstream reform efforts.

Ted Sizer's (1992) *Coalition of Essential Schools* took a similar path. Grounded in research on adolescent development and school culture, Sizer advocated for smaller, more personalized schools that focused on depth over breadth. His work challenged the norms of the time and opened space for schools to rethink structure and purpose.

Today, that same spirit of innovation continues. WestEd's *Four Domains for Rapid School Improvement* offers a more current example of evidence-informed innovation. Designed for schools facing chronic underperformance, the framework is grounded in research but emphasizes real-time learning and adaptation. It doesn't prescribe one-size-fits-all solutions but instead guides leaders to make strategic changes that respond to their unique contexts (Center on School Turnaround at WestEd, 2017).

Similarly, Linda Darling-Hammond et al.'s (2023) work on redesigning high schools points to the need for equitable, deeper learning environments that respond to today's student needs. Their framework builds on decades of educational research and pushes into new terrain, challenging outdated models while encouraging school systems to reimagine what learning can look like.

This mindset—of honoring what works while pushing toward what's needed—helps thought leaders stay focused on real-world problems. It keeps them grounded in evidence yet not limited by it, creating space for solutions that are both credible and forward-thinking.

A Critical Eye on Evidence Gaps

Even the strongest research has blind spots. Influential thought leaders don't just use evidence—they interrogate it. They ask what's missing, who's left out, and what questions haven't yet been asked. Rather than treating evidence as the final word, they see it as a starting point for further exploration.

Linda Darling-Hammond (2006, 2017), for instance, has long acknowledged the limitations in teacher preparation research. While she draws on available studies, she also calls for more robust and nuanced approaches that capture the complexity of how teachers learn, develop, and impact student outcomes. Her leadership contributes not only to improved practice but also to the evolution of the research itself.

Carol Dweck, known for her work on the growth mindset, has likewise emphasized the need for ongoing investigation into how her theory is applied in real-world settings. She has cautioned against oversimplified interpretations of her work and calls for more clarity around how mindset interventions affect students across different disciplines and demographics (Dweck, 2015; Yeager & Dweck, 2020). Her openness to critique and further refinement ensures that growth mindset research continues to evolve in useful, responsible ways.

This critical stance is what drives research-based innovation forward. Thought leaders who engage with evidence gaps don't settle for what's already known—they remain curious, reflective, and committed to deepening the field's understanding.

The Balancing Act

The most impactful educational thought leaders walk a careful line. They neither dismiss research, nor let it limit them. They build ideas that are both rooted in evidence and open to experimentation. They honor what we've learned—and ask what we still need to discover.

Their influence lies not just in what they know but also in how they think. They use research as a foundation, not a ceiling, and that's what allows them to lead with both insight and imagination.

The Role of Academic Inquiry in Developing Thought Leadership

Academic inquiry—systematic investigation grounded in theory and rigorous methodology—plays a foundational role in shaping educational thought leadership. While thought leadership moves beyond traditional scholarship to influence policy and practice, its most impactful ideas often emerge not from intuition or anecdote but from disciplined research and theoretical exploration. Understanding this relationship between inquiry and influence reveals how transformative educational ideas take shape. Let's look at several dimensions that define this relationship.

Conceptual Clarity as a Foundation

Through precise definitions, careful analysis, and structured frameworks, scholarly work offers conceptual tools that deepen understanding and allow ideas to be communicated with accuracy. As such, academic inquiry brings clarity to complex ideas.

Some of the most enduring conceptual contributions continue to serve as anchors for educational thought leadership. Howard Gardner's (1983) theory of multiple intelligences, for example, didn't just challenge traditional notions of intelligence but also offered a clearly articulated alternative. By naming and defining distinct intelligences, Gardner gave educators a more nuanced vocabulary to describe student strengths and learning beyond standardized metrics.

Likewise, Lee Shulman's (1987) introduction of pedagogical content knowledge brought new specificity to the conversation around teaching expertise. By distinguishing this form of knowledge from both subject matter understanding and general pedagogy, he reframed how teacher preparation and instructional effectiveness could be understood and developed.

These foundational frameworks continue to shape how we think about expertise, cognition, and instructional design. However, conceptual clarity isn't static; it evolves as new scholars take up the challenge of refining our understanding of complex educational realities. Looney et al. (2023) build on this legacy by emphasizing the role of developmental thinking in teacher education. Their analysis argues for clarity not just in definitions but also in how we grapple with complexity as a necessary part of educator preparation.

This kind of conceptual clarity enables thought leaders to move beyond buzzwords and slogans. It allows for the construction of frameworks that are intellectually rigorous, practically useful, and capable of evolving over time. Therefore, it's not just about coining new terms but also about deepening the profession's capacity to understand and act on what matters. This kind of conceptual clarity enables thought leaders to move beyond buzzwords and slogans.

Methodological Discipline as a Source of Credibility

Good ideas are not enough. Academic inquiry lends credibility through disciplined methods, whether experimental, qualitative, historical, or philosophical. This rigor strengthens the foundation of thought leadership, grounding it in more than just opinion or selective observation.

Take Robert Marzano's work on instructional strategies. By conducting meta-analyses across hundreds of studies, Marzano identified approaches with consistent evidence of effectiveness. His frameworks are trusted not because they sound appealing but because they're backed by a comprehensive review of what works across settings (Marzano Research Laboratory, 2011).

Marilyn Cochran-Smith's research on teacher education demonstrates a different kind of methodological depth. She blends quantitative data with qualitative insights to capture both outcomes and learning processes. This multifaceted view supports more holistic, actionable approaches to teacher development (Cochran-Smith & Lytle, 1990).

Thought leadership informed by methodological discipline inspires and equips educators with tools that are tested, refined, and ready for adaptation.

Theoretical Perspective as a Source of Depth

Academic inquiry helps thought leaders think more deeply. Engaging with core questions about learning, development, knowledge, and justice brings assumptions to the surface and invites more intentional design of educational practices.

James Banks (2004), for instance, didn't simply advocate for multicultural education; he also grounded it in epistemological and sociocultural theory. His work addresses how knowledge is constructed and who gets to define it, connecting classroom practice to broader issues of equity and representation.

Nel Noddings' (1984) ethics of care is another example. Rather than framing education as a neutral transmission of content, she examined its moral dimensions, arguing that relationships and care are central to effective teaching. Her theoretical framing continues to influence how educators think about classroom culture and student well-being.

This kind of theoretical grounding helps thought leaders avoid superficial fixes and address root causes. It encourages strategies that are not only effective but ethically and philosophically sound.

Critical Analysis as a Tool for Nuance

Finally, academic inquiry sharpens thought leadership through critical analysis. Identifying blind spots, unintended consequences, and implementation challenges helps thought leaders avoid oversimplification.

David Berliner's (2011) work on high-stakes testing, for example, didn't just critique accountability systems; it also documented how they reshape instruction, narrow curriculum, and distort measures of success. His analysis urged for a more measured, thoughtful approach to assessment reform.

Diane Ravitch's (2013) historical analysis of reform cycles similarly serves as a cautionary tale. She traced how ambitious initiatives often falter when enthusiasm outpaces evidence, reminding educators to ask hard questions before jumping into the next big thing.

This kind of critical engagement strengthens ideas by exposing their limits. It encourages thought leadership that is realistic, sustainable, and aware of complexity.

Academic Inquiry and the Practice Gap

While academic inquiry strengthens thought leadership, scholarship alone isn't enough. The most effective thought leaders bridge the gap between theory and practice, translating insights without diluting them, communicating ideas without losing depth, and influencing practice without abandoning nuance.

Their role is to make rigorous ideas usable, bring research into conversation with real-world constraints, and ensure that educational change is grounded in both what we know and what we continue to learn.

In doing so, they extend the reach of academic inquiry, ensuring its value goes beyond journal articles to live where it matters most: in the hands of those shaping the future of education.

Balancing Theoretical Knowledge With Practical Application

One of the core challenges in educational thought leadership is navigating the space between theory and practice. Theory without application risks becoming detached from reality, whereas practice without a strong theoretical foundation can be scattered, inconsistent, or hard to replicate. Thought leaders work at this intersection, bridging ideas and action in ways that respect the complexity of both.

Using Theory as a Lens, Not a Script

Thought leaders often treat theory as a way of looking at educational practices, not as a step-by-step manual. Theoretical frameworks highlight important aspects of teaching and learning, but they never capture the whole picture. The goal isn't to prescribe every move but to help educators see their work with new clarity.

Etienne Wenger's *Communities of Practice* theory offers one such lens. It describes how learning happens through social participation and shared activity, without dictating how to structure those communities (Jakopovic & Johnson, 2023). Recent work in faculty development has built on this idea, showing how communities of practice can support educators in reimagining instructional practices with equity and research in mind.

Similarly, situated learning theory—originally proposed by Lave and Wenger—explains how people learn best through experience and context. While the theory emerged decades ago, it continues to shape practice today, particularly in areas like clinical teaching, workplace learning, and project-based environments (Farnsworth et al., 2016). The key insight is that theory should clarify, not control.

Building Middle-Range Theories That Connect the Dots

Some thought leaders work in the space between sweeping theory and narrow technical advice. These "middle-range" theories offer just enough structure to guide practice without locking educators into a rigid model.

Wiggins and McTighe's (2005) *Understanding by Design* is one such example. It blends research on backward planning and authentic assessment with a user-friendly framework for curriculum design— clear enough to apply, flexible enough to adapt.

More recently, work in learning sciences has advanced middle-range frameworks for personalized learning and formative assessment, offering models that help educators translate core principles into instructional routines (Pellegrino, 2022). These frameworks aren't blueprints—they're bridges between theory and practice.

Using Examples to Make Theory Real

Theories can be powerful, but they need grounding. Thought leaders often use vivid, specific examples to show how ideas come alive in classrooms.

Lisa Delpit's (2006) writing is especially effective here. Her work on power and communication in culturally diverse classrooms illustrates how abstract ideas like "the culture of power" show up in day-to-day teacher-student interactions. She doesn't just explain—she shows.

Carol Ann Tomlinson does something similar with differentiated instruction. She draws on learning theory and research on student diversity, but the heart of her work is in the examples—how a teacher might adjust tasks, groupings, or materials to meet students where they are. Recent studies have affirmed the impact of differentiation, not just on achievement but on student engagement and emotional well-being (Deunk et al., 2018; Pozas et al., 2021).

Engaging Educators in Meaning-Making

Rather than treating educators as passive recipients of theory, strong thought leaders bring them into the meaning-making process.

Ann Lieberman's work on teacher learning emphasized this long before it was widely accepted. She viewed professional development as a collaborative, reflective process where educators shape models as much as they apply them (Lieberman & Miller, 2001).

Michael Fullan's (Fullan et al., 2021) ongoing work builds on this, especially in system-level change. His theory of action includes space for practitioner wisdom—what he calls "leading from the middle"—and acknowledges that implementation is a generative act, not a mechanical one.

Addressing the Realities of Implementation

The most promising ideas can fall apart if they overlook the practical challenges of real schools. That's why thought leaders must anticipate implementation, not just as logistics but as culture, history, and politics.

Anthony Bryk's research on relational trust is a case in point. His work explores how change in schools depends on ideas and on the social fabric in which those ideas live (Bryk & Schneider, 2002). Trust isn't a side condition but the main one for learning to take root.

Recent work on systems transformation echoes this. Studies point to the need for leadership stability, collaborative cultures, and aligned policies to make even well-supported reforms stick (Weritz et al., 2024). It's a reminder that theory must travel through human systems, and those systems are anything but simple.

These five moves—treating theory as a lens, developing middle-range frameworks, grounding concepts in examples, engaging educators in meaning-making, and addressing implementation challenges—are hallmarks of high-impact thought leadership.

The most influential educational ideas live in the space between abstraction and application: clear enough to understand, grounded enough to try, and flexible enough to evolve.

Contribution to the Knowledge Base through Original Thinking

Educational thought leadership isn't just about applying what's already known—it's about pushing the boundaries of that knowledge. Thought leaders don't merely echo the research; they build on it, connecting dots others haven't noticed and reshaping how we think about long-standing educational challenges. This capacity for original thinking is what separates transformative ideas from recycled ones.

Recognizing Patterns Across Disconnected Findings

Thought leaders often recognize connections that others overlook. Where most see isolated findings or fragmented insights, they identify underlying patterns—linking research across disciplines, methodologies, and policy arenas to develop new, coherent frameworks.

Take the work of Linda Darling-Hammond (2021). Her analyses of teacher preparation, development, and systemic equity reforms don't rest on a single dataset. Instead, she synthesizes evidence from diverse studies to build comprehensive models for advancing teaching quality across contexts (Darling-Hammond, 2021). Her thought leadership lies not just in data collection but in framing that data within a compelling, actionable vision.

Mehta and Fine (2019) have brought this kind of pattern recognition to school improvement. In their deep, ethnographic study of American high schools, they identified recurring practices and mindsets that support deeper learning, even when those schools looked very different on the surface (Mehta & Fine, 2019). Their contribution wasn't just empirical—it was interpretive. They helped educators see the "hidden infrastructure" of powerful learning environments.

Similarly, Thomas Guskey (2020) has contributed significantly by drawing connections between professional development practices, assessment policies, and student outcomes. His integrated frameworks help educators trace how system-level decisions ripple through teacher practices and ultimately affect student learning (Guskey, 2020).

This kind of meaning-making relies on intellectual synthesis—the ability to bring scattered pieces together into a sharper, more usable picture—than on groundbreaking discoveries. The result is not more noise but deeper clarity.

Applying Concepts From Other Disciplines

Great thought leaders think across boundaries. They draw from psychology, sociology, neuroscience, economics, and organizational theory—not to borrow jargon but to borrow lenses. This interdisciplinary thinking allows them to reframe persistent problems in education and explore new pathways forward.

Howard Gardner's (2011) theory of multiple intelligences exemplifies this approach. Grounded in cognitive science, developmental psychology, and brain research, Gardner didn't just critique standardized notions of intelligence but also offered a new conceptual map for how we understand student potential. His work didn't stay in the realm of theory; it helped reshape how schools think about talent, learning, and inclusion.

Richard Elmore (2004) similarly turned to organizational theory to unpack the challenges of school reform. By treating schools as complex systems with layered incentives and power structures, he revealed why surface-level changes often fail and why deep instructional improvement requires shifts in culture, relationships, and leadership.

Interdisciplinary thinking like this expands what's possible. It breaks education out of its own silos and opens up new intellectual tools, allowing thought leaders to approach problems with greater creativity and insight. It's not just about knowing more but about seeing things differently.

Reconceptualizing Familiar Problems

Sometimes, the breakthrough isn't in what's being studied but in *how* it's being understood. Thought leaders often flip the script on conventional ideas, revealing hidden dynamics or reframing old problems in more illuminating ways.

Lisa Delpit's (1988) concept of "the culture of power" does just that. Her work critically examined how educational systems often reinforce power dynamics that go unnoticed, especially in marginalized communities. By spotlighting the unspoken rules and dynamics of classroom communication, Delpit challenged surface-level discussions about diversity and framed equity as a curriculum *and* power issue.

Carol Dweck's (2006) research on mindsets similarly redefined how we think about student achievement. Rather than seeing it solely as a reflection of innate ability or hard work, Dweck argued that success is deeply influenced by students' beliefs about intelligence—beliefs that shape their motivation and resilience.

While these kinds of insights add to the list of educational challenges, they also help us see challenges in new ways, ultimately leading to more effective responses and approaches.

Developing New Methodologies

Sometimes, it's not enough to generate new ideas—you also need new ways to investigate them. Methodological innovation is another powerful tool in a thought leader's arsenal.

Ann Brown's (1992) development of "design experiments" created space for iterative, in-context research that bridged the gap between laboratory studies and classroom realities. Her methods reshaped how learning processes could be studied in real-time, emphasizing the importance of context and flexibility.

Anthony Bryk's (2015) "improvement science" took this a step further. Borrowing from healthcare and engineering, he introduced structured approaches to testing small changes in educational systems. Rather than waiting years for results, educators could learn and adapt quickly, turning research into a real-time problem-solving tool.

When traditional research methods fall short, thought leaders work around the problem and invent better tools for understanding it.

Synthesizing Across Knowledge Domains

Educational thought leadership often involves integrating multiple sources of knowledge—research findings, practitioner insights, philosophical perspectives, and policy contexts—into coherent, actionable frameworks.

James Comer's (2004) School Development Program stands out here. By weaving together child development theory, organizational change models, and school-level practice, he built a holistic model for school reform that was both theoretically grounded and practically effective.

Linda Darling-Hammond's (2010) work on equity similarly reflects a synthesis across domains—combining insights from pedagogy, policy, and organizational behavior to propose system-wide solutions to entrenched inequalities. Her frameworks emphasize the need for policies that support teacher preparation, professional development, and equitable access to resources.

This synthetic thinking addresses the full complexity of education. Rather than cherry-picking ideas from different sources, it forges a unified approach from them.

Educational thought leaders use these strategies to expand the field while working within it. Their influence stems from their ability to move the conversation forward, offering not only new strategies but new ways of thinking about what's possible in education.

Developing a Scholarly Voice While Maintaining Accessibility

Educational thought leadership requires a communication style that balances scholarly rigor with broad accessibility. This dual aim can be challenging: Academic writing often leans on specialized jargon and dense phrasing, while simplifying ideas too much can strip away nuance. Thought leaders navigate this tension by crafting messages that are both intellectually grounded and widely understandable.

In addition to including jargon, scholarly writing also tends to be dense, often needing to be unpacked. It may also describe skills and concepts that are not readily accessible. These challenges often prevent teachers, administrators, and hands-on educational leaders from fully engaging with academic texts.

Precision Without Pretension

Thought leaders choose their words carefully. They use technical terms when necessary, such as when no simpler term captures the idea, but avoid using language that serves only to sound academic. Their goal is clarity, not gatekeeping.

Carol Dweck (2006) exemplifies this in her work on mindsets. She introduces terms like "fixed mindset" and "growth mindset" but defines them clearly and supports them with relatable examples. The terminology is precise, but never alienating.

John Hattie (2009) does the same with statistical terms like "effect size." Rather than dropping the phrase and moving on, he explains what it means, why it matters, and how it connects to what teachers do every day.

This approach respects the reader's intelligence without assuming prior expertise. It shows that scholarly communication doesn't need to be cryptic to be credible.

Making the Abstract Concrete

Even complex theories become more approachable when they're tied to real-world examples. The best thought leaders present ideas *and* show others how those ideas play out in practice.

Lisa Delpit's (2006) writing on *The Culture of Power* is a powerful case in point. She uses specific classroom examples to illustrate how power dynamics operate between teachers and students, especially across cultural lines. The theory gains weight because readers can see it in action.

Carol Ann Tomlinson (2001) takes a similar approach to differentiated instruction. Instead of just defining it, she shares stories and vignettes from classrooms that show differentiation in real time— what it looks like, how it works, and why it matters.

These examples aren't decorative—they're integral to understanding. They bridge the gap between concept and application.

Visualizing Complexity

Sometimes, the clearest way to explain something isn't with words but with images. Diagrams, matrices, and visual tools help convey how multiple parts of a system interact, especially when relationships are nonlinear or layered.

Wiggins and McTighe (2005) built visual thinking into their *Understanding by Design* framework. Templates and charts help educators plan backward, connecting goals, assessments, and learning activities in a way that's easy to grasp.

Robert Marzano (2007) also leans on visual formats—his models often map out how different instructional strategies relate to student outcomes. These visuals don't dumb things down; they clarify what might otherwise remain abstract.

Visuals can make dense content more navigable without sacrificing depth. When used well, they're a form of rigorous thinking, not a substitute for it.

Metaphors That Illuminate, Not Obscure

Metaphors and analogies make unfamiliar ideas feel familiar. Great thought leaders use them to explain and reveal so readers can see something in a new way.

David Perkins (1992) compares knowledge to design, framing understanding as something purposeful and adaptive rather than stored information. This metaphor brings philosophical ideas about learning into a sharper, more relatable focus.

Michael Fullan's (2001) phrase "the implementation dip" captures a reality many educators recognize: Things often get harder before they get better. It's a simple image, but one that resonates deeply.

These metaphors stick because they reveal core truths. They don't oversimplify; they clarify.

Story as Strategy

Stories pull people in. They humanize abstract concepts and help readers remember what they've learned. Thought leaders often weave narrative elements into their work alongside analysis.

Ted Sizer (1992) used a fictional teacher, Horace, to show how policy and structure impact real classrooms. His stories made systemic critiques more tangible, emotional, and urgent.

Deborah Meier (2002), drawing on her own school leadership experiences, tells stories that highlight democratic education in action. Her narratives illustrate ideas that might otherwise feel purely theoretical.

In each case, storytelling deepens the message. It helps readers see the "why" and the "who" behind the "what."

Structuring for Multiple Audiences

Not every reader approaches a text the same way. The best thought leaders build their writing with multiple entry points: a newcomer can get the gist, while a scholar can dig deeper. This kind of layered communication respects different levels of expertise and interest.

Richard Elmore's (2004) writing often includes conceptual overviews, policy critiques, and practice-focused recommendations, all within the same piece. He gives each reader a way in.

Linda Darling-Hammond (2000) does the same in her policy work. She offers summaries, detailed evidence, and real-world applications, letting readers engage at the depth they choose.

This multilevel approach makes ideas portable: useful to policymakers, researchers, school leaders, and teachers alike. It's how ideas travel without getting lost in translation.

In short, thought leaders craft a voice that's both scholarly and inclusive. They don't trade depth for simplicity or clarity for complexity. Instead, they balance the two using precise language, relatable examples, visual tools, metaphors, stories, and strategic structure to make their ideas resonate across audiences.

This is the kind of communication that moves ideas beyond academic circles into practice, policy, and public conversation. It's not just about saying something smart but about saying something that matters in a way others can understand and use.

Methods for Translating Research Into Actionable Insights

Educational thought leadership produces research-based ideas and makes them usable. One of its defining features is the ability to bridge the gap between what we know and what we do. Thought leaders don't leave the possibility of good ideas trickling into classrooms or leadership meetings to chance. Instead, they develop structured, intentional methods for translating knowledge into practice. The following six common methods stand out in this process.

Building Coherent Frameworks

One of the hallmark traits of thought leadership is the creation of frameworks that pull together disparate research findings into something more usable. Educators often lack the time and resources to sift through individual studies. A well-designed framework highlights essential connections, clarifies the most important takeaways, and shows how various pieces of research fit together.

Robert Marzano's (2007) synthesis of research into nine categories of high-yield instructional strategies is a good example. This comprehensive framework provides teachers with a clear map to navigate evidence-based practices. Similarly, Charlotte Danielson's (2007) *Framework for Teaching* organizes the complex nature of effective instruction into four domains, helping educators understand how different aspects of their work interconnect. These frameworks are practical tools that make research both relevant and actionable.

Designing Decision Tools

Even the best frameworks require careful judgment to be applied effectively. Educational environments are filled with unique variables—students, resources, time constraints, and more. Thought leaders often respond by creating tools that help educators make informed decisions in their specific contexts.

An example of this is the *Understanding by Design* templates developed by Wiggins and McTighe (2005). These templates offer a structured planning process rooted in research that is adaptable to any subject or grade level. Carol Ann Tomlinson's (2001) matrices for differentiated instruction serve a similar purpose—they guide educators in tailoring their approaches to meet the needs of diverse learners without prescribing one-size-fits-all solutions. These decision tools provide flexibility and nuance, helping educators turn theory into action.

Mapping Implementation Progressions

Adopting new practices doesn't happen overnight; it's a developmental process. As a result, many thought leaders offer implementation progressions—clear sequences that guide educators as they build their capacity over time.

Dylan Wiliam's (2011) work on formative assessment is a prime example. Rather than expecting immediate mastery, Wiliam outlines stages of adoption, allowing educators to progress and refine their practice over time. Lucy Calkins (n.d.) has developed similar progression models in writing instruction, offering both teachers and students step-by-step guides for growth. These progression models recognize the learning curve inherent in educational change and support long-term growth.

Creating Practical Protocols

Some ideas are too complex to be explained simply; they require step-by-step processes to ensure consistent application. Thought leaders often develop protocols—structured routines and processes—that help educators implement research-based principles in their everyday practice.

Richard DuFour's (2006) work on professional learning communities (PLCs) offers a clear example. He shows how collaborative inquiry can be operationalized through specific structures and meeting routines. Similarly, Ron Berger's (2014) protocols for peer critique and student-led conferences help educators put big ideas about assessment into practice. These protocols strike a balance between structure and adaptability, giving educators clear steps without stifling their flexibility.

Sharing Cases and Examples

Abstract principles become far more meaningful when grounded in real-world examples. Thought leaders often use detailed cases to illustrate how their ideas play out in practice.

Ted Sizer (1992), through the *Coalition of Essential Schools*, demonstrated how principles like personalization could be applied in diverse educational settings. Deborah Ball (2003) has done the same for the concept of mathematical knowledge for teaching, using classroom examples to make complex research tangible. These real-world cases make research accessible, providing concrete ways to apply theoretical ideas in specific contexts.

Providing Self-Assessment Tools

The implementation of new practices is an ongoing process that requires regular reflection and adjustment. Many thought leaders support this by offering self-assessment tools that allow educators to evaluate their progress and identify the next steps in their development.

Danielson's (2007) rubrics, embedded within her *Framework for Teaching*, provide a structured tool for educators to reflect on their practice. Leithwood et al. (2004) have created similar self-assessment instruments for school leaders, helping them evaluate their effectiveness based on research. These self-assessment tools encourage continuous improvement, grounded in research, by enabling educators to track their development and adapt their practices accordingly.

Together, these methods form the backbone of how thought leadership translates theory into practice. Influential leaders rarely rely on a single approach. Instead, they create comprehensive toolkits that offer multiple entry points for practitioners working in diverse environments.

By focusing on usability as much as originality, thought leaders ensure that their ideas don't remain confined to academic discourse; they become practical instruments that shape classrooms, influence decisions, and drive meaningful change.

Looking Ahead

In future chapters, we will explore how these methods of translation appear in specific educational domains such as systems thinking, technology, curriculum design, and collaborative networks. We will also examine how aspiring thought leaders can build their own capacity to connect research with practice in ways that are both rigorous and responsive.

By grounding ourselves in these scholarly foundations, evidence-based thinking, research-driven innovation, and practical translation, we gain a clearer understanding of what educational thought leadership truly entails.

Chapter 4:
Systems Thinking and Organizational Transformation

Educational institutions are among the most complex systems we interact with. They include layered webs of people, policies, routines, cultures, and internal and external pressures. Classrooms don't operate in isolation; they sit within schools, which sit within districts, all influenced by state mandates, community expectations, funding structures, and shifting societal demands. It's no wonder that efforts to improve education often feel like pushing on one part of a balloon—address one issue, and another part bulges out.

Traditional improvement efforts often zero in on individual components: a new curriculum, tech platform, or leadership training. But when these changes happen without giving attention to the system as a whole, progress is fragile at best and counterproductive at worst. That's where systems thinking comes in—not as a buzzword, but as a serious lens for educational thought leadership.

This chapter explores how systems thinking reshapes our understanding of educational change by allowing us to step back far enough to see the patterns beneath the problems. It also helps us recognize that schools are not machines to be fixed part by part but dynamic systems that adapt, evolve, and sometimes, resist change in surprising ways.

We'll dive into the following:

- Frameworks that help leaders analyze the interdependence of roles, routines, and resources within schools and districts.

- Strategies for leading systemic change across multiple levels of an organization without losing sight of the people at the center of it.

- Approaches for cultivating cultures of innovation, where continuous improvement isn't a mandate but a mindset.

We'll also look at real-world case studies where systems thinking has made a difference in raising test scores and implementing new tools while transforming how schools function at their core.

At its best, systems thinking doesn't just help us respond to complexity—it helps us design for it. For educational thought leaders, it's a mindset that turns fragmented reforms into coherent, sustainable change.

Understanding Educational Institutions as Complex Adaptive Systems

Educational institutions are not machines; they are living systems, shaped by culture, relationships, and feedback loops that cannot be easily reduced to linear processes. The predictability of unpredictability is a constant. Attempts to impose rigid change, such as top-down mandates, quick-fix reforms, or standardized interventions, often fall short because they fail to account for this complexity. This is why systems thinking matters.

Systems thinking provides a powerful framework for understanding and transforming educational organizations. It encourages us to view schools, districts, and higher education institutions as complex adaptive systems (CAS), which are dynamic environments consisting of interdependent agents—students, educators, administrators, policies, and community members—whose interactions create unpredictable outcomes.

Key Characteristics of Complex Adaptive Systems

Unlike mechanical or bureaucratic models, CAS are complex. This means that they exhibit behaviors and outcomes that cannot be fully understood by analyzing individual parts in isolation. Below are the defining characteristics of a complex adaptive system:

1. **Interdependence:** In CAS, agents such as teachers, students, families, and community stakeholders do not function in isolation. Their actions and behaviors are interconnected. For example, a change in curriculum affects not only classroom practices but also student engagement, assessment methods, and even parent expectations. The ripple effect of any change is felt across multiple parts of the system, making it difficult to predict outcomes based solely on isolated actions.

2. **Emergent Properties:** The outcomes in a CAS emerge from the interactions between its agents, rather than from top-down design or control. A school's culture, for example, is not just a product of its mission statement or policies. It arises from the daily interactions, rituals, and the shared meaning-making of the people within the system. As Seymour Sarason (1996) argued, lasting change can only happen when it works with, not against, these emergent norms. The very essence of a school's culture is forged through these collective, bottom-up processes.

3. **Feedback Loops:** Feedback loops—both positive and negative—drive the behavior of the system. For instance, policies that reward innovation may foster more experimentation, while punitive accountability systems might suppress creativity and risk-taking. These feedback loops can

either create virtuous cycles, where success breeds more success, or vicious cycles, where failure perpetuates further challenges. The design and perception of these feedback mechanisms play a significant role in shaping the system's trajectory.

4. **Non-linearity:** In a CAS, change is rarely proportional to effort. Small actions can have disproportionate effects, while large investments may yield minimal outcomes. Michael Fullan's work on educational change highlights this non-linearity, proving how a single charismatic leader can drive a schoolwide transformation, whereas a multi-million-dollar reform initiative might falter if it fails to connect with the local context. This unpredictability is a hallmark of complex systems.

5. **Adaptation and Learning:** Agents within CAS learn and adapt over time. Students modify their learning strategies, teachers refine their teaching practices, and educational systems evolve in response to both internal dynamics and external pressures. Peter Senge (1990) emphasized the concept of the "learning organization," one that continuously adapts to its environment, ensuring it remains responsive to change and ready to evolve in line with emerging needs.

6. **Distributed Control:** In complex adaptive systems, no single agent or leader exerts complete control over the system. While leadership is undeniably crucial, influence is distributed across a network of relationships. Leadership in these systems is less about command and control and more about creating the right conditions for emergence. Leaders in a CAS serve as facilitators, enabling coherence and fostering an environment where positive change can arise naturally.

Recognizing educational institutions as complex adaptive systems is foundational for understanding how change works within them. It underscores the idea that schools and other educational entities are not machines that can be easily adjusted through directive actions or standardized interventions. Instead, they are evolving systems where relationships, interactions, and feedback dynamics shape the future.

However, knowing that educational institutions are CAS is just the first step. To truly transform these systems, educational leaders need practical frameworks that help identify leverage points—places within the system where small changes can lead to significant impacts. Systems thinking highlights the complexity of educational organizations and provides the tools to work with that complexity, leveraging the natural dynamics of the system to guide meaningful and sustainable change.

Applying Systems Thinking to Educational Transformation

For educational leaders, the central question is not only how to implement change but also how to create the conditions that allow for meaningful, sustainable transformation to emerge. Several systems thinking frameworks offer valuable guidance in this regard.

Peter Senge's Five Disciplines

Senge's (1990) framework includes five key disciplines: personal mastery, mental models, shared vision, team learning, and systems thinking. These disciplines foster a culture of collective learning and inquiry. In educational settings, this might involve creating PLCs where teachers reflect on their underlying assumptions (mental models), co-create visions, and experiment with new practices.

The Cynefin Framework

The Cynefin Framework, developed by Snowden and Boone (2007), is a sensemaking model that helps leaders distinguish between simple, complicated, complex, and chaotic contexts. In complex domains, such as curriculum design or equity initiatives, leaders are encouraged to probe, sense, and respond, supporting safe-to-fail experiments rather than imposing best practices.

Fullan's Drivers of Whole System Reform

Fullan (2011) identifies several key drivers that are crucial for deep, sustainable change, including capacity building, collaborative work, and pedagogy. While he emphasizes the importance of alignment in the system, he argues that coherence, ensuring that all parts of the system work together toward a shared purpose, is even more critical. Fullan cautions against accountability systems that undermine intrinsic motivation, instead advocating for a system-wide approach that aligns with the system's internal logic. His work underscores the idea that effective change efforts must not only align various components but also create a coherent, integrated system that supports long-term transformation.

Meadows' Leverage Points

Donella Meadows (1999) introduced the concept of leverage points— places within a system where a small change can lead to significant shifts. In education, one powerful leverage point is shifting the dominant narrative from one of sorting and ranking to one of equity and learning. Systems thinking urges educational leaders to focus not only on policies and practices but also on changing the mindsets and metaphors that shape educational systems.

Heifetz's Adaptive Leadership

Ronald Heifetz (1994) distinguishes between technical problems, which can be solved through expertise, and adaptive challenges, which require shifts in beliefs and values. Educational transformation often involves addressing adaptive challenges: mobilizing individuals to confront uncomfortable realities, experiment, and learn through change.

Networked Improvement Communities

Bryk et al. (2015) developed the concept of networked improvement communities (NICs), which use improvement science within collaborative networks to solve complex educational problems. NICs emphasize the importance of context-sensitive solutions and the iterative development of knowledge through shared learning and testing.

These frameworks help educational leaders move from isolated reforms to systemic transformation. They equip leaders to work *with* complexity rather than against it, reducing implementation friction and reform fatigue and fostering sustainable change.

Frameworks for Analyzing and Redesigning Educational Structures

Educational thought leaders have developed a range of frameworks to help make sense of—and improve—how schools and systems are organized. These frameworks offer more than surface-level reform strategies. They help leaders think in systems: how structural elements interact with one another, how they impact teaching and learning, and how to design more coherent, adaptive, and equitable systems.

Loose Coupling

The concept of loose coupling, originally introduced by Karl Weick (1976) and later applied to educational systems by scholars such as Richard Elmore, describes how various components of an organization may be only loosely connected. In education, this framework helps explain why structural or policy reforms often fail to affect classroom practice in meaningful ways. While administrative functions may be tightly integrated, instructional practices often remain insulated and loosely coupled from broader organizational changes (Weick, 1976; Elmore, 2004).

Elmore's (2004) research emphasizes the importance of intentionally redesigning these connections to strengthen the relationship between instructional practice and the structures meant to support it. For educational thought leaders, this means acknowledging that simply altering organizational charts or governance structures does not necessarily influence what happens in classrooms. Effective transformation requires a more strategic approach—one that focuses on aligning the relationships across system levels in ways that directly support teaching and learning.

Organizational Learning

Chris Argyris and Donald Schön helped establish the foundation for the concept of organizational learning—the idea that institutions, like schools, can adapt and grow by learning collectively. Later educational researchers, such as Karen Seashore Louis, extended this work to the school context.

Organizational learning emphasizes how schools evolve through shared reflection, continuous improvement, and the development of collective knowledge.

Richard DuFour's (2004) work on PLCs offers one of the most influential applications of this concept in education. He argued that lasting school improvement doesn't come from top-down mandates but from fostering cultures of collaboration, where educators routinely examine their practice, analyze student data, and solve problems together.

PLCs are more than structural adjustments—they represent a shift in how educators work together. By prioritizing shared responsibility for student outcomes and continuous learning, PLCs foster the kind of feedback loops and collective inquiry that drive sustained improvement. Leaders who apply this framework understand that meaningful change requires collective capacity to be built instead of enforced compliance.

Leadership

The distributed leadership framework, developed by Spillane et al. (2004), shifts attention away from individual leaders toward leadership as a system-wide function. Leadership, from this perspective, is spread across formal roles, informal relationships, and everyday interactions.

In practice, this framework helps explain why leadership transitions can derail progress: When leadership is concentrated in a few individuals, change becomes fragile. Spillane's (2006) research encourages one to redesign school structures to support shared responsibility and collaborative decision-making, making leadership a function of the system, not just a title.

Coherence

Fullan and Quinn (2016) introduced the coherence framework to address a common challenge: Schools often adopt new initiatives without aligning them with existing structures. When efforts conflict—when one initiative pushes for student-centered learning while another reinforces rigid scheduling or top-down accountability—progress is stalled.

This framework helps leaders examine how structures, processes, and priorities fit together. Fullan's work encourages the building of coherence across system layers so that strategic goals, daily routines, and resource allocations reinforce, rather than contradict, one another.

Equity

The equity framework—advanced by scholars such as Pedro Noguera (2003) and Linda Darling-Hammond (2010)—focuses on how educational structures shape access to opportunity. Course tracking, discipline policies, and funding formulas can reduce or exacerbate disparities.

Thought leaders who center equity examine who benefits from system improvements. Noguera's work highlights the need for redesigning systems so that every student, not just those already positioned for success, has access to rigorous and meaningful learning. Equity-focused structural change challenges leaders to confront who the system is serving and who it may be leaving behind.

Complexity Leadership

Uhl-Bien et al.'s (2007) complexity leadership framework, extended into education by scholars like Deborah Netolicky, brings a systems-thinking lens to leadership. It distinguishes between administrative leadership (which maintains operations), adaptive leadership (which drives change), and enabling leadership (which creates conditions for innovation).

Traditional school structures often support administrative leadership but fall short in enabling adaptive practices. Netolicky's (2021) work argues that leaders must reconfigure structures to foster creativity and responsiveness. In complex systems, leadership is less about control and more about shaping the conditions for emergence and evolution.

Using Multiple Frameworks in Tandem

No single framework fully captures the complexities of school systems. Effective educational leaders often draw on multiple lenses depending on context. Loose coupling explains why policies don't always influence classroom practice. Distributed leadership reveals how influence flows beyond job titles. Coherence highlights alignment across initiatives. Equity grounds structural change in justice. Complexity leadership guides adaptive responses in dynamic environments.

In this view, structural redesign isn't about moving boxes on an org chart. It's about recognizing the deeper patterns that shape a system's behavior—and shifting those patterns to support meaningful change.

Leading Change Across Multiple Organizational Levels

Educational systems are layered and dynamic. What happens in a single classroom is shaped by decisions made at the school, district, state, and even federal levels. Each level operates with its logic, priorities, and constraints, yet each one constantly influences others. Thought leaders who understand this complexity don't settle for surface-level fixes. They think across layers and build strategies that align and connect efforts rather than allowing them to compete or cancel each other out (Fullan, 2016).

Coherence Through Vertical Alignment

A core task of multilevel leadership is creating coherence, ensuring a shared sense of purpose across all system levels. Often, initiatives launched at the school level fall short because they are unsupported by district or state policies. Misalignment leads to frustration and burnout.

Richard Elmore's (Marion et al., 2004) concept of *reciprocal accountability* addresses this challenge directly. He argued that every level of the system must not only hold others accountable but also provide the support needed to enable change. This reciprocity is key to vertical alignment: mutual responsibility backed by meaningful resources.

Michael Fullan (2010, 2016) has also emphasized the importance of coherence. He argues that system-wide reform requires alignment across schools, districts, and governments and that leaders must build bridges between levels rather than reinforce silos. His approach moves systems beyond fragmented efforts toward unified, systemic improvement.

Communication That Connects

Cross-level communication isn't just about sharing information—it's also about building understanding. Disconnects occur when educators and leaders at different levels don't grasp each other's realities, stalling momentum.

Bryk et al. (2010) found that trust in schools is built through authentic relationships, not compliance-driven directives. Honest dialogue fosters mutual understanding and lays the groundwork for collaborative problem-solving.

Karen Seashore Louis (2006) expanded on this by showing that communication structures influence system coherence. Systems that foster two-way communication and feedback loops tend to be more aligned and effective in implementing change.

Building Capacity Across the System

Real change requires every level of the system to be well-equipped. Teachers need tools for instruction, principals need leadership development, and district leaders need systemic frameworks.

Linda Darling-Hammond (2010) has long advocated for aligned professional learning. Her work shows that improvement doesn't come from policy mandates alone but also from sustained investment in teacher and leader development across the system.

Leithwood et al. (2004) demonstrated that leadership effects cascade: district leaders shape principals, principals influence teachers, and teachers impact students. Building leadership capacity at each layer is essential for long-term system improvement.

Creating Policy That Doesn't Fight Itself

One of the most common challenges of education is conflicting policies. A state might push for project-based learning while a district enforces rigid assessment schedules. The result is confusion and compliance over innovation.

Cohen and Moffitt (2009) highlight the problem of incoherent policy design. They argue that even well-intended reforms fail if they aren't coordinated. Policy alignment, from their view, is a critical ingredient for effective change.

Paul Manna (2006) extends this thinking through his work on federalism in education. He argues that education governance requires collaboration across levels and that misalignment between local, state, and federal actors often undermines reform efforts.

Making Learning a System-Wide Habit

Good ideas often don't travel. A breakthrough in one classroom or district may never influence the broader system. Thought leaders create mechanisms that help learning scale.

Ann Lieberman (2000) emphasizes the role of teacher leadership in spreading innovation. Teacher leaders act as connectors between practice and policy, ensuring that insights from classrooms inform broader strategies.

Amy Anderson (2016) provides a complementary lens with her work on research-practice partnerships. These partnerships connect practitioners, policymakers, and researchers, enabling evidence-based innovations to circulate across the system and inform change at every level.

Change Moves at Different Speeds

Every level of the system moves at its own pace. Teachers need time to try, adapt, and refine new practices. Districts may implement structural reforms more quickly. State-level policy might change faster or remain stagnant. Change doesn't flow evenly across the system, and that's okay. What matters is thoughtful sequencing and coordination.

Michael Fullan (2010) has written extensively about the rhythms of change. His work on implementation phases emphasizes that successful reform takes timing seriously. You can't expect classroom practice to shift overnight while leaving leadership structures untouched. Change that lasts respects the unique realities and timelines of each system level.

Milbrey McLaughlin (1987) adds another important layer. Her research on policy implementation reveals how policies often morph as they travel through different layers of the system. What's designed at the top can look very different when it reaches the classroom. Thought leaders anticipate these shifts and design strategies that are flexible enough to adapt as they go.

Bringing It All Together

Leading meaningful change across educational systems requires more than isolated strategies. It calls for an integrative approach that connects coherence, capacity-building, communication, and alignment across all levels of the system. Effective leaders understand that no single framework is sufficient; instead, they draw from multiple perspectives to respond to complex and evolving contexts. This kind of leadership treats education as a system—interconnected, layered, and dynamic. Progress in one part of the system influences others, so initiatives must be designed not just for local impact but with system-wide coherence in mind. The goal is not to perfect one part of the structure but to ensure that all parts work together.

Ultimately, leading at scale means building change that flows across layers, connecting efforts rather than allowing them to compete or collapse. It's not about mastering one strategy but about orchestrating many in a way that sustains momentum and deepens impact over time.

Creating Cultures of Innovation and Continuous Improvement

Transformational change in education involves more than innovation, funding, and policies. Real and lasting improvement depends on something deeper: culture. Educational thought leaders understand that the beliefs, values, and everyday norms within a school or district often determine whether change efforts truly change practices or just check a box.

Instead of episodic fixes, they cultivate sustainable cultures where continuous learning and improvement are embedded into how people work, think, and collaborate. Below are six key approaches used by thought leaders to build these improvement-focused cultures.

Psychological Safety: Building Environments Where It's Safe to Grow

Improvement requires risk. It means asking tough questions, admitting when something isn't working, and trying new approaches that might not succeed on the first try. For that to happen, educators need to feel psychologically safe.

Amy Edmondson's (1999) foundational research on psychological safety has been widely applied in education. Her work shows how environments that encourage open voice, experimentation, and learning from failure create the conditions necessary for growth. When educators feel safe enough to take risks, the door opens for honest reflection and innovation.

Similarly, Anthony Bryk's (2010) research on relational trust shows how meaningful change is rooted in the quality of relationships. Trust enables vulnerability—without it, improvement efforts often fall short. Bryk's insights help leaders see that sustainable change starts with how people treat and respect one another.

Key Insight: Without psychological safety and trust, even the best-designed initiatives can collapse under fear or defensiveness. Creating space for openness is foundational.

Inquiry Orientation: Making Investigation a Daily Habit

In too many schools, decisions are driven by tradition or assumption. Thought leaders flip this script by embedding inquiry into the culture, making evidence-based reflection part of the everyday rhythm.

David Perkins' (2000) work on cultures of thinking emphasizes schools as communities of inquiry. His approach encourages evidence, reasoning, and shared investigation as central features of professional life.

Likewise, Elmore and City's (2007) instructional rounds adapt a medical model to schools, supporting systematic observation and analysis of teaching practice. Their work makes inquiry visible, structured, and collaborative, no longer something extra but something essential.

Key Insight: Inquiry-driven cultures help schools move from reacting to problems to proactively learning from them.

Collaborative Responsibility: Shifting From Isolation to Collective Improvement

Real change doesn't happen in silos. Educational thought leaders foster authentic collaboration, which involves shared ownership of goals and problems, not just team meetings.

Judith Warren Little (1990) distinguished between surface-level sharing and deep, joint work on teaching practice. Her research helps schools move beyond collegial niceties to genuine, purposeful collaboration.

Andy Hargreaves (2014) takes this further with collaborative professionalism, challenging leaders to replace contrived collegiality with relationships built on trust, shared purpose, and ongoing dialogue.

Key Insight: Collaboration that matters is built on mutual accountability and shared goals. It is not just a form of proximity or polite conversation.

Learning Orientation: Embracing Growth as Identity, Not Just a Strategy

In improvement-focused schools, learning doesn't stop at the students. It's part of how adults define their professional identities. Leaders build cultures where continuous development is expected, encouraged, and supported at every level.

Carol Dweck's (2006) growth mindset work, though aimed at students, has significantly influenced adult learning in schools. When educators believe they can grow, they're more likely to engage in meaningful development.

Ellie Drago-Severson (2009) expands this view through her research on adult development, showing how leaders can support educators at different developmental stages. Her work pushes beyond one-size-fits-all professional development to more responsive, supportive learning environments.

Key Insight: Growth-oriented cultures treat professional learning as core work instead of just a fix for weaknesses.

Balanced Use of Evidence: Data-Informed, Not Data-Driven

Data matters. However, if it becomes the only thing that matters, education risks becoming narrow and mechanical. Thought leaders use data as a mirror, not a hammer, helping educators see patterns and make informed decisions without reducing learning to test scores.

Paul Bambrick-Santoyo's (2010) data-driven instruction model demonstrates how schools can use data to guide teaching while keeping student understanding at the center.

Karin Chenoweth's (2007) research on high-performing, high-poverty schools shows how data can support equity and excellence when used thoughtfully. While these schools don't ignore data, they also don't let it define their purpose.

Key Insight: Evidence supports judgment—it doesn't replace it. The most effective cultures use data to inform, not dictate.

Innovation Diffusion: Spreading What Works Without Forcing It

Successful change doesn't stay confined to one classroom. Thought leaders develop cultures that spread effective practices while encouraging smart adaptation.

Everett Rogers' (2003) diffusion of innovations theory explains how new practices spread through networks over time. Leaders who understand this process can nurture innovation organically rather than forcing it top-down (Rogers, 2003).

Frank Spillane's (2006) work builds on this by showing how innovations inevitably adapt as they spread. The key isn't copying but honoring the core idea while allowing flexibility in application.

Key Insight: Innovations spread best through trusted relationships and shared ownership rather than through mandates.

Pulling It All Together

These six approaches aren't separate checkboxes. They interact, reinforce, and build on each other. The most effective educational thought leaders understand that sustainable improvement doesn't come from a single program or philosophy. It comes from shaping a culture where growth is constant, learning is communal, and change is part of the DNA.

In other words, it's not about launching the next big thing but about creating environments where the next big thing can emerge, take root, and thrive.

Addressing Resistance and Building Coalitions for Change

Alongside new policies and practices, change in education also involves navigating complex and dynamic systems. Educational thought leaders understand that resistance is not inherently negative but that it often signals valid concerns.

Understanding Resistance as a Signal

Change in education disrupts routines, challenges identities, and often introduces uncertainty. Educators, students, and families may push back, not because they reject progress but because they're trying to protect something they value or avoid repeating past failures. Thoughtful educational leaders listen for what's underneath that resistance.

Rather than labeling opposition as obstructionist or fearful, thought leaders explore the legitimate concerns it often masks—worries about vulnerable students, skepticism from failed reforms, or discomfort with losing practices that once worked. Michael Fullan (2007) calls this the "implementation dip," a predictable downturn in performance during change as people adjust. Recognizing this helps leaders reframe resistance as part of the process.

Similarly, Andy Hargreaves (2005) highlights the emotional toll of change. For many teachers, reforms feel personal, touching on professional identity, relationships, and a sense of purpose. By attending to these emotional undercurrents, Hargreaves' work helps leaders navigate resistance with empathy rather than force.

Designing Change With Educators

When people help shape an initiative, they're more likely to support it. Thought leaders know this isn't just about a buy-in but about building better solutions. Inclusive design invites educators into the change process early, tapping their insights and expertise and reducing the sense of external imposition.

Ann Lieberman's (2000) work on teacher leadership emphasizes this participatory approach. Rather than positioning teachers as passive implementers, she promotes structures where they co-create change. Likewise, Helen Timperley's (2008) research on professional learning reinforces that agency matters: when teachers are treated as professionals with valuable expertise, engagement improves and so does effectiveness.

An inclusive and participatory design helps shift the culture from "doing what we're told" to "doing what we believe in." This kind of engagement is essential for changes that last. It builds a shared vision and makes implementation feel like a collective mission.

Building Coalitions That Carry the Work Forward

Educational change doesn't move far on individual charisma alone. It needs coalitions—diverse, committed groups that carry the message and help implement ideas across systems.

John Kotter's (1996) concept of a guiding coalition highlights this. While his work is rooted in business, his insights have influenced education leaders who understand that mandates fade but movements grow. Similarly, Mark Warren's (2005) work on community organizing in schools shows how coalitions that include families, activists, and educators can push meaningful reforms forward, especially in underserved communities.

Coalitions help shift change from isolated efforts to broad-based movements. They make it easier for schools and districts to maintain momentum even when leadership changes or challenges arise and help ensure that initiatives reflect the needs of those they're meant to serve.

Honoring the Protective Function of Resistance

Sometimes, what looks like resistance is an effort to protect something people believe is still worth holding on to. Thought leaders pay attention to what educators are clinging to and ask why. Is it just a habit, or does it serve a deeper purpose?

Tyack and Cuban's (1995) concept of the *grammar of schooling* explores this. They argue that many structures persist because they meet unspoken needs, like stability or safety, even if they seem outdated. Similarly, Milbrey McLaughlin's (1987) research on reform implementation suggests that local adaptations are often about protecting students or tailoring ideas to fit complex realities, not simply rejecting reform.

Effective thought leaders don't bulldoze over these protective instincts. They learn from them. When efforts to change honor what's working and address what's not, they feel less like loss and more like evolution.

Bridging Capacity Gaps Before Demanding Change

Some resistance stems from a fear of failure. Educators may hesitate, not because they oppose change but because they don't feel prepared to implement it well. As such, thought leaders respond with support, not pressure.

Darling-Hammond et al.'s (2017) work on professional development emphasizes the need to build real capacity, not just explain new rules. They advocate for learning experiences that are ongoing, collaborative, and grounded in practice. In the same vein, Dylan Wiliam (2011) shows how formative assessment takes time and support to implement effectively.

By building capacity up front, leaders reduce anxiety and increase trust. Teachers are more likely to try something new if they believe they can succeed and if they know mistakes will be part of the learning process. The competence they develop through sustained support builds confidence, making them more willing to engage with change and better able to implement it with greater fidelity.

Making Change Make Sense

When change feels disconnected from core values or overloaded on top of existing demands, resistance grows. However, when people can see how new efforts support their purpose, they're more likely to get behind them.

Fullan and Quinn's (2016) work on coherence underscores this. Leaders who connect new initiatives to deeper educational goals help staff navigate complexity. Viviane Robinson's (2011) research on student-centered leadership echoes this: By anchoring decisions in what's best for students, leaders build stronger rationales for change.

Coherence helps educators answer, "Why are we doing this?" When the answer connects to what matters, like equity, learning, or student well-being, support grows organically. Change stops feeling like another initiative and starts feeling like a shared purpose.

Thought Leadership in Action

Addressing resistance is about understanding, involving, supporting, and aligning people instead of neutralizing dissent. The most influential educational thought leaders don't rely on a single tactic; they weave these approaches together into what we can frame as the BRIDGE Framework:

- **Build Coalitions With Shared Values:** Change gains strength when it's carried by diverse groups committed to a common purpose.

- **Respect Existing Efforts:** Honoring what's already working builds trust and helps preserve valuable practices.

- **Invite Inclusive Participation:** Lasting change is co-created, not imposed. Broad involvement builds ownership.

- **Develop People First:** Supporting professional growth lays the foundation for successful implementation.

- **Gather Insights Through Deep Listening:** Thoughtful leaders surface concerns not to dismiss them but to learn from them.

- **Elevate to Greater Purpose:** The most resonant reforms are those tied to core educational values like equity, student learning, and well-being.

In doing so, they turn potential resistance into a source of insight and create movements strong enough to transform systems.

Measuring and Evaluating Systemic Transformation

Educational thought leaders understand that systemic transformation can't be captured by simplistic evaluation tools. Traditional approaches often zero in on narrow outcomes, missing the deeper, interconnected changes across educational systems. Instead of relying on checkboxes or rigid metrics, thought leaders turn to more sophisticated ways of evaluating change—ways that reflect the complexity and dynamics of real educational environments.

Multilevel Measurement Approaches

Effective thought leadership recognizes that transformation happens at multiple levels—classroom practices, school cultures, district structures, and community partnerships. These layers interact. Change in one affects the others. So, rather than evaluating any single level in isolation, thought leaders build multilevel frameworks that track these interconnected shifts.

Patton's (2011) developmental evaluation model, though not designed solely for education, has heavily influenced how leaders assess systemic change. His approach, which is suited for complex adaptive systems, helps leaders design evaluations that are responsive, flexible, and grounded in real-time feedback. Bryk et al.'s (2015) improvement science also reflects this multilevel logic by focusing on how shifts in infrastructure and organizational support ultimately translate to better teaching and learning. These perspectives remind us that transformation is not linear, so evaluation shouldn't be either.

Mixed-Methods Evaluation

Numbers alone rarely tell the full story, and while stories can be powerful, they need structure and evidence. Educational thought leaders combine quantitative and qualitative data to capture a fuller picture of transformation.

Greene's (2007) work on mixed methods has been especially influential. She highlights how different data sources complement each other—numbers provide scope and general patterns, while narratives reveal depth and meaning. Similarly, Guskey's (2000) evaluation of professional development shows how layering data, from teacher feedback to student outcomes, offers a richer view of what's working and why. Mixed-methods approaches help leaders balance measurable results with the lived experiences behind them.

Process-Focused Evaluation

Outcomes matter, and so does the process. Educational thought leaders care deeply about how implementation unfolds. Is the initiative being adapted well to different contexts? Are schools and educators supported throughout the change?

McLaughlin's (2006) research shows how policies evolve as they're implemented on the ground. Coburn (2003) studied how innovations scale, not just in terms of reach but also in terms of depth, sustainability, and ownership. These process-oriented views help leaders move beyond the black box of inputs and outcomes to uncover the pathways of transformation.

Contribution Analysis

In education, simple cause-and-effect explanations often fall flat. Real change happens within complex systems where multiple initiatives, policies, and conditions interact. That's why thought leaders lean toward contribution-focused evaluations.

Mayne's (2001) contribution analysis and the realistic evaluation model by Pawson and Tilley (1997) both offer tools for examining how an initiative contributes to outcomes, not in isolation but in context. These approaches embrace complexity. They explore how mechanisms work differently depending on the setting. Rather than claiming to prove direct causation, they ask," What role did this effort play in the broader picture of change?"

Learning-Oriented Evaluation

Evaluation isn't just about accountability; it's also a learning tool. Thought leaders design evaluation systems that help schools, districts, and communities *learn* and *adapt.* This aligns with the principles of learning organizations, where continuous learning and improvement are at the heart of the system. By adding evaluation into these ongoing cycles of reflection and growth, educational leaders ensure that the process isn't only about assessing performance but also about fostering deeper insights that drive further progress.

Patton's (2008) utilization-focused evaluation emphasizes the need to design evaluations with the end-user in mind. What information will be used? How can it support reflection and improvement?. Bryk et al. (2015) similarly weave measurement into continuous improvement cycles, treating data not as a judgment tool but as feedback for learning. These approaches shift evaluation from a one-time report card to an ongoing dialogue. It's crucial, however, to first clarify the purpose and intent behind the evaluation before answering any subsequent questions. Understanding the "why" behind the evaluation ensures that the data gathered will be meaningful and aligned with the goals of continuous learning and improvement.

Participatory Evaluation

The most impactful evaluations are those that engage the people most affected by them. Educational thought leaders involve educators, families, students, and community members, not just as sources of data but also as co-creators of the evaluation process.

King (2004) advocates for participatory evaluation methods that increase relevance, trust, and the use of findings. House (2004), whose work connects evaluation with social justice, underscores the need to include multiple voices, especially those historically marginalized, to ensure evaluations are equitable and meaningful. These participatory approaches foster buy-in, improve implementation, and surface deeper insights.

As such, the following six approaches form the foundation of how educational thought leaders measure transformation: multilevel, mixed-methods, process-focused, contribution-based, learning-oriented, and participatory. No single method tells the whole story. But used together, they reflect the real complexity of educational systems and the nuanced, ongoing nature of change.

The most influential thought leaders don't lock themselves into a single model. They draw on multiple strategies, building evaluation frameworks that are flexible, inclusive, and deeply informed by context. In doing so, they support systems that are not just accountable but continually evolving and improving.

Case Studies of Successful Organizational Redesigns Through Thought Leadership

Examining specific cases of successful organizational redesign through thought leadership highlights how the frameworks, strategies, and approaches discussed above manifest in practice. These cases demonstrate both common patterns and distinctive applications across diverse educational contexts.

Long Beach Unified School District

If you're looking for a real-world example of how thought leadership and systems thinking can drive lasting change, Long Beach Unified School District (LBUSD) is a great one. This California district—serving a diverse, high-poverty student population—has been a national standout for over two decades. Its success wasn't built on a flashy initiative or a single superstar leader. It was built on a deep, thoughtful, and sustained systems transformation.

Leadership That Outlasts Leaders

One of the most impressive things about LBUSD is how it has managed leadership over time. Under superintendents like Carl Cohn and Christopher Steinhauser, the district created something rare: leadership that didn't fall apart with each new administration. Instead of relying on a single visionary, LBUSD built a culture of distributed leadership, developing capacity across roles and levels. More than charisma, their leadership was about shared responsibility, and this kind of leadership resilience is a hallmark of systems thinking (Harris, 2013).

Coherence Over Chaos

Another core part of LBUSD's approach is coherence. While many districts launch initiative after initiative—each one disconnected from the last—LBUSD took a different path. They built a cohesive strategy where curriculum, professional development, assessment, and leadership training were all aligned and spoke the same language. This wasn't just good planning; it was systems thinking at work. The district understood that piecemeal efforts often cancel each other out. However, when initiatives are designed to reinforce one another, you get momentum instead of burnout (Fullan, 2010).

Structure Meets Flexibility

LBUSD also struck a smart balance between direction and autonomy. The central office set clear expectations and provided robust support, but schools weren't boxed in. They had room to adapt strategies to their own context. This is what Fullan (2010) refers to as "permeable connectivity"—strong links between the central and local levels but with enough flexibility to adapt. In systems thinking, this kind of balance is critical.

Data That Drives Learning

The district's data systems also stand out. Instead of focusing solely on high-stakes test results, LBUSD built systems that helped educators make timely, targeted decisions. Teachers and administrators had access to real-time information about student progress, information they could use. This is systems thinking in the form of feedback loops. Rather than waiting for end-of-year scores, the district gave its educators the tools to make mid-course corrections to focus on learning rather than judgment.

Partnerships That Matter

LBUSD didn't try to do everything alone. They built strong, meaningful partnerships with local universities, community groups, and businesses, and they didn't keep these partners at arm's length; instead, they made them part of the core work, which speaks to another systems principle: organizations don't exist in isolation. LBUSD treated its boundaries as flexible in a way that allowed valuable knowledge and resources to flow in, not in a way that lost focus. They developed what researchers call "absorptive capacity"—the ability to take in new ideas and make them their own (Cohen & Levinthal, 1990).

High Tech High

Where LBUSD shows what it looks like to improve an existing system, High Tech High (HTH) in San Diego offers a different story—what happens when you build something entirely new from scratch with systems thinking baked in from day one? Founded by Larry Rosenstock and a team of like-minded educators, HTH set out to redesign secondary education around project-based learning, interdisciplinary teaching, real-world assessment, and deeply embedded teacher learning. It's not just a school but a living, breathing experiment in reimagining what education can be.

Built for the Learning They Wanted to See

HTH didn't try to shoehorn new ideas into old frameworks. Instead, they created structures that supported the kind of teaching and learning they believed in. This meant no traditional departments, no rigid age-grouping, and no factory-model classrooms. Students learn in multi-age groups, and teachers work in cross-disciplinary teams. This kind of structural innovation reflects a key systems thinking insight: If you want different outcomes, you need different conditions (Senge, 1990).

Learning Systems That Include the Adults

One of the most powerful things HTH did was refuse to separate student learning from adult learning. They built their own Graduate School of Education right into the school's structure. As such, teacher preparation and ongoing development happen alongside and in direct connection with what's happening in classrooms. This creates a feedback loop between teaching practice and professional growth. Teachers aren't just attending workshops; they're part of a continuous cycle of learning, inquiry, and refinement (Rosenstock, 2007).

Leadership That's Shared, Not Shelved at the Top

HTH didn't default to traditional top-down leadership. They designed governance around shared responsibility. Teacher-led teams, collaborative leadership structures, and participatory decision-making are the norm. They build leadership capacity throughout the organization. In systems thinking, that's a big deal. When leadership lives in many places, it's more sustainable, responsive, and resilient (Senge, 1990).

Making Learning Visible—Inside and Out

HTH also invested heavily in systems that make learning public and transparent. Students regularly share their work through exhibitions and digital portfolios. Teachers engage in action research and share their findings. The school doesn't just produce results—it shows the process. This approach creates what some call "organizational memory." Instead of every teacher or team starting from scratch, knowledge is captured, documented, and shared. That kind of visibility allows other schools and communities to learn from HTH's model. It's a way of scaling influence without scaling the school itself (Rosenstock, 2007).

Learning That Spills Over the Edges

HTH doesn't believe learning stops at the school's front door. Through partnerships with businesses, universities, and community groups, they've created real-world opportunities for students to do meaningful work and explore different pathways beyond high school. These partnerships reflect a systems mindset about organizational boundaries—specifically, that there don't need to be walls. By intentionally building relationships across sectors, HTH expands what's possible for its students and brings fresh ideas and resources into its learning ecosystem (Senge, 1990).

HTH didn't just tweak the system—it redesigned it, and while its model looks different from LBUSD's, the underlying principles of systems thinking, design thinking, and improvement science are just as strong. HTH shows that when thought leadership meets bold design, you can build schools that break the mold entirely without losing clarity, coherence, or results.

Similarly, LBUSD's transformation relied heavily on design thinking principles, ensuring that changes were user-centric and adaptable to real-world conditions. Both models reflect the idea that continuous improvement is key to educational innovation. It's a powerful reminder that, sometimes, the most transformative work isn't about fixing what's broken but about building something better from scratch.

Tomball Independent School District

Tomball Independent School District (TISD), located in Southeast Texas, is a powerful example of how thought leadership, systems thinking, and community engagement can work together to drive meaningful educational transformation. Unlike highly centralized systems, TISD's story is grounded in distributed leadership, local innovation, and a culture of collaborative improvement, making it an especially relevant case for those seeking change that is both systemic and sustainable.

A Shared Vision Built on Relationships

TISD's transformation didn't start with a top-down mandate. It began with intentional relationship-building and an articulated belief in "Destination Excellence," the district's guiding vision. This wasn't a generic slogan but a north star embedded into every layer of the organization. Leaders worked to align strategy with culture, ensuring that every initiative was connected to shared community values and long-term goals.

This reflects a key tenet of systems thinking: Coherence emerges not from uniformity but from alignment (Fullan & Quinn, 2016). Rather than controlling every variable, TISD created clarity of purpose and trusted its people to move in concert.

Leadership as a Distributed Capacity

Under the leadership of Dr. Martha Salazar-Zamora, TISD has cultivated a leadership model that empowers educators at all levels. Principals, teacher leaders, instructional coaches, and district administrators are seen not as implementers but as co-leaders of transformation. The emphasis is on developing leadership as a shared organizational capacity, not a role held by a few at the top (Spillane, 2006).

This distributed approach enables faster adaptation, greater ownership, and more context-sensitive decision-making, which is an essential feature of systems thinking in action.

Learning-Centric Design and Feedback Loops

TISD's approach to innovation is deeply informed by learning science and continuous improvement. Rather than imposing fixed solutions, the district engages in ongoing cycles of inquiry, feedback, and redesign (Bryk et al., 2015). This is evident in their focus on student-centric learning environments, real-time data use, and collaborative professional development.

Feedback isn't reserved for summative evaluations; it's built into the daily rhythms of the organization. Teachers and leaders engage in reflective practice, supported by systems that help them iterate and improve. These feedback loops mirror the core of systems thinking: using real-time learning to steer the system adaptively (Senge, 2006).

Strong Community Partnerships

TISD's success is rooted not just in what happens inside schools, but in how schools interact with the wider community. The district has forged deep partnerships with parents, local businesses, higher education institutions, and civic organizations. These aren't peripheral connections but those central to the district's strategy (Wenger-Trayner & Wenger-Trayner, 2015).

This kind of boundary-crossing collaboration speaks to another systems principle: Organizations are open systems, not closed silos. TISD's ability to draw in external perspectives and resources enhances its capacity to innovate and serve its students more holistically.

Intentional Structures That Support

TISD offers a smart balance between structure and flexibility. There are clear frameworks in place around curriculum, instructional practice, and professional growth, but those frameworks are intentionally designed to support adaptability. Schools have space to make strategic choices, but those choices are aligned with district-wide goals (Fullan & Quinn, 2016).

This mirrors Michael Fullan's concept of "permeable connectivity": the right mix of direction and local autonomy. It's the kind of structural thinking that prevents fragmentation without falling into rigidity.

A Culture of Trust and Empowerment

Perhaps most importantly, TISD has built a culture rooted in trust between schools and families, teachers and administrators, and the district and the broader community. Change doesn't feel imposed. It feels shared.

This kind of cultural groundwork is often overlooked in reform efforts, yet it's foundational. Systems change doesn't happen without the human relationships that hold it together (Senge et al., 2012; Bryk & Schneider, 2002). TISD understands that, and their progress is proof.

Connecting the Case Studies

The three case studies—LBUSD, HTH, and TISD—illustrate distinct yet equally powerful ways in which systems thinking can be used to design meaningful educational transformations. While they differ in structure, geography, and governance, each represents a *Coherent District*, one in which strategy, culture, leadership, and practice are integrated into a unified system of improvement.

These districts are more than collections of schools. They function as coherent learning organizations. Places where purpose is clear, feedback loops are strong, and leadership is distributed. The following shared themes emerge:

- **Coherence across system elements:** Whether through policy alignment, instructional models, or leadership pipelines, each system links its components so they reinforce one another instead of going in different directions.

- **Balance between direction and adaptation:** Clear goals and strategic frameworks guide the work, but there's also space for local problem-solving and innovation. Flexibility is an intentional design feature.

- **Distributed leadership:** Leadership isn't concentrated in a few roles. Teachers, principals, and central office staff all contribute to shaping the system. Efforts to change are stronger and more sustainable because they're shared.

- **Feedback and continuous learning:** These systems don't rely on one-time fixes. They embed structures for reflection, data-informed iteration, and real-time learning. Feedback is part of the routine.

- **Open boundaries:** Whether through community partnerships, research-practice collaborations, or engagement with industries, each system is intentionally porous. Ideas and energy move in and out, keeping the work dynamic and connected.

These case studies make it clear: Systems thinking is a design strategy for real transformation. It allows educational leaders to look beneath surface-level symptoms and engage with the underlying structures and mental models shaping their schools.

When thought leaders adopt systems thinking, they don't just intervene in broken processes—they redesign the systems that gave rise to them in the first place. That's what sets coherent districts apart, and that's how they become engines of deep, sustained change.

Looking Ahead

In the next chapters, we'll explore how systems thinking interacts with other dimensions of educational thought leadership, from digital transformation to content creation and edupreneurship to collaborative networks. As we move forward, you'll see how these ideas can work together to fuel sustainable, meaningful change.

The systems thinking lens gives us the foundation to understand complexity so we can design for lasting impact. Whether you're working within a school, leading a network, shaping policy, or sparking new conversations, this perspective can help you move from insight to action.

Chapter 5:
Digital Transformation and
Educational Thought Leadership

The digital revolution has dramatically reshaped the world of education. It has brought with it a mix of exciting possibilities and complex challenges, from the introduction of classroom technologies and the rise of learning management systems to the growth of data analytics and the expansion of artificial intelligence (AI). Digital tools have changed not just how educators teach but also how students learn and how institutions function as a whole.

This transformation requires new forms of thought leadership— leadership that understands the intersection of technology and education, that envisions how digital tools can enhance learning rather than automating it, and that can guide thoughtful implementation that integrates technology, pedagogy, and organizational culture.

In this chapter, we'll explore how digital transformation intersects with educational thought leadership. We'll look at how forward-thinking educational leaders have conceptualized the role of technology in the learning process. We'll also explore how they've navigated the fine line between technophobia (fear of technology) and techno-utopianism (overenthusiasm for technology) while tackling the ethical dilemmas that arise with digital tools. Through both theoretical insights and real-world examples, this chapter will show how effective thought leadership can guide the use of technology in education, pushing beyond technical efficiency to ensure it serves meaningful educational purposes.

Conceptualizing Technology's Role in Learning and Teaching

Educational thought leaders have developed various frameworks to understand how technology integrates into learning and teaching. These frameworks move beyond the simplistic question of whether technology "works," focusing instead on aligning technological approaches with educational goals, contexts, and pedagogical philosophies. They serve as valuable tools for integrating technology in ways that prioritize educational values over mere technical features.

Substitution, Augmentation, Modification, and Redefinition

We can analyze how technology can transform educational practices using Puentedura's Substitution, Augmentation, Modification, and Redefinition (SAMR) model. It distinguishes between uses of technology that enhance existing practices (substitution and augmentation) and those that transform the learning experience (modification and redefinition). This model explains why many technology initiatives fail to create significant educational change when technology merely substitutes traditional tools without altering the learning process. Educators who understand SAMR recognize that the value of technology lies in reshaping the learning experience, not just its presence in the classroom.

Connected Learning

The Connected Learning framework, developed by Ito et al. (2013), examines how digital tools can bridge different learning contexts. It focuses on connecting formal and informal learning, school and community activities, and academic and interest-driven pursuits to create integrated learning environments. This perspective highlights the limitations of technology confined solely to the classroom, emphasizing the importance of connecting learning across various contexts to engage students deeply. Educators who understand connected learning recognize that technology's true value lies in its ability to connect disparate parts of students' lives.

Knowledge Building

Scardamalia and Bereiter (2012) developed the Knowledge Building framework to conceptualize how digital technologies can support collaborative knowledge creation. It encourages viewing students as active contributors to knowledge, emphasizing collective cognitive responsibility and progressive dialogue to support deeper learning processes. This focus explains why technology applications that emphasize content delivery often fall short of achieving real learning gains. Educators who adopt this perspective see technology as a tool to foster collective learning and critical thinking, not just content absorption.

Computational Thinking

Wing (2006) introduced the concept of Computational Thinking, highlighting the importance of thinking skills that apply broadly across disciplines, not just in computer science. This approach teaches students to decompose problems, recognize patterns and abstract complex ideas, and develop algorithmic solutions. It explains why technology-focused education targeting specific tools quickly becomes outdated. Educators who embrace this framework understand that technology education should develop broad thinking skills beyond vocational training.

Critical Digital Literacy

Lankshear and Knobel (2006) developed the Critical Digital Literacy framework, emphasizing the need for students to critically assess the digital world. It involves understanding how digital tools work and their underlying power structures, ideological assumptions, and social consequences. This perspective explains why technology education focusing solely on technical skills doesn't adequately prepare students for the digital world. Educators in this field emphasize teaching digital literacy that includes evaluation and critical thinking, not just functional skills.

Networked Educational Systems and Technology Framework

I developed the Networked Educational Systems and Technology (NEST) framework to offer educators and institutions a comprehensive approach to digital transformation in education. The framework provides a structured yet flexible pathway for integrating advanced technologies, strong pedagogy, and digital literacy through five core components:

- **Knowledge Integration Sphere:** This component brings together digital skills and traditional subject matter, helping students develop both simultaneously.

- **Transformative Implementation Ladder:** It supports educators as they move from using basic digital tools to more advanced technologies, making the transition more approachable and sustainable.

- **Connected Learning Ecosystem:** This element connects classroom learning with online resources and real-world applications, expanding the boundaries of traditional learning environments.

- **Cognitive Development Framework:** It focuses on building essential thinking skills like computational thinking and problem-solving, skills students need to navigate complexity across disciplines.

- **Critical Evaluation Layer:** This ensures that technology integration remains aligned with learning goals through regular assessment and responsive feedback loops.

NEST's balance between embracing innovation and maintaining a focus on student learning sets it apart. While incorporating cutting-edge technologies, the framework ensures that technology enhances rather than replaces quality teaching. In districts using similar approaches, teachers report greater confidence in integrating digital tools, and students develop both technical and critical thinking abilities.

Guiding Implementation: Beyond Technophobia and Techno-Utopianism

When bringing technology into education, the key is finding the sweet spot—avoiding both the knee-jerk rejection of digital tools and the overly optimistic belief that technology is a quick fix or the ultimate solution to every problem. The best educational thought leaders have figured out how to navigate these extremes by focusing on thoughtful, purposeful approaches to tech integration. They know that technology can be a powerful ally in education, but only if it's used the right way and with the right intentions.

Start With the Why

Effective technology integration begins with aligning digital tools to clear learning goals. As Jonassen (2006) emphasizes, technology should serve to enhance students' thinking and learning processes. Similarly, the Understanding by Design (UbD) framework advocates for backward planning from desired learning outcomes, ensuring that instructional methods and tools are purposefully selected to achieve those goals (Wiggins & McTighe, 2011).

Put Teachers at the Center

Teachers play a pivotal role in the successful implementation of technology in education. Darling-Hammond et al. (2017) highlight the importance of providing teachers with the autonomy to adapt technological tools to their unique classroom contexts, fostering innovation and responsiveness to student needs. Rogers (2013) further supports this view, suggesting that when teachers are empowered to shape technology use, they can create more effective and meaningful learning experiences.

Consider the Context

Technology does not function uniformly across all educational settings. Warschauer (2004) notes that the effectiveness of technological interventions can vary significantly based on factors such as community resources, student demographics, and existing infrastructure. Mitra (2016) also emphasizes that understanding the specific context of each classroom is essential, as technology's impact is influenced by the unique needs and circumstances of the learners.

Take It Slow

Transforming educational practices through technology is a gradual process. Cuban (2016) observes that successful technology integration often involves incremental changes that build upon existing practices. Rogers' (2003) Diffusion of Innovations theory also supports the idea that adoption of new technologies follows a phased approach, requiring time and adaptation to achieve meaningful change.

Let the Evidence Guide You

Decisions about the use of technology in education should be grounded in empirical evidence. Means (n.d.) advocates for the use of research-based strategies to inform technology integration, ensuring that tools are selected based on their demonstrated effectiveness. Hattie's (2009) synthesis of educational research further underscores the importance of evidence-based practices, highlighting the impact of various interventions on student achievement.

Make Sure Everyone Has a Fair Shot

Equity is a critical consideration in the implementation of educational technology. Reich (2019) discusses the "second digital divide," where disparities exist not only in access to technology but also in the quality of its use among different student populations. Watkins (n.d.) emphasizes the need to address these inequities, ensuring that all students, regardless of background, have the opportunity to benefit from technological advancements in education.

Putting It All Together

What makes these approaches so powerful is that they're multidimensional. The best educational thought leaders don't just pick one strategy and stick with it; they blend these elements to create a well-rounded, thoughtful approach to technology implementation. They understand that technology is not a one-size-fits-all solution but a tool that, when used wisely, can transform education. The goal is to focus on purpose, support teachers, consider context, take gradual steps, rely on evidence, and most importantly, ensure that everyone has a fair chance to succeed.

Addressing Ethical Questions in Educational Technology

Integrating technology into education necessitates a thoughtful examination of the ethical implications involved. Rather than uncritically embracing new tools or dismissing them due to potential risks, educational leaders advocate for frameworks that align technological adoption with core educational values, student development, and societal responsibilities.

Privacy: Who Owns the Data?

A significant ethical concern in educational technology is student data privacy. Modern digital learning platforms often collect extensive data, ranging from academic performance to behavioral patterns. While such data can enhance personalized learning, it also poses risks related to misuse or exploitation.

Julie E. Cohen (2013) emphasizes that privacy transcends individual preferences, serving as a safeguard for fundamental human and social rights. Her perspective urges educational institutions to critically assess data collection practices, ensuring they uphold students' rights and freedoms. Building upon this, Elana Zeide (2015) focuses on student data governance, advocating for policies that protect student information while enabling beneficial educational outcomes.

Autonomy: How Much Control Should Tech Have?

Educational technologies increasingly influence student decisions through algorithms and gamified elements. While these features can guide learning, they may also undermine student autonomy.

Cathy O'Neil (2016) discusses how algorithms, often perceived as neutral, can perpetuate biases and reinforce inequalities if not properly scrutinized. Audrey Watters (2015) further critiques the impact of educational technologies on agency, highlighting how they can shift power dynamics within educational settings.

Equity: Does Everyone Have Equal Access?

The digital divide remains a pressing issue, with unequal access to technology exacerbating existing educational disparities.

Kentaro Toyama (2011) introduces the concept of "technology as amplifier," suggesting that technology tends to magnify existing inequalities instead of mitigating them. Tressie McMillan Cottom (2012) examines how technological implementations in education can reinforce systemic inequities, particularly when profit motives overshadow educational equity.

Attention: How Does Tech Affect Focus?

While technology can enhance engagement, it may also detract from students' ability to maintain sustained attention and engage in deep learning.

James Williams (2018) explores the ethics of attention in the digital age, arguing that persuasive design in technology can undermine users' autonomy and focus. Maryanne Wolf (2018) investigates how digital reading environments affect cognitive processes, noting a decline in deep reading capabilities among students accustomed to digital formats. These thought leaders not only raise critical concerns about how educational technology might encourage distraction over deep intellectual engagement but also offer strategies and insights to help mitigate these effects. Their work guides educators in designing and selecting technologies that support sustained attention and cognitive depth.

Dependency: Are We Losing Our Cognitive Skills?

The convenience of technology raises concerns about over-reliance and the potential erosion of essential cognitive skills.

Nicholas Carr (2010) contends that excessive dependence on digital tools can lead to superficial thinking and diminished concentration. Conversely, Barbara Rogoff (1990) emphasizes the role of guided participation, suggesting that technology, when used appropriately, can support cognitive development through collaborative learning experiences.

Commercialization: Who's Behind the Tech?

The involvement of private companies in educational technology prompts questions about the alignment of commercial interests with educational goals.

Joel Spring (2012) critiques the influence of corporate entities in shaping educational policies and technologies, cautioning against the commodification of education. Audrey Watters (2015) also highlights the potential conflicts arising from profit-driven motives in the development and implementation of educational technologies.

Bringing It All Together

The best educational thought leaders know that these ethical issues—privacy, autonomy, equity, attention, dependency, and commercialization—are interconnected. They don't just pick one issue to focus on; they see the whole picture and understand that these challenges often overlap, requiring a nuanced and balanced approach.

The ethical frameworks these leaders develop go beyond easy answers, aiming to create solutions that respect student rights, promote equity, and align with the educational mission. Rather than just accepting or rejecting tech, they encourage us to think critically about how it fits into the broader goals of education.

Case Studies in Digital Transformation Through Thought Leadership

Examining specific cases of digital transformation through thought leadership reveals how frameworks, approaches, and ethical considerations can manifest in practice. These cases highlight both common patterns and distinctive applications across diverse global educational contexts.

Khan Academy's Evolution

Khan Academy's evolution from a collection of YouTube tutorials to a sophisticated learning platform highlights how thought leadership can guide the development of educational technology. The organization's focus on accessibility, learning science, learner agency, and ethical concerns shaped its transition from content delivery to an adaptive learning environment.

Commitment to Accessibility

From its inception, Khan Academy prioritized making learning resources accessible to as many learners as possible. The platform focused on removing financial, geographical, and institutional barriers to education. This commitment to equity prevented the platform from becoming a tool exclusive to a privileged few, ensuring broad access to high-quality educational materials (Khan Academy, 2023).

Integration of Learning Science

While initially offering simple video tutorials, Khan Academy progressively incorporated evidence-based learning strategies such as mastery learning and knowledge mapping. This shift transformed the platform from a passive content repository into an adaptive, research-based learning environment.

Balance Between Algorithmic Guidance and Learner Agency

Khan Academy developed sophisticated algorithms to guide students through personalized learning paths while allowing substantial learner control over their pace and trajectory. This balance between structure and freedom empowered learners to take ownership of their educational journeys.

Integration With Social and Classroom Learning

Initially a self-study resource, Khan Academy gradually incorporated features for classroom use, enabling teachers to track student progress and facilitate collaborative learning. This evolution reflected an understanding of the importance of social learning, moving beyond individual study to include group interactions.

Ethical Data Practices

As the platform expanded, Khan Academy developed careful data governance policies, balancing the use of learning data to improve personalized experiences with protecting user privacy. This ethical approach to data ensured that student information was handled responsibly while still providing benefits for personalized learning.

Khan Academy's success demonstrates how thoughtful leadership can guide the evolution of educational technology toward increasingly sophisticated and student-centered applications.

Fundación Proacceso (Mexico): Bridging the Digital Divide Through Community-Centered Innovation

Fundación Proacceso, a non-profit organization in Mexico, established the Red de Innovación y Aprendizaje (RIA), a network of digital inclusion centers providing educational tools to underserved communities. The initiative prioritizes accessibility, lifelong learning, and community empowerment.

Commitment to Community Access

RIA centers are strategically located in marginalized areas, offering low-cost courses in areas like digital literacy, English, math, and science. This approach directly addresses geographic and socioeconomic barriers to learning (Fundación Proacceso, 2023).

Focus on Lifelong Learning

The RIA centers cater to a wide demographic, including children, youth, and adults. By embracing lifelong learning principles, the initiative supports diverse learners throughout their educational journeys.

Integration With Local Needs

The centers were designed in consultation with local communities to ensure alignment with real-world needs. This localized approach supports relevance, cultural responsiveness, and stronger engagement.

Sustainability and Design Innovation

Fundación Proacceso invested in sustainable architectural design and infrastructure to ensure that centers were both environmentally responsible and inviting learning spaces.

Impact Measurement

Through longitudinal research, RIA centers have demonstrated measurable educational outcomes, improved academic performance, and increased digital fluency, underscoring the initiative's efficacy.

The Quantitative Undergraduate Biology Education and Synthesis (USA)

Advancing STEM education through open educational resources, the Quantitative Undergraduate Biology Education and Synthesis (QUBES) project exemplifies digital transformation through scholarly collaboration and open-access platforms.

Accessibility to Professional Resources

QUBES (2023) provides open educational resources (OER), including customizable teaching modules and interactive tools, to lower faculty barriers to reform in undergraduate biology education.

Community-Centered Learning Design

QUBES fosters professional learning communities, enabling educators to co-develop, revise, and disseminate curricular materials. This participatory approach nurtures shared expertise and pedagogical innovation.

Support for Authentic Science Learning

By offering tools and content aligned with real-world scientific practices, QUBES promotes authentic learning experiences that prepare students for research and careers in STEM.

Scalable Dissemination Models

Through partnerships with universities, societies, and government agencies, QUBES scales its impact without compromising quality or accessibility.

Evidence-Informed Practice

Evaluation and feedback loops are central to QUBES' model. Resources are continuously refined based on instructor and student input, allowing for iterative improvement.

Geekie (Brazil)

A form of personalized learning to address educational inequities, Geekie, an educational technology company in Brazil, developed a dynamic, personalized learning platform aimed at improving outcomes for under-resourced students.

Commitment to Equity

Geekie (2023) targets low-income students, many of whom lack access to high-quality instruction. The platform's adaptive approach helps level the playing field by customizing content to individual learners.

Personalized Learning Paths

Using learning analytics, Geekie identifies gaps in knowledge and creates individualized learning trajectories. Students can work at their own pace, improving engagement and outcomes.

Teacher Integration

Geekie provides educators with dashboards and tools to track student progress, making it easier to support personalized instruction within the classroom.

Focus on Measurable Outcomes

Geekie's model emphasizes data-driven accountability. Pilot programs have shown improved performance in national exams and reduced dropout rates, supporting the efficacy of its adaptive approach.

Blended and Remote Learning Models

The platform supports both blended learning in schools and independent learning at home, increasing its flexibility and reach, particularly during disruptions like the COVID-19 pandemic.

What We Can Learn

These case studies illustrate how thought leadership drives meaningful digital transformation in education. While the settings vary, from classrooms in the US to innovations in countries like Mexico and Brazil, all reflect a shared set of guiding principles that can inform efforts here in the US:

- **Educational Purpose Over Technological Features:** In every case, technology serves well-defined learning goals instead of being an end in itself.

- **Balance Between Structure and Flexibility:** Initiatives maintain coherence while allowing room for student agency and personalized learning.

- **Integration With Broader Educational Processes:** Technology isn't isolated; it's embedded in systems of instruction, curriculum, and assessment.

- **Equity and Inclusion:** Each approach seeks to reduce barriers and meet the needs of diverse learners, particularly those historically underserved.

- **Continuous Evolution Based on Evidence:** These programs adapt over time, using feedback and research to refine practices and ensure sustainability.

Together, these global patterns reinforce the power of digital thought leadership to ensure that technology enhances core educational values. By linking innovation with educational wisdom, leaders around the world are transforming learning in ways that are accessible, responsive, and relevant. These lessons offer valuable direction as we shape the future of education in the US.

Chapter 6:
Content Creation and Thought Leadership in Education

In today's world, where information is everywhere, the ability to create engaging, meaningful content has become a hallmark of educational thought leadership. Whether through scholarly articles, practitioner-focused pieces, keynote speeches, or social media posts, educational thought leaders stand out for the strength of their ideas and their ability to share those ideas in ways that connect with diverse audiences. From books to blogs, effective content creation is often the key to transforming valuable insights into widespread influence.

This chapter dives into the link between content creation and educational thought leadership. It explores how leading educational thought leaders develop unique voices, adapt their message to different platforms and audiences, and maintain intellectual integrity while doing so. By examining both theoretical frameworks and real-world examples, this chapter shows how thoughtful content strategies can elevate ideas, broadening their reach and deepening their impact across educational communities.

Developing a Distinctive Voice and Communication Approach

Educational thought leaders' unique communication styles make their work recognizable and memorable, often becoming a hallmark of their thought leadership. These distinctive voices reflect both conscious stylistic choices and deeper intellectual orientations—ways of framing questions, structuring arguments, employing evidence, and engaging with audiences.

Over time, these approaches will become signature elements across different publications and presentations. Understanding how educational thought leaders develop these unique communication strategies sheds light on the connection between content creation and thought leadership.

Characteristic Framing Approaches

One of the key ways thought leaders differentiate themselves is through the way they frame educational questions and challenges. For example, some consistently examine issues through an equity lens, considering how different student populations are affected by educational practices (Ladson-Billings, 1994). Others may use a historical framing, placing current challenges within a larger, longitudinal context (Tyack & Cuban, 1995).

Systems thinking is another popular approach, where the focus is on the interconnections between various elements of the education system (Senge, 1990). These consistent approaches not only reflect the thought leader's intellectual identity but also provide readers with a framework for understanding educational issues more profoundly.

Howard Gardner's (1983) work, particularly through his theory of multiple intelligences, illustrates this well. He consistently applies this framework to a variety of educational topics, from assessment practices to curriculum design, creating a recognizable intellectual signature across different subjects. Similarly, Gloria Ladson-Billings (1995) often uses critical race theory to examine educational dynamics, adding depth and coherence to her work on topics ranging from teacher preparation to literacy development.

Characteristic Narrative Approaches

Beyond framing, thought leaders often develop distinctive narrative techniques, which influence how they tell the story of educational practice. Some use detailed classroom vignettes to immerse readers in specific teaching moments, others weave biographical narratives to trace the development of ideas over time, and others still focus on case studies of organizational change, helping readers understand how theories manifest in real-world settings. These storytelling techniques create a unique experience for readers, making abstract ideas more tangible and relatable (Schmoker, 2006).

Mike Schmoker (2006) often uses real classroom examples to illustrate effective educational practices, grounding his theoretical discussions in the realities of day-to-day teaching. Similarly, Deborah Meier (1995) employs extended narratives to show how educational ideas play out over time in school development processes. These approaches make her work engaging while emphasizing the importance of implementation in the development of educational ideas.

Characteristic Evidence Approaches

The way educational thought leaders support their arguments also plays a key role in shaping their distinctiveness. Some leaders rely on quantitative data, using statistical analyses to conclude educational practices (Hattie, 2009). Others prefer qualitative methods, using detailed descriptions of classroom interactions or student experiences (Paley, 1990). Some may focus on historical analysis, tracing the evolution of educational practices over time (Tyack & Cuban, 1995). These consistent methods of evidence gathering become a hallmark of their intellectual credibility.

John Hattie's (2009) work, particularly his use of meta-analysis, demonstrates a characteristic evidence-based approach. By synthesizing data from numerous studies, he provides an empirical foundation for his arguments about effective teaching strategies. In contrast, Vivian Gussin Paley (1990) uses qualitative observational data to build her insights into early childhood education, offering a rich, descriptive view of how children interact in classroom settings.

Characteristic Structural Approaches

Thought leaders also develop distinctive ways of organizing their arguments. Some prefer a problem-solution structure, clearly defining educational challenges before presenting solutions. Others may begin with theoretical concepts before moving to practical applications or use a narrative-analytical approach, telling stories first and then extracting lessons. These organizational patterns create a predictable reading experience that helps audiences engage with and understand complex ideas.

Robert Marzano's (2007) work often follows a hierarchical structure, breaking down complex educational issues into clear categories and subcategories. This approach provides clarity and makes his ideas more accessible. Parker Palmer (1998) tends to structure his writing through a progression that starts with personal experience, moves into philosophical reflection, and ends with practical application. This approach provides an integrative and engaging structure that resonates with readers on multiple levels.

Characteristic Stylistic Approaches

The writing style itself is another signature of thought leadership. Some leaders write in formal, scholarly prose, using complex sentence structures and specialized vocabulary. Others take a more conversational approach, opting for accessible language and direct address. Others still may use poetic or metaphorical language, creating a rhythm that enhances the emotional impact of their work (Rose, 2009).

Nel Noddings (2003), for example, uses thoughtful, measured prose that aligns with the care ethics she advocates. This stylistic choice allows her writing to embody the very principles she is promoting. Similarly, Mike Rose (2009) uses richly descriptive language to capture the experiences of marginalized students, giving his writing a humanistic quality that connects with readers on a personal level.

Characteristic Engagement Approaches

Finally, thought leaders engage with alternative perspectives in unique ways. Some consistently integrate multiple viewpoints into their work, creating a dialogic approach that reflects diverse perspectives (Hooks, 1994). Others may use critical frameworks to analyze opposing arguments in depth, or they might synthesize different perspectives into new, integrated ideas. These engagement strategies create a distinctive intellectual texture and allow thought leaders to position themselves within broader educational debates.

David Berliner's (2006) work in educational policy, for instance, often includes thorough and direct engagement with counterarguments, adding depth and rigor to his analyses. Similarly, Bell Hooks (1994) incorporates diverse voices within her writing, ensuring that multiple perspectives are represented. This approach enriches her work and fosters inclusive discourse.

Building a Distinctive Thought Leadership Voice

All of these dimensions—framing, narrative, evidence, structure, style, and engagement—come together to form the distinctive voice of an educational thought leader. The most influential thought leaders manage to develop consistency in these areas without falling into formulaic repetition. Their voices become recognizable, yet remain flexible enough to evolve as they address new topics and contexts.

This ability to create a unique intellectual and stylistic signature is essential to thought leadership. It allows thought leaders to shape how others engage with educational issues, not just by presenting ideas but also by providing communication models that influence the broader discourse. Through their distinctive voices, these leaders leave an indelible mark on the field of education.

Adapting Content for Different Platforms and Audiences

Educational thought leaders excel at generating meaningful ideas and adapting them across varied communication contexts. Their ability to move fluidly between platforms, tailor messages to distinct audiences, and present ideas at varying levels of complexity without losing their core message is central to their influence (Beetham & Sharpe, 2013). This kind of multidimensional adaptability allows thought leaders to sustain intellectual integrity while expanding their reach and relevance.

Platform-Specific Content Strategies

Different platforms come with unique rhythms, expectations, and limits. Educational thought leaders adjust accordingly, recognizing that a dense academic article, a blog post, and a TED-style talk all require different framing and tone.

Linda Darling-Hammond (2017) exemplifies this skill. Her research on teacher preparation appears in peer-reviewed journals, policy briefs, practitioner-friendly resources, and keynote presentations, each shaped by the norms and needs of the target platform yet unified by her research-backed principles.

Similarly, Dylan Wiliam (2011) adapts his work on formative assessment across media, ranging from academic publications to interactive workshops and tweets, offering different access points for educators without diluting the rigor of his ideas.

Audience-Centered Adaptation

Reaching different audiences involves more than simplifying content; you need to understand the values, roles, and concerns of each group. Whether researchers, teachers, administrators, policymakers, or parents, they all have different perspectives.

Carol Ann Tomlinson's (2001) work on differentiated instruction shifts subtly depending on whether she's addressing teachers with practical classroom strategies or administrators seeking scalable implementation frameworks.

Richard Elmore (2004) uses a similar approach, tailoring his discussions on instructional improvement to suit researchers' needs for theory, leaders' needs for systems thinking, and practitioners' needs for immediate application.

Progressive Complexity Strategies

Thought leaders often present their work at varying levels of depth. They design accessible entry points for general audiences and deeper explorations for those seeking more complexity.

Howard Gardner's (2011) theory of multiple intelligences spans introductory texts for general readers and technical discussions that address neurobiological underpinnings and academic critiques.

Likewise, John Hattie's (2009) work on visible learning is available in simplified summaries, mid-level practitioner texts, and advanced statistical papers, each offering access to his research at a different level.

Temporal Adaptation Over Idea Lifecycles

Thought leaders also adapt their content over time, updating their work as feedback, implementation challenges, and new evidence emerge.

Wiggins and McTighe (2005) evolved their UbD framework over years of dialogue with educators, revising and expanding the model to address real-world questions and critiques.

Robert Marzano's (2007) early research on effective instruction has similarly grown into a body of work that includes implementation tools and cross-disciplinary applications.

Media-Specific Communication Approaches

Thought leaders choose media formats—text, audio, video, or visuals—based not on trendiness but on communicative purpose.

Ken Robinson's (2015) advocacy for creativity in education took different forms: TED Talks rich in visual humor, books with strong narrative and metaphors, and animated videos that visualized systemic change.

Michael Fullan's (2016) work similarly spans static texts, interactive digital tools, and video case studies, each chosen for its potential to illuminate a specific concept or practice.

Cultural Responsiveness Across Contexts

Cultural adaptation is key to ensuring that messages resonate globally. Thought leaders tailor language, references, and case examples to align with local values and educational systems.

Andy Hargreaves (2003) adjusts his change management frameworks when speaking to U.S., European, and Asian audiences, choosing culturally grounded examples while preserving the core architecture of his thinking.

Yong Zhao (2009) likewise adapts his discussions of innovation and global competitiveness to different national contexts, drawing on local data and cultural references to support his ideas.

Adapting content for different platforms and audiences isn't about branding or simplification but about intellectual agility. Educational thought leaders like Darling-Hammond, Wiliam, Gardner, and Zhao don't just change how they say things but thoughtfully recalibrate their strategies to ensure that their messages are both rigorous and resonant, regardless of the context. This multidimensional adaptability is a hallmark of impactful thought leadership, allowing it to move across boundaries, bridge communities, and evolve.

Building Content Ecosystems and Extending Influence

Thought leadership is rarely built on isolated publications or one-off presentations. Thought leaders create *content ecosystems*—networks of interconnected works that reinforce and extend core ideas across contexts, media, and audiences. These ecosystems allow for both depth and accessibility, encouraging long-term engagement rather than passive consumption.

Content Progression Strategies

One hallmark of effective content ecosystems is *developmental progression*. Thought leaders intentionally design pathways through their work, beginning with introductory content, moving through intermediate engagement, and culminating in advanced treatments of core ideas.

Robert Marzano (2007) exemplifies this approach. His widely used instructional strategies appear in entry-level articles, practitioner-oriented guides, and advanced theoretical analyses. Each level builds on the last, enabling educators to move from basic awareness to deep implementation and understanding.

Carol Dweck's (2006) work on mindset theory follows a similar arc. Her early presentations introduced the fixed and growth mindset distinction in accessible terms, while her later works explored complex neurological bases and context-specific challenges. This progression accommodates a diverse readership while encouraging sustained learning over time.

By designing content with different levels of complexity, thought leaders support both broad dissemination and scholarly rigor. They acknowledge that engagement cannot mean the same thing for all and create space for audiences to grow intellectually alongside their ideas.

Content Diversification Strategies

Effective ecosystems also reflect *diversity of format and focus*. Rather than presenting their ideas through a single genre or lens, thought leaders develop theoretical foundations, practical tools, contextual case studies, and reflective analyses.

Howard Gardner's (2011) theory of multiple intelligences spans conceptual works, instructional guides, school case studies, and philosophical explorations. This diversified treatment allows different audiences to connect with the theory in ways most relevant to their needs and roles.

Michael Fullan's (2016) work on educational change takes a similar approach. He develops conceptual models, outlines practical strategies, and presents leadership philosophies together, constructing a more holistic vision of transformation.

This strategy deepens understanding by recognizing the multifaceted nature of complex educational issues. Theoretical insights gain practical resonance, and pragmatic actions remain connected to larger conceptual frameworks.

Collaborative Extension Strategies

Educational thought leaders rarely operate alone. Through *collaborative extension*, they co-author publications, curate edited volumes, work with practitioners on field-based projects, and welcome derivative interpretations of their core ideas.

David Perkins' (2009) thinking routines extend through co-authored research, practitioner partnerships, and adaptations across domains, from early childhood to workplace training. These collaborations not only expand his reach but enhance the relevance of his ideas.

Ann Lieberman, known for her work on teacher leadership, consistently partners with educators, curates diverse perspectives, and supports school-based applications. Her influence grows not by replicating her ideas but by allowing others to adapt and evolve them (Lieberman & Miller, 2008).

Collaboration strengthens thought leadership by embedding ideas in real-world contexts and distributing the work of refinement and dissemination across broader intellectual communities.

Multimedia Extension Strategies

Modern educational leaders understand that the *medium matters*. A book and a podcast don't just differ in length or tone but offer fundamentally different ways of engaging with an idea.

Ken Robinson's (2015) advocacy for creativity in education spanned written works, animated talks, live presentations, and workshops. Each format emphasized different strengths—narrative, humor, clarity, and interaction.

Dylan Wiliam (2011) has extended his work on formative assessment through books, podcasts, videos, and online platforms. These media-specific strategies ensure his ideas reach educators in formats that resonate with their learning preferences and professional needs.

This approach treats media as part of the message. It recognizes that how ideas are communicated is inseparable from how they are understood and applied.

Institutional Embedding Strategies

Ideas gain power when they influence systems, not just individuals. Through *institutional extension*, thought leaders embed their concepts within professional development programs, consulting partnerships, certification systems, and organizational change efforts.

Robert Marzano's (2007) instructional frameworks are supported by district-level training programs, evaluation tools, and partnerships, enabling systemic adoption of his ideas.

Richard DuFour's (2008) work on professional learning communities similarly gained traction through structured implementation supports and institutional partnerships that moved his ideas from vision to practice.

This strategy acknowledges that meaningful change often requires organizational infrastructure. By aligning ideas with systems of support, thought leaders enhance both fidelity and scale.

Digital Extension Strategies

In an increasingly connected world, thought leadership must also be *digitally persistent*. Leading educators build online ecosystems that house resources, foster dialogue, and support ongoing application.

Wiggins and McTighe's (2005) UbD framework lives on through a robust website, digital tools, social media channels, and community forums.

Jo Boaler's (2016) work on mathematical mindsets similarly thrives through digital modules, teaching tools, video libraries, and global online communities. These platforms ensure her ideas remain accessible and evolving.

Digital infrastructure allows educational ideas to outlast any single publication. It supports ongoing learning, flexible access, and global reach.

The most influential educational thought leaders don't just publish; they construct ecosystems. They layer content in developmental progressions, diversify their formats, collaborate with others, embrace multimedia, build institutional support, and establish a digital presence. These interconnected strategies amplify their influence and ensure their ideas are not just heard but sustained, adapted, and applied.

Ultimately, what sets enduring thought leadership apart is its ability to move beyond isolated brilliance. It thrives in networks of people, platforms, and practices that extend the life, relevance, and impact of big ideas.

Balancing Accessibility and Intellectual Depth

Influential educational thought leaders generate big ideas and make them usable. They understand that to create real impact, complex thinking must be both respected by scholars and understood by practitioners. It's a balancing act: keep the rigor but remove the barriers. The best thought leaders don't dumb things down; they open things up.

Scaffolding Ideas

Rather than throwing readers into the deep end, thought leaders build understanding gradually. They introduce foundational ideas in clear, simple language and then add layers of complexity over time. It's not simplification—it's pacing.

Richard Elmore (2004), for example, doesn't start with theory-heavy analysis. He begins with tangible ideas like the "instructional core" and then unpacks more complex interactions between teachers, students, and content. Similarly, City et al (2009). walk readers through data use step by step, starting with basic concepts and then moving into deeper territory like multiple data types and the subtleties of implementation.

This kind of scaffolding helps readers build capacity. It treats them with respect, neither overwhelming them with jargon nor assuming they need spoon-feeding.

Turning Concepts Into Concrete Examples

Abstract ideas only go so far. Thought leaders often make their work come alive through specific examples: a teacher's decision in a classroom, a student's project, or a school's journey. These details ground the theory and make it stick.

Deborah Ball is a master at this. Her work on the specialized knowledge teachers need to teach math becomes real through her use of classroom moments—when a teacher navigates a student's misconception or chooses one representation over another (Ball et al., 2008). Ron Berger (2003) does something similar. His big ideas around student work and engagement are always anchored in tangible projects and stories from classrooms.

This strategy keeps ideas honest. If you can't show what a theory looks like in practice, maybe it's not ready.

Making the Complex Visible

Visuals often do what words alone can't: make structure visible, show how pieces connect, and give abstract systems a clear shape. The best thought leaders use diagrams, maps, charts, and models not as decoration, but as explanation.

Michael Fullan's (2011) work on change is often accompanied by simple, powerful visuals that organize complex relationships. Jay McTighe's curriculum design frameworks become accessible when they're laid out in clear templates and planning tools (Wiggins & McTighe, 2005).

Visuals don't dumb ideas down—they give them shape. They're scaffolding in another form.

Using Metaphors to Make Ideas Click

Sometimes, the best way to explain something new is by connecting it to something familiar. Thought leaders often use metaphors and analogies to make abstract concepts more relatable.

David Perkins (2009) does this with his "thinking in the zoo" versus "thinking in the wild" metaphor, helping readers see the difference between artificial and authentic thinking environments. Ron Ritchhart (2015) draws on cultural metaphors to explain classroom dynamics in ways that resonate deeply.

Done well, metaphors provide insight. They give readers a bridge to new territory.

Writing in Layers

The best educational writing often works on multiple levels. It invites casual readers in, gives practical guidance to educators, and satisfies academics looking for depth: one piece of writing, multiple entry points.

Mike Rose's (2009) work is a great example—stories about individual students are wrapped in a deeper analysis of education and equity. Lisa Delpit (2006) does something similar: her writing speaks powerfully to teachers while unpacking broader questions of power and culture in education.

This layered writing respects the fact that readers come with different goals and backgrounds. It meets them where they are but doesn't stop there.

Translating Technical Language Without Losing Precision

Many of the most important ideas in education use specialized language. Thought leaders don't avoid it—they explain it. They define key terms, walk you through methods, and translate dense concepts in ways that keep their integrity intact.

John Hattie's (2009) work with effect sizes is a perfect example. He breaks down statistical ideas without stripping them of their meaning. Carol Ann Tomlinson (2001) does the same with differentiated instruction, staying true to the complexity while making the ideas usable.

They don't dumb things down; they open the door.

The most impactful educational thought leaders don't sacrifice depth for accessibility—or vice versa. They know that influence depends on doing both well. That's why they build content that scaffolds ideas, grounds them in real-world examples, visualizes relationships, leans into metaphors, writes in layers, and translates technical language with care.

This multidimensional approach focuses on creating work that travels further, lands deeper, and stays useful across time and context.

Case Studies in Content Creation and Thought Leadership

To understand how educational ideas gain traction and influence, it helps to look at specific cases where content creation played a central role in that process. The strategies discussed earlier come alive through the work of prominent thought leaders—Carol Dweck, Grant Wiggins, Jay McTighe, and Linda Darling-Hammond—who didn't just share good ideas but developed ways of communicating them that made those ideas stick. Their stories show us what effective content creation looks like in action: clear framing, layered engagement, concrete examples, responsiveness to misunderstanding, and collaborative amplification.

Carol Dweck and the Power of Mindset

Carol Dweck's mindset theory has become one of the most widely adopted concepts in education, from early childhood classrooms to university lecture halls. What made her work so impactful was the strength of her research and how she communicated it.

Dweck (2006) didn't try to explain all of attribution theory at once. Instead, she framed the core idea around a simple, memorable distinction: some people believe intelligence is fixed; others believe it can grow. That clarity gave educators something they could immediately grasp and use. It opened the door to deeper learning rather than overwhelming readers with complexity upfront.

However, it wasn't just the framing. Dweck created a whole ecosystem of content: peer-reviewed studies, practitioner-friendly books like *Mindset*, tools for assessing beliefs about learning, and workshop materials for schools. Each piece spoke to a different audience and served a different purpose (Dweck, 2006; Yeager & Dweck, 2012). This layering allowed educators to start wherever they were and go as deep as they needed.

She also used vivid examples—stories of students reacting to failure, classroom dialogues, and teacher feedback practices. These stories made abstract psychology visible in everyday interactions, helping educators see where mindsets show up and how they could respond (Boaler, 2013).

Importantly, Dweck (2015) stayed involved as her work spread. When the growth mindset started being misunderstood, like reducing it to "just praise effort," she addressed those misconceptions directly in articles and talks. She also collaborated with teachers and researchers to refine and extend the work, keeping it grounded and responsive.

UbD: Wiggins and McTighe

When Wiggins and McTighe (2005) introduced the UbD framework, they weren't just offering a new way to plan curriculum. They were changing how educators thought about planning altogether: start with the end in mind, figure out what counts as evidence, and then plan instruction accordingly.

What made UbD powerful was its structure. The three-stage model—backward design—was easy to follow but rich enough to support deep instructional planning. It provided clarity without being prescriptive, giving educators a way to organize their thinking without locking them into a formula.

They also developed tools to make this abstract process concrete. Graphic organizers, templates, and visual models helped educators map out enduring understandings and essential questions, making complex curriculum design more approachable (Wiggins & McTighe, 2011).

Their books were full of real-world examples, spanning subjects and grade levels. This wasn't just theory—it was visible in unit plans and classroom strategies. Teachers could see how the model played out across different contexts, which helped them adapt it to their own.

Wiggins and McTighe also built a deep content ecosystem: comprehensive books, guidebooks for specific subjects, workshop materials, and digital supports. They didn't stop at the classroom level. They partnered with districts and organizations, developed certification programs, and helped schools implement the framework at scale.

Like Dweck, they also paid attention to how their work was being used. When UbD was misunderstood as a rigid formula or assessment-first approach, they responded by clarifying resources and providing professional learning support (Wiggins & McTighe, 2011). They stayed engaged in the ongoing learning process, and their framework was inspired.

Linda Darling-Hammond and the Future of Teacher Quality

Linda Darling-Hammond's work on teacher quality is a model for how research can inform policy and practice through strategic communication. Her writing and advocacy shaped debates about how teachers are prepared and supported, influencing everything from licensure systems to district hiring practices.

What set her apart was the rigor of her evidence base. Her arguments were always grounded in large-scale, multi-study syntheses that connected teacher preparation to student outcomes (Darling-Hammond, 2000). This gave her work credibility in both academic and policy circles.

She didn't stop at scholarly journals. Darling-Hammond adapted her messages for different audiences—publishing policy briefs, practitioner pieces, and public commentary that maintained core messages while adjusting the tone, detail, and format (Darling-Hammond, 2017). Her work traveled because it was accessible without being oversimplified.

She also used international comparisons to challenge the status quo. Rather than just saying American systems needed improvement, she pointed to countries with strong teacher development pipelines, places like Finland and Singapore, to show what was possible (Darling-Hammond, 2010).

Another powerful aspect of her communication was the integration of data and narrative. Her work often combined statistical findings with personal stories of teachers and schools, creating an emotional and intellectual case for change. This made the research feel real and relevant.

Finally, she engaged others—policymakers, teacher educators, and researchers—to carry her ideas forward. The Learning Policy Institute, which she founded, became a hub for collaborative inquiry and implementation. Her work didn't stay confined to academic journals; it lived in real policies, classrooms, and conversations.

Patterns Across the Case Studies

What ties these stories together isn't just the content—it's how the content was built, adapted, and communicated. Across these three leaders, we see common strategies:

- Clear framing of complex ideas in a way that's both memorable and meaningful.

- Layered ecosystems of content that serve multiple audiences at different depths.

- Concrete examples that ground abstract concepts in lived experience.

- Ongoing responsiveness to how ideas are used, misused, or evolve.

- Collaborative amplification that turns individual ideas into shared movements.

These aren't just communication strategies but mechanisms of influence. They show that thought leadership is more than publishing a great idea. It's about building the conditions for that idea to take root, grow, and make a difference.

As we move into the next chapters, we'll explore other dimensions of thought leadership: building communities, shaping policy, influencing institutions, and staying grounded in ethical purpose. Content is where it starts, but it's only the beginning.

Chapter 7:
Building Networks and
Communities of Practice

Educational thought leadership rarely happens in a vacuum. The people whose ideas end up shifting practice or influencing policy aren't usually working alone in an office or publishing from an ivory tower. More often, they're part of a network, a community of practice (CoP), where ideas are tested, shaped, and refined alongside others who are also thinking, experimenting, and trying to make things better.

These communities do more than offer support or cheer from the sidelines. They're active partners in the process. New ideas often start as hunches, get challenged and improved through conversation, and only then start to take shape as something more fully formed. Whether it's through informal discussions, collaborative research, or school-based trials, thought leaders rely on others to help them see what works, what doesn't, and what needs more time to grow.

This chapter explores the deep connection between thought leadership and community building. It looks at how influential educational leaders don't just write or speak about big ideas—they build ecosystems around those ideas. These ecosystems include trusted colleagues, teacher collaborators, early adopters, and critical friends who push the thinking forward and carry it outward.

Understanding CoPs in Educational Contexts

Effective educational thought leadership often rests on a deep understanding of how professional communities function in educational environments. Unlike formal organizations with top-down hierarchies or informal networks with loose affiliations, CoPs represent a distinct form of social learning structure. These communities bring together professionals with shared domain interests who engage in ongoing, meaningful interactions. Within these spaces, knowledge is not just exchanged—it's developed, refined, and embedded in shared practices.

A range of theoretical frameworks helps clarify how these communities work and why they matter.

CoPs: Etienne Wenger

Wenger's (1998) theory of CoPs is foundational. It defines them as groups characterized by a shared domain of interest, mutual engagement in joint activities, and a developed repertoire of resources and practices. This model moves beyond organizational charts and professional titles to highlight how real learning communities evolve. According to Wenger, it's not enough to have a shared topic; without genuine interaction and ongoing practice development, a group cannot function as a CoP.

This model helps explain why some professional learning communities thrive while others stagnate. Thought leaders who understand this framework recognize that building community requires intentionally cultivating all three elements—domain, community, and practice. Wenger's (1998) influence lies in offering conceptual clarity that empowers leaders to foster genuine communities rather than defaulting to top-down initiatives or superficial networking.

Situated Learning: Jean Lave

Lave's situated learning theory further clarifies the picture by positioning learning as inherently social. Through "legitimate peripheral participation," newcomers gradually become full members of a community, learning not by absorbing content in isolation but by engaging in shared practice (Lave & Wenger, 1991). This explains why stand-alone workshops or individual professional development sessions often fail to change classroom practice: they lack the community context that anchors and sustains meaningful change.

Educational thought leaders draw on this insight to design environments that embed professional learning in real-world, collaborative activity rather than treating it as an individual, cognitive event.

Cultural Theory: Mary Douglas

Douglas's (1982) cultural theory adds another layer by exploring how different community structures shape knowledge cultures. Her framework uses the concepts of "group" (the strength of group boundaries) and "grid" (the extent of role differentiation and regulation) to describe how cultural biases influence the way communities function. This helps explain why similar professional groups can approach the same problem in vastly different ways depending on their underlying social structures.

For thought leaders, Douglas's work offers a reminder: there is no one-size-fits-all model for professional communities. Effective community-building must account for cultural context and structural variation. It shouldn't just adopt a preferred model wholesale.

Structural Holes: Ronald Burt

Burt's theory of structural holes focuses on how the architecture of professional networks influences access to knowledge and innovation.

He argues that individuals and groups who bridge disconnected networks, those who occupy structural holes, can access diverse perspectives and serve as catalysts for innovation (Burt, 2004). In other words, it's not just who you know but also who your connections don't know.

This theory supports the idea that diversity in professional connections can be a key driver of creative thinking and adaptive leadership. For educational thought leaders, it points to the value of cultivating cross-boundary relationships, not just deep ties within a single group.

Knowledge Creation: Ikujiro Nonaka

Nonaka's theory of organizational knowledge creation focuses on how communities convert tacit knowledge (deep, experiential, and context-bound) into explicit knowledge (codified and transferable), and vice versa, through a model with a dynamic cycle of socialization, externalization, combination, and internalization (SECI) (Nonaka & Takeuchi, 1995).

This model helps clarify why communities that emphasize only formal training or only lived experience may struggle. Real innovation and deep learning occur when both forms of knowledge are actively integrated. For thought leaders, the lesson is clear: effective professional learning must blend theory and experience, not privilege one at the expense of the other.

Systems Model of Creativity: Mihaly Csikszentmihalyi

Csikszentmihalyi's systems model of creativity reframes innovation as a product of social systems, not just individual genius. It emphasizes the role of "fields"—networks of experts who evaluate and validate new ideas—and "domains"—the existing cultural frameworks into which innovations must fit (Csikszentmihalyi, 1999). Creativity, in this view, depends on structures that can recognize and support valuable contributions, not just the talent of the contributor.

This insight pushes thought leaders to think not only about idea generation but also about how their communities validate, support, and institutionalize innovation.

Together, these frameworks provide a rich, multidimensional understanding of how professional communities function in education. The most effective educational thought leaders don't rely on a single perspective. They draw from multiple lenses to build communities that support professional growth, knowledge development, and innovation.

Whether by cultivating shared practices, embedding learning in social participation, adapting to cultural contexts, building cross-boundary networks, integrating tacit and explicit knowledge, or strengthening evaluative structures for innovation, these leaders understand that community is not just a backdrop for educational change but the engine that drives it.

Developing and Nurturing Professional Networks

Educational thought leadership doesn't emerge in isolation. It grows within carefully cultivated professional networks—webs of relationships that support the evolution of ideas and the expansion of influence. These networks go far beyond the simple accumulation of contacts or social media followers. They are deliberately structured, multidimensional ecosystems that enable feedback, collaboration, implementation, and resilience. Educational thought leaders understand that the quality of their networks shapes the reach and relevance of their work.

Diversity-Oriented Networking

Thought leaders intentionally build networks that span different roles, regions, and perspectives. Rather than surrounding themselves with like-minded peers, they seek out cognitive diversity—connecting across institutional, cultural, and ideological boundaries to challenge their thinking and strengthen their ideas.

Andy Hargreaves exemplifies this strategy through his cross-role and cross-national collaborations. His professional relationships include teachers, administrators, researchers, and policymakers across North America, Europe, and Asia, creating a multidimensional view of educational change (Hargreaves & Fullan, 2012). This diversity helps ensure his ideas are robust and context-sensitive.

Linda Darling-Hammond (2010) similarly bridges research, policy, and practice. Her ability to move between these spaces—linking universities, K–12 schools, and government agencies—has made her one of the most influential voices in education reform. Her work shows that enduring educational change requires one to dissolve boundaries between domains rather than reinforcing them.

This approach aligns with the idea of "boundary spanning" in leadership theory, which highlights the benefits of connecting disparate groups to facilitate innovation and systems change (Ernst & Chrobot-Mason, 2011).

Reciprocity-Based Networking

Sustainable professional networks are grounded in mutual benefit. Thought leaders who create durable influence don't simply broadcast ideas; they engage in meaningful exchanges where all participants contribute and benefit.

Ann Lieberman's work reflects this ethos. Through her collaborations with teachers and school leaders, she consistently frames knowledge creation as a two-way street, where academics and practitioners co-construct professional knowledge (Lieberman & Miller, 2001). Her relationships are marked by shared inquiry, not one-directional expertise.

Michael Fullan also exemplifies reciprocity through his partnerships with school districts, which function as living laboratories for innovation. These partnerships feed back into his theoretical frameworks, ensuring they remain grounded and adaptable (Fullan, 2016). Such models resonate with the concept of "generative reciprocity" in organizational learning, where knowledge exchange drives mutual growth.

Depth-Balanced Networking

Effective networks balance strong, trust-based relationships with loose, information-rich connections. Sociologist Mark Granovetter's (1973) seminal theory on "the strength of weak ties" explains why both types of relationships matter—strong ties provide support and deep collaboration, while weak ties introduce new perspectives and extend influence.

Richard Elmore's network demonstrates this balance. He maintained close partnerships with research colleagues and practitioners while engaging broadly with school leaders and policymakers. This dual structure allowed his ideas to evolve with depth and spread with breadth (Elmore, 2004).

Dylan Wiliam follows a similar model, developing both tight-knit research teams and broad practitioner communities interested in formative assessment. This structure supports both deep conceptual development and wide-scale application.

Technology-Enhanced Networking

Digital platforms have expanded the possibilities for professional connection, enabling educators to sustain and scale networks beyond geographical and institutional constraints.

Will Richardson harnesses this potential through online learning communities, blogs, social media, and virtual events. His digital presence doesn't replace in-person relationships but enhances them, enabling a hybrid professional identity that spans physical and virtual contexts (Richardson & Mancabelli, 2011).

Yong Zhao also uses digital tools to build global networks. His virtual engagements connect educators across continents, offering a truly international perspective on educational transformation (Zhao, 2009). These examples reflect the shift toward "networked professionalism" enabled by digital tools (Trust, 2012).

Implementation-Connected Networking

The most impactful networks are those that bridge the gap between theory and practice. Thought leaders recognize that ideas must be tested in real-world settings to be refined and sustained.

Anthony Bryk's work with improvement science embodies this principle. His partnerships with schools and districts enable theory to evolve through practical application, creating a continuous feedback loop between research and reality (Bryk et al., 2015).

Carol Ann Tomlinson similarly maintains close connections with schools implementing differentiated instruction. Her frameworks continue to evolve based on practitioner insights, avoiding the pitfall of becoming detached from the classroom.

This strategy echoes Donald Schön's (1983) concept of the "reflective practitioner," emphasizing iterative learning between theory and action.

Regenerative Networking

Lasting influence depends on building networks that can grow and adapt without constant central leadership. Thought leaders who prioritize sustainability cultivate distributed leadership and independent relationships within their networks.

Richard DuFour's work on PLCs showcases this regenerative approach. His emphasis on shared leadership and peer-to-peer structures allowed PLCs to flourish beyond his direct involvement, creating a movement rather than a personality cult (DuFour et al., 2010).

Deborah Meier also built networks that outlasted her leadership. Her emphasis on democratic school structures and educator autonomy enabled the creation of communities capable of sustaining progressive education long after her departure.

This model reflects Wenger's (2002) concept of "stewardship" in CoPs, where leadership is distributed and the community takes collective responsibility for its ongoing development.

Integrating the Strategies

These six strategies don't operate in isolation. The most effective educational thought leaders weave them together, developing layered networks that support both intellectual rigor and practical application.

By understanding professional networks as dynamic systems rather than static lists of contacts, thought leaders build the social infrastructure needed to seed new ideas, refine them through dialogue and feedback, and extend their influence across complex educational landscapes.

Creating CoPs Around Educational Ideas

Educational thought leaders have a unique way of building CoPs that help their ideas grow and spread. They know that the most impactful educational concepts aren't usually born from just one person's work but rather through the collective efforts of a group. By fostering communities that explore, implement, and expand ideas together, these leaders create an environment where ideas can evolve in ways that individual efforts alone just can't achieve.

Clarifying the Focus

The first strategy these leaders use is ensuring everyone in the community agrees on what's being focused on. They create a clear framework around the core idea, ensuring everyone understands the domain they are working within. This clarity allows for diverse contributions while staying true to the shared purpose (DuFour, 2004; Wiggins & McTighe, 2005).

Take Richard DuFour's work on PLCs, for example. He set clear guidelines for what made an authentic PLC—things like a focus on learning, a collaborative culture, and a results-driven mindset. This clarity helped shape communities that were focused on the right goals, even while allowing for flexibility depending on the local context. Wiggins and McTighe (2005) did the same with UbD, making sure their community was built around backward design and a focus on understanding.

This focus-driven approach helps thought leaders build communities that are well-defined and purposeful. It keeps things from getting too narrow or too vague, ensuring that the group has a clear direction without limiting participation.

Building Multiple Ways to Engage

Next, thought leaders create communities where people can engage at different levels. Not everyone has the time or resources to dive in deeply, and that's okay. These leaders design their communities so that newcomers and experts alike can find a role that suits them (Dweck, 2006; Berger, 2003).

Carol Dweck's mindset community shows how this works. She designed multiple ways to participate, from research collaborations for academics to practical networks for teachers. This allowed a broad range of educators to engage in ways that made sense for them, without losing sight of the core concept.

Ron Berger's Expeditionary Learning community used a similar strategy, offering everything, from school partnerships for intensive work to resource networks for teachers looking for specific tools. By creating these varied pathways, both Dweck and Berger ensured that their ideas had a wider reach and more impact.

Focusing on Real Practice

Another key strategy is ensuring that the community doesn't just discuss theory but develops concrete tools and practices. Effective thought leadership prioritizes real-world solutions—approaches that educators can apply, test, and adapt in their settings (Lemov, 2010).

Doug Lemov's *Teach Like a Champion* community is a strong example. Rather than staying in the realm of abstract pedagogy, Lemov and his collaborators have focused on codifying clear, practical techniques that teachers can implement immediately. From checking for understanding to managing transitions, the strategies are field-tested and refined based on feedback from classrooms across the country. This focus on concrete, usable practices makes their work especially valuable to educators looking for clarity and effectiveness in their teaching.

By producing tangible tools and continuously iterating based on real-world conditions, thought leaders like Lemov ensure their communities stay anchored in the day-to-day work of teaching, not just in theory or aspiration.

Creating Lasting Resources

Thought leaders also know that successful communities don't just have good conversations—they produce valuable resources that can be used long after the community's meetings end. These resources can be anything from tools to examples, all designed to support continued learning and improvement (Gardner, 2008; PBLWorks, 2014).

For instance, Project Zero developed thinking routines and classroom examples that became resources educators could use and adapt in their teaching. The Buck Institute did something similar with project-based learning, creating detailed rubrics and planning templates that captured their community's collective knowledge.

These tangible artifacts help keep the community's ideas alive, even when the group isn't physically together. They provide ongoing value that extends beyond the community's interactions.

Sharing Stories of Success and Struggles

Another powerful tool in these communities is the sharing of stories, not abstract theories but real accounts of how ideas were put into practice in different schools. By sharing the successes, failures, and adaptations of others, communities can learn from each other's experiences in a way that's richer than just reading about principles (Sizer, 1992; Calkins, 2001).

Ted Sizer's Coalition of Essential Schools is a great example of this. The coalition shared detailed stories of how different schools implemented their ideas, providing a richer, more contextually grounded understanding of what worked and what didn't. The National Writing Project (NWP) also emphasized teacher stories to show how writing instruction played out in real classrooms, offering valuable insights into the complexities of implementation.

These stories help communities learn and grow in a way that theory alone can't, as they provide the context needed to understand how ideas work in practice.

Distributing Leadership Across the Community

Finally, educational thought leaders understand that the most sustainable communities are those that don't rely on one central figure. They work to distribute leadership, making sure that others in the community have opportunities to lead and take ownership of the work (DuFour, 2004; Reading Recovery Council of North America, 2002).

Richard DuFour's PLC model is a great example of this distributed leadership approach. Instead of keeping all the leadership with him, DuFour set up systems that trained others to take on leadership roles within the community. This approach meant the community could continue to grow and evolve even without him being directly involved. The Reading Recovery program took a similar approach, developing leadership structures at multiple levels so the community could thrive independently.

By spreading leadership throughout the community, these thought leaders ensure their ideas will last long after they've moved on to other projects.

These strategies are the foundation of how educational thought leaders build CoPs. Through these strategies, they create spaces where ideas can evolve, be implemented, and spread in ways that go beyond what one person could accomplish alone. The most successful thought leaders recognize that creating these communities isn't a one-size-fits-all process. They use a combination of approaches, ensuring their communities can grow, adapt, and make a lasting impact.

Leveraging Communities to Extend Influence

Educational thought leaders employ sophisticated strategies for leveraging CoPs to extend their influence beyond what individual efforts alone could achieve. They recognize that the most influential educational ideas typically spread through community networks rather than through direct communication from originators to adopters. By thoughtfully engaging communities in both idea development and dissemination, thought leaders create conditions for both concept improvement and influence expansion that isolated publication or presentation rarely accomplishes.

Implementation Laboratory Strategies

First, educational thought leaders develop implementation laboratory strategies that engage communities in testing and refining ideas through diverse applications. They recognize that theoretical concepts inevitably require adaptation when implemented in different contexts and that these implementation experiences provide essential feedback for concept development. They create structures for systematically gathering and analyzing implementation experiences to strengthen their frameworks (Bryk et al., 2015; Tomlinson, 2001).

Anthony Bryk's improvement science community illustrates this implementation laboratory approach. By engaging networked improvement communities in testing change ideas across diverse contexts, systematically documenting implementation variations and outcomes, and analyzing patterns across these experiences, Bryk (2015) created a community-based learning system that strengthened improvement methods beyond what his research alone could achieve.

This collective implementation testing enabled more robust framework development.

Similarly, Carol Ann Tomlinson engages differentiated instruction implementation communities in documenting and analyzing how differentiation principles manifest in different grade levels, subject areas, and student populations, thus allowing her frameworks to develop through diverse application experiences (Tomlinson, 2001).

This implementation of laboratory strategy enables educational thought leaders to develop more robust ideas through community-based testing and refinement. It acknowledges that significant educational concepts develop through implementation experience rather than emerging fully formed from theoretical work alone. It supports the development of thought leadership that addresses practical complexities instead of offering untested theoretical constructs (Wiggins & McTighe, 2005).

Adaptation Documentation Strategies

Second, educational thought leaders develop adaptation documentation strategies that capture how communities modify core ideas for different contexts. They recognize that educational approaches inevitably require contextual adaptation and that these adaptations provide valuable knowledge about both implementation requirements and concept boundaries. They create systems for documenting these adaptations to guide future implementation (Berger, 2003; Sizer, 1992).

Ron Berger's Expeditionary Learning community illustrates this adaptation documentation approach. By systematically collecting and analyzing how schools adapt project-based learning principles to different grade levels, subject areas, student populations, and resource contexts, Berger's (2003) community created a knowledge base about contextual adaptation that guides implementation while maintaining core principles.

Similarly, the Responsive Classroom community documents how teachers adapt core practices for different grade levels, school structures, and student needs, creating detailed knowledge about contextual implementation while maintaining essential principles, thus creating valuable implementation guidance beyond generic descriptions (Charney, 2002).

This adaptation documentation strategy enables educational thought leaders to develop more nuanced implementation guidance through community-based collections of experience and supports the development of thought leadership that guides thoughtful adaptation (Bryk et al., 2015).

Evidence Collection Strategies

Third, educational thought leaders develop evidence collection strategies that engage communities in gathering implementation outcomes across diverse contexts. They recognize that educational approaches produce different results in different settings and that comprehensive evidence requires data from diverse implementations. They create systems for collecting and analyzing outcome evidence across community implementations (Hattie, 2009; Slavin, 2009).

John Hattie's Visible Learning community illustrates this evidence collection approach. By engaging practitioner networks in documenting implementation processes and outcomes across diverse settings, Hattie's community creates an evidence base far more extensive than traditional research studies alone could produce. This collective evidence gathering enables a more comprehensive understanding of what works, for whom, and under what conditions (Hattie, 2009).

Similarly, the Reading Recovery community systematically collects implementation data from all participating schools, creating a massive evidence base about the effectiveness of interventions across diverse contexts, thus providing implementation credibility beyond what limited research sites alone could establish (Pinnell & Fountas, 2009).

This evidence collection strategy enables educational thought leaders to develop a more comprehensive understanding through community-based data gathering. It acknowledges that educational evidence requires diverse contextual data and supports the development of thought leadership that addresses implementation variation (Hattie, 2009).

Problem-Solving Network Strategies

Fourth, educational thought leaders develop problem-solving network strategies that engage communities in addressing implementation challenges collectively. They recognize that educational innovations inevitably encounter obstacles during implementation and that these challenges require diverse perspectives and experiences to be resolved effectively. They create collaborative structures for identifying and addressing implementation problems (Elmore, 2004; National Writing Project, 2020).

Richard Elmore's instructional rounds networks illustrate this problem-solving approach. By engaging educator communities in collaborative examination of implementation challenges, bringing diverse perspectives and experiences to problem analysis, and developing collective solutions, Elmore (2004) created problem-solving capacity far beyond what individual practitioners or consultants alone could achieve.

Similarly, the NWP creates teacher inquiry communities that collectively address writing instruction challenges, from ensuring diverse classroom experiences to analyzing problems and developing solutions, thus developing more effective responses than isolated practitioners could create individually (National Writing Project, 2020).

This problem-solving network strategy enables educational thought leaders to develop more effective implementation support through community-based collaboration. It acknowledges that educational implementation challenges require collective intelligence and supports the development of thought leadership that addresses implementation complexity (Elmore, 2004).

Diffusion Channel Strategies

Fifth, educational thought leaders develop diffusion channel strategies that leverage community networks for idea dissemination. They recognize that educational ideas spread more effectively through trusted professional relationships than through official channels or commercial marketing alone. They thoughtfully engage community members as idea ambassadors who can translate concepts for their local contexts and relationships (Wiliam, 2011; Buck Institute for Education, 2014).

Dylan Wiliam's formative assessment community illustrates this diffusion channel approach. By developing teacher leaders who understand both the technical aspects of formative assessment and the specific contexts of their colleagues, Wiliam created a dissemination system that translates his ideas through trusted relationships. This networked diffusion enables a more extensive and effective spread than individual efforts alone could achieve (Wiliam, 2011).

Similarly, the Buck Institute for Education develops project-based learning coaches within school districts who serve as local implementation guides and advocates, translating general project-based learning principles for specific district contexts and relationships, thus creating a more effective spread than external expertise alone (Buck Institute for Education, 2014).

This diffusion channel strategy enables educational thought leaders to extend their influence through community-based dissemination. It acknowledges that educational ideas spread through trusted relationships and support the development of thought leadership that reaches diverse contexts through local translation (Wiliam, 2011).

Identity Formation Strategies

Sixth, educational thought leaders develop identity formation strategies that engage communities in creating shared professional identities around core ideas. They recognize that sustainable educational change often requires an identity shift, with practitioners coming to see themselves differently concerning their work. They create experiences and narratives that support this identity development within communities (Sizer, 1992; National Writing Project, 2020).

Ted Sizer's Coalition of Essential Schools illustrates this identity formation approach. By developing rich descriptions of what it means to be an "essential school educator," creating experiences that reinforce this identity, and fostering community narratives that celebrate this professional self-concept, Sizer's coalition created an identity-based community rather than a mere technique-sharing network. This identity focus enabled deeper and more sustainable commitment than technical compliance alone (Sizer, 1992).

Similarly, the NWP develops a strong "teacher-writer" identity among participants, creating a professional self-concept that fundamentally shapes how they approach both their writing and teaching, thus creating a deeper transformation than technique training alone could achieve (National Writing Project, 2020).

This identity formation strategy enables educational thought leaders to create more sustainable influence through community-based professional identity development. It acknowledges that significant educational change often requires an identity shift and supports the development of thought leadership that transforms how educators understand themselves rather than only changing what they do (Sizer, 1992).

Case Studies in Community Building and Thought Leadership

Exploring case studies of successful community building by educational thought leaders reveals how the strategies discussed earlier come to life in practice. These examples highlight both common approaches and unique adaptations across various educational domains.

NWP

This project is a prime example of community building around educational ideas. Founded by James Gray in 1974 at the University of California, Berkeley, NWP has expanded to nearly 200 university-based sites across the US, engaging thousands of teachers in the development and dissemination of effective writing instruction techniques.

The project's impressive growth and ongoing influence are a testament to its well-crafted community-building strategies, which have transformed initial concepts of writing instruction into a powerful professional movement.

Here are the key elements of NWP's community-building approach:

1. **Teacher-Writer Identity Formation:** NWP cultivated a sense of identity among participants through the "teachers as

writers" concept. Instead of merely positioning teachers as instructors of writing, NWP encouraged them to see themselves as writers, actively engaging in the writing process while developing instructional practices. This focus on identity led to a deeper transformation in teaching than traditional technique-based training could achieve (Whitney, 2008).

2. **Distributed Leadership:** NWP's "teachers teaching teachers" model distributed leadership across its network. By developing teacher-leaders to facilitate professional development sessions, the NWP expanded its capacity far beyond what a centralized leadership model could have accomplished (Lieberman & Wood, 2003). This distributed leadership helped sustain and scale the initiative.

3. **Practice-Centered Focus:** NWP organized its community around concrete writing practices rather than abstract principles. This approach, which addressed specific techniques like prewriting strategies, revision methods, and assessment approaches, helped teachers implement and refine practices across various educational contexts (National Writing Project, n.d.-b).

4. **Adaptation Documentation:** NWP emphasized documenting how writing instruction strategies were adapted across different grade levels, subjects, and student demographics. This approach not only allowed for contextualized guidance but also acknowledged the variations in classroom settings, making the implementation more realistic and effective (Whitney, 2008).

5. **Evidence-Based Practices:** Rather than relying solely on standardized assessments, NWP developed strategies to document qualitative growth in student writing. This evidence, collected from diverse contexts, enhanced the

credibility of the project and informed its ongoing development (National Writing Project, n.d.-b).

6. **Hybrid Network Structure:** NWP's collaboration between university and K–12 schools created a unique hybrid structure. This networked approach bridged the gap between academic research and classroom practice, fostering the flow of knowledge across institutional boundaries (Lieberman & Wood, 2003).

Through its teacher-writer identity, distributed leadership, practical focus, adaptation documentation, evidence-based practices, and hybrid network, NWP successfully transformed educational ideas into a thriving, influential movement.

Project Zero's Visible Thinking

This initiative, developed by researchers at the Harvard Graduate School of Education, provides another notable example of effective community building. Initially designed by David Perkins, Ron Ritchhart, and Shari Tishman, the initiative has evolved into a global community of educators implementing thinking routines and documentation strategies across diverse educational settings (Ritchhart et al., 2011). This wide adoption speaks to the success of the community-building strategies that transformed cognitive research into a globally influential educational movement (Tishman et al., 1993).

Here are the key elements of Visible Thinking's community-building approach:

1. **Practice-Centered Focus:** Visible Thinking's community is built around specifically named thinking routines such as *See-Think-Wonder* and *Claim-Support-Question*. These routines provided educators with immediate, actionable tools that

allowed for rapid adoption and adaptation across different educational contexts (Ritchhart et al., 2011).

2. **Artifact Documentation:** The initiative emphasized documenting student thinking through various methods, such as maps, reflections, and visual representations. This rich collection of artifacts provided evidence of thinking development, guiding implementation and offering valuable feedback for instructional refinement (Ritchhart, 2015).

3. **Cultural Adaptation:** Visible Thinking's cultural framework acknowledged the role of classroom dynamics—time, environment, and discourse patterns—in shaping thinking development. This understanding allowed for better contextual adaptation of the thinking routines, ensuring their effectiveness across diverse cultural and educational contexts (Ritchhart, 2015).

4. **Multiple Participation Pathways:** Visible Thinking encouraged broad participation by offering various entry points for educators, from intensive research collaborations to resource-sharing networks. This flexibility accommodated different levels of involvement, making it accessible to a wide range of educators (Project Zero, n.d.).

5. **Distributed Diffusion:** Rather than centralizing all implementation efforts, the initiative created "intellectual outposts"—local hubs and partner schools—that served as support centers for contextualized guidance and training. This distributed approach helped extend the reach of the initiative more effectively than a centralized model would have (Ritchhart et al., 2011).

6. **Collaborative Evidence Collection:** Visible Thinking leveraged the collaborative documentation of thinking

development across various educational contexts to create a robust evidence base. This collective effort not only validated the initiative's approach but also provided ongoing insights for refinement and improvement (Tishman & Palmer, 2007).

Through its practice-centered focus, artifact documentation, cultural adaptation, multiple participation pathways, distributed diffusion, and collaborative evidence collection, Visible Thinking successfully translated educational research into impactful practice.

Professional Learning Communities

The PLC movement, popularized by Richard DuFour, exemplifies another robust model of community building in education. What began as a small initiative at Adlai Stevenson High School in Illinois has grown into a global movement, influencing thousands of schools worldwide. This expansion reflects the effectiveness of DuFour's community-building strategies in transforming school improvement concepts into a widely adopted educational model (DuFour & Eaker, 1998; DuFour et al., 2010).

Here are the key elements of the PLC community-building approach:

1. **Definitional Clarity:** DuFour established clear boundaries for what constitutes a true PLC, emphasizing a shared mission, vision, and values centered on learning, collective responsibility, and results orientation. This clarity helped prevent the dilution of the concept as it scaled and maintained its integrity across diverse educational settings (DuFour et al., 2010).

2. **Practice-Centered Focus:** The PLC movement focused on concrete collaborative practices—goal-setting, common formative assessments, data analysis, and structured interventions—to drive improvements in teaching and

learning (DuFour et al., 2006). These processes empowered educators to take collective ownership of student success.

3. **Structured Artifacts:** DuFour et al. (2002) developed specific tools, protocols, and templates to guide PLC implementation, including meeting agendas, SMART goals worksheets, and assessment templates. These artifacts served as both structure and scaffold, enabling replication and adaptation in various contexts.

4. **Multi-Level Leadership Development:** The movement emphasized cultivating leadership across multiple levels—classroom, school, district, and beyond. By developing teacher-leaders and building administrative capacity, the PLC model promoted sustainability and adaptability over time (DuFour et al., 2006).

5. **Results-Based Evidence:** Central to the PLC framework is the use of student learning evidence to guide and evaluate practice. This data-driven approach reinforced the movement's focus on results, distinguishing it from more compliance-oriented or conceptual models of school improvement (DuFour et al., 2010).

6. **Story-Centered Communication:** DuFour frequently used storytelling—case studies, school profiles, and personal narratives—to convey the PLC process in action. These stories offered practical insights and made the work relatable, helping educators envision how PLCs might function in their settings (DuFour, 2004).

Through its focus on definitional clarity, practice-centered approaches, structured tools, leadership development, results-based evidence, and story-centered communication, the PLC movement successfully expanded the reach and impact of its model for school improvement.

Common Patterns Across Case Studies

Despite the differing domains and strategies of the NWP, Project Zero's Visible Thinking, and Professional Learning Communities, several common patterns emerge:

- **Identity Development:** All three initiatives prioritize the transformation of educators' professional identities, encouraging them to see themselves as technicians and active participants in the educational process.

- **Practice-Centered Focus:** The focus on concrete, actionable practices that educators can immediately implement is a central theme across all three cases.

- **Distributed Leadership:** Each initiative involves a model of leadership development that goes beyond the founders, ensuring sustainability and growth.

- **Adaptation Documentation:** The systematic documentation of how strategies are adapted to various contexts ensures that implementation remains flexible and responsive.

- **Evidence Collection:** Whether through qualitative or quantitative data, each case emphasizes the importance of gathering evidence to demonstrate effectiveness and guide improvement.

- **Narrative Sharing:** Each movement uses stories of implementation to communicate lessons learned and share wisdom across the community.

These case studies illustrate how effective community-building strategies amplify the influence of educational thought leadership. By creating communities around ideas, thought leaders can extend their impact far beyond the classroom or the page, fostering ongoing refinement and real-world application of educational concepts.

The examples demonstrate how thoughtful community-building can transform educational ideas into influential movements. The strategies used in these cases offer valuable insights into how educators, researchers, and leaders can create and sustain communities that drive educational improvement.

The next chapters will delve into other aspects of educational thought leadership, including policy influence, ethical foundations, and emerging trends, while continuing to explore the vital role of community building in the success of these efforts.

Chapter 8:
Thought Leadership in Educational Policy and Reform

The relationship between thought leadership and educational policy represents one of the most consequential yet complex dimensions of educational influence. While classroom innovations and school-level practices can transform individual educational experiences, policy changes can reshape entire educational systems, affecting millions of students across diverse contexts. Educational thought leaders who effectively engage with policy processes can extend their influence far beyond what direct practitioner engagement alone could achieve, creating systemic conditions that either support or hinder educational improvement at scale.

This chapter explores the intricate relationship between educational thought leadership and the influence of educational policies. It examines how influential educational thought leaders engage with policy development, how they navigate political complexities while maintaining intellectual integrity, and how they translate research and practice insights into viable policy frameworks. Through analysis of both theoretical perspectives and historical examples, educational thought leadership illustrates how thoughtful policy engagement can amplify educational ideas while addressing the distinctive challenges that policies present.

Understanding Educational Policy Processes

Educational thought leaders draw upon a sophisticated understanding of how policy processes function within educational systems. They recognize that these processes differ significantly from both academic knowledge development and practitioner implementation, operating through distinctive dynamics, constraints, and opportunities. Policy development involves multiple stakeholders with diverse interests, functions through formal and informal channels, and relies on different forms of evidence and arguments than academic or practitioner ones. Understanding these distinctive characteristics forms the foundation for effective policy engagement.

Multiple Streams Framework

John Kingdon's Multiple Streams Framework provides conceptual tools for understanding how policy windows open and close. This framework explains how three relatively independent streams—problems (issues needing attention), policies (available solutions), and politics (public mood and institutional dynamics)—must align for significant change to occur. It highlights the role of policy entrepreneurs who actively couple these streams during moments of opportunity (Kingdon, 2011).

This perspective helps explain why certain educational ideas gain policy traction while others do not, despite similar merit. When educational proposals align with recognized problems, seem politically viable, and emerge during favorable conditions, they can gain sudden momentum. Thought leaders who understand this dynamic recognize the need to monitor and engage across all three streams and advocate for the quality of a solution.

Advocacy Coalition Framework

Paul Sabatier's Advocacy Coalition Framework (ACF) emphasizes how actors coalesce around shared core beliefs and compete for influence over extended periods. Within these coalitions, policy learning occurs primarily internally, and policy debates often reflect deep-seated values rather than just technical disagreements (Sabatier & Jenkins-Smith, 1993).

This helps explain why educational policy debates often resist resolution through data alone—issues like school choice or standardized testing tap into fundamental beliefs about education, authority, and equity. Educational thought leaders who understand the ACF know how to engage belief systems.

Argumentative Turn Framework

Frank Fischer's (2003) Argumentative Turn Framework adds an interpretive dimension, analyzing how policy arguments function across levels, from technical evidence to ideological narratives. This framework reveals that successful policy advocacy depends not only on empirical support but also on the capacity to justify policies morally, contextually, and ideologically.

This helps explain why some empirically supported policies fail— they lack resonance with public values or don't address systemic concerns. Thought leaders who understand this framework craft arguments that speak to multiple dimensions of justification, not just technical efficacy.

Street-Level Bureaucracy Theory

Michael Lipsky's (1980) Street-Level Bureaucracy theory focuses on the implementation stage, revealing how frontline educators— teachers, principals, and administrators—exercise discretion and often adapt policy to context. Policy is thus made not only in legislature but also in classrooms.

This helps explain discrepancies between policy design and educational practice. Thought leaders who understand Lipsky's perspective prioritize implementer buy-in and design for adaptation.

Policy Paradox Framework

Deborah Stone's Policy Paradox Framework highlights the strategic nature of policy discourse. It reveals how problems, solutions, and causal explanations are framed to serve political goals instead of emerging from objective analysis (Stone, 2012).

This framing explains why equity-oriented reforms can be portrayed as threats to excellence or accountability systems can be pitched as tools for justice. Thought leaders fluent in Stone's insights shape narratives intentionally, challenging dominant frames and advancing alternatives that align with their values.

Research Utilization Framework

Carol Weiss's (1979, 1991) Research Utilization Framework outlines how research affects policy not only through direct application but also through conceptual shifts, symbolic uses, and process contributions.

This helps explain why research may influence long-term thinking or the terms of debate even if it isn't cited directly. Thought leaders who understand Weiss's framework communicate research in ways that influence policy discourse and decisions.

Together, these frameworks provide powerful tools for understanding and navigating policy processes in education. They help thought leaders move beyond idealized rational models and engage more effectively with the complex realities of policy-making.

The most influential educational thought leaders typically draw on multiple frameworks. They understand that no single lens can capture the full complexity of educational policy. Their engagement becomes more strategic and impactful by considering political timing, belief systems, discourse framing, implementation variability, and research influence in tandem.

Navigating Political Complexities While Maintaining Intellectual Integrity

Educational thought leaders face the unique challenge of engaging in politically charged environments while staying true to their core intellectual commitments. Unlike academic settings, where the emphasis is on the depth of analysis and peer-reviewed credibility, policy engagement demands responsiveness to competing interests, value conflicts, and power dynamics. However, sacrificing intellectual integrity for political gain undermines both credibility and lasting influence. The most effective thought leaders navigate this terrain through deliberate strategies that allow them to operate politically without compromising their intellectual principles.

Principle-Priority Strategies

Educational thought leaders define clear boundaries around core values, allowing flexibility on the "how" while holding firm on the "why." They know when to compromise on timelines, assessment methods, or governance structures, but they don't waver on their foundational beliefs. For instance, Linda Darling-Hammond (2006) consistently champions equity and teacher professionalism, demonstrating flexibility on how these ideas are implemented across different political contexts, while her core values remain intact. Similarly, James Comer's (2005) commitment to child development as the foundation of school reform allows his work to adapt across districts and systems without diluting its essence.

This strategy keeps the door open to political compromise without losing sight of essential commitments. It enables sustained influence across diverse policy environments while preserving a coherent intellectual stance.

Evidence-Framing Strategies

To influence policy, you need more than just good data; you must frame evidence in ways that resonate with political audiences. Educational thought leaders translate research into policy-relevant terms without oversimplifying or distorting the findings. For example, Robert Slavin (2008) aligns research on educational programs with policymakers' concerns about accountability and costs, all while maintaining methodological rigor. Likewise, Claude Steele (2010) brings the complexity of stereotype threat into conversations about achievement gaps, balancing accessibility with scientific accuracy.

This approach acknowledges that policy communication is not the same as academic writing but insists on preserving the integrity of research, even when adapting it to meet the needs of different audiences.

Coalition-Building Strategies

Policy influence often depends on coalitions. However, this doesn't mean saying different things to different groups. Instead, thought leaders find common ground by crafting messages and positions that resonate across diverse audiences while remaining consistent at their core. For instance, Ted Sizer's (1992) Coalition of Essential Schools brought together a broad spectrum of educators, from progressive to more traditional advocates, through a shared commitment to intellectual rigor and student-centered learning. Similarly, Howard Gardner's (2011) work on multiple intelligences succeeded across political lines by expanding definitions of intelligence without undermining academic seriousness.

These coalitions don't require you to abandon core ideas. They succeed by articulating a vision that invites multiple interpretations while maintaining conceptual coherence.

Implementation-Realistic Strategies

Aspirations matter, but so do constraints. Educational thought leaders engage with the messy realities of implementation, crafting proposals that are both visionary and workable. Anthony Bryk's (2015) work on networked improvement communities acknowledges capacity gaps and institutional limitations while still pushing for deep change. Similarly, Lauren Resnick (2010) advocates for cognitively ambitious learning while addressing the day-to-day challenges of instructional change.

This strategy reflects a mindset of "practical idealism," which is about holding on to ambitious goals while developing realistic plans to achieve them. It's not about settling but about solving.

Timing-Sensitive Strategies

Timing matters. The most effective thought leaders adapt their engagement based on where the policy process stands, whether it's agenda setting, design, adoption, implementation, or reform. Michael Fullan (2016) tailors his strategies across phases, defining the problem at one stage, building capacity at another, and showing results when it's time for evaluation. Similarly, David Berliner (2009) changes how he communicates findings based on whether policymakers are identifying problems or evaluating existing programs.

Policy isn't a static game—it moves in cycles. Leaders who adapt to those cycles extend their influence over the long term.

Multi-Level Engagement Strategies

Educational governance isn't centralized—it's layered. Thought leaders who work across federal, state, and local levels build more comprehensive and coordinated influence. Linda Darling-Hammond (2006) engages at every level, from advising national commissions to working directly with local districts. James Comer's (2005) model works within schools and districts while shaping policy discussions at the state and national levels.

This strategy embraces the complexity of educational systems. Rather than trying to change the system from one angle, it addresses it holistically.

Sophistication Over Simplicity

These six strategies—principle prioritization, evidence framing, coalition building, implementation realism, timing sensitivity, and multi-level engagement—aren't checkboxes. They're habits of mind. They reflect a way of engaging with politics that is strategic and principled and responsive and grounded.

What distinguishes influential educational thought leaders is not just their ideas but how they position those ideas in the world. They don't avoid politics, and they don't get swallowed by it. Instead, they navigate it with clarity, consistency, and craft.

Translating Research and Practice Into Policy Frameworks

Educational thought leaders understand that turning research findings into effective policy is a complex process. It's not simply about presenting data or recommending best practices. To influence meaningful change, these leaders must bridge the gap between academic research, everyday classroom practices, and the often-chaotic world of policy. Successful policy development requires thoughtful translation—transforming research insights into relevant, actionable, and viable solutions for policymakers.

Framing Problems With Research Insights

The first step in translating research into policy is recognizing that policymakers are primarily concerned with solving problems, not just implementing research. Educational thought leaders frame their findings around issues that are already top of mind for policymakers. Instead of simply presenting research, they connect it to the problems already on the policy agenda, or they help reshape existing problems to demonstrate how research can offer solutions.

For example, David Berliner and Bruce Biddle's work on educational achievement redefined the problem of underachievement by focusing on the impact of socioeconomic factors and resource disparities, rather than reinforcing the narrative of an educational "crisis." This reframing didn't just present data—it changed how policymakers understood the issue, offering a new perspective on educational achievement (Berliner & Biddle, 1995). Similarly, Claude Steele's (2010) research on stereotype threat was framed to address achievement gaps by emphasizing the psychological factors that contribute to disparities, making his findings more relevant to policy discussions on equity and achievement.

By framing the problem in terms that policymakers care about, these thought leaders don't just add to the conversation—they reshape it.

Scaling Solutions to Fit the System

Once a promising practice or idea has been identified, the next step is translating it into a policy that can work on a larger scale. Moving from a successful small-scale pilot program to a large-scale policy requires thoughtful scaling, ensuring that key elements are consistent while allowing for adaptation to local contexts.

Anthony Bryk's work on school improvement exemplifies this balance. He emphasizes the importance of maintaining core principles while adapting solutions to fit different school contexts. Rather than advocating for a one-size-fits-all approach, Bryk's (2015) strategy ensures that policies can scale up without losing the effectiveness of the original practices. Linda Darling-Hammond's (2006) approach to teacher development also reflects this balance, focusing on embedding essential principles in policy while allowing for contextual flexibility in implementation.

Design thinking offers another powerful tool for scaling educational solutions. Rooted in the work of Herbert Simon and popularized by David Kelley and the Stanford d.school, design thinking emphasizes iterative, human-centered problem-solving. Its process—empathy, definition, ideation, prototyping, and testing—helps education leaders co-create solutions with stakeholders while preserving core intentions (Simon, 1969; Kelley & Kelley, 2013). Used in initiatives like IDEO's school redesign projects and the d.school's K12 Lab Network, this approach has helped scale reforms that are both principle-driven and locally responsive.

Scaling solutions effectively involves understanding the balance between consistency and flexibility. By creating frameworks that allow for local adaptation while maintaining key principles, educational thought leaders ensure that successful practices can be applied across diverse contexts.

Building Capacity for Implementation

A policy may look excellent on paper, but it will only succeed if those responsible for implementing it have the necessary capacity, knowledge, skills, and resources. Educational thought leaders recognize this reality, which is why they focus not only on creating policies but also on building capacity for successful implementation.

Michael Fullan's approach to school reform highlights this focus on capacity. He stresses that it's not just about identifying what needs to change but also about supporting educators in making those changes. Fullan's (2016) emphasis on professional development, collaborative structures, and leadership development provides a foundation for effective policy implementation. Similarly, Richard Elmore (2004) underscores the importance of reciprocal accountability, where teachers and administrators are not only held to standards but are also supported with the resources and training necessary to meet those standards.

Without building the capacity for implementation, policies are at risk of becoming mere mandates that fail to resonate with those tasked with carrying them out.

Aligning Incentives With Policy Goals

For a policy to be effective, it must align with the motivations of those expected to implement it. This alignment includes both external incentives, such as funding or regulations, and internal motivations, such as a teacher's intrinsic desire to improve student outcomes. Educational thought leaders understand that lasting change happens when policies tap into both types of motivation.

Research by Ryan and Deci (2000) on self-determination theory highlights how policies can support intrinsic motivation by addressing psychological needs for autonomy, competence, and relatedness. When policies respect these needs, they foster deeper commitment to the goals of the policy. Daniel Pink's (2009) work on motivation reinforces this concept, emphasizing that autonomy, mastery, and purpose are key drivers for motivating educators and students alike. By aligning policy incentives with these intrinsic motivators, policymakers can create conditions for lasting, meaningful change.

Addressing Resource Realities

No matter how well-designed a policy is, it cannot succeed without adequate resources. Educational thought leaders recognize the importance of integrating resource considerations into their policy recommendations. They don't simply develop idealistic solutions; they consider what it will take to make those solutions work in the real world.

Henry Levin's (2001) work on cost-effectiveness analysis provides a framework for understanding how educational interventions can be both effective and cost-efficient. Levin's research helps policymakers weigh the financial implications of different policy options, ensuring that policies are not only aspirational but also economically viable. Allan Odden's (2009) work on school finance reform emphasizes that funding must be aligned with educational strategies, showing that financial resources should directly support the educational goals of the policy.

Integrating Evaluation and Feedback

Finally, educational thought leaders understand that policy development is not a one-time event but an ongoing process of improvement. For this reason, they stress the importance of evaluation systems that provide continuous feedback on both the implementation process and the outcomes.

Michael Patton's utilization-focused evaluation is an excellent example of how evaluations can be used to improve programs, rather than simply assess their success. By focusing on feedback that supports continuous improvement, policies can evolve based on real-world experiences (Patton, 2008). Similarly, Black and Wiliam's (1998) work on assessment for learning demonstrates how assessment systems can support ongoing growth and improvement, rather than just measuring outcomes.

By integrating evaluation into policy frameworks, these thought leaders ensure that policies remain adaptable and responsive to changing needs.

These strategies—framing the problem, scaling solutions, building capacity, aligning incentives, addressing resources, and integrating evaluation—represent how educational thought leaders translate research and practice into actionable, viable policies. Through these strategies, they ensure that policies are not only grounded in research but are also practical enough to be successfully implemented.

The most influential educational thought leaders understand that effective policy development is complex, requiring careful attention to various factors. By employing a combination of these strategies, they ensure that their work has a lasting, meaningful impact on the educational landscape.

Historical Examples of Influential Policy Engagement

Let's look at how the strategies discussed earlier play out in practice. These historical examples highlight common strategies while showcasing unique adaptations in different educational contexts.

Jerome Bruner and the Curriculum Reform Movement

Jerome Bruner's impact on U.S. education post-Sputnik (1957) illustrates how educational thought leadership can shape national priorities. Bruner's work, notably from the 1959 Woods Hole Conference and *The Process of Education*, changed the course of American education:

- **Reframing the Problem:** shifting the focus from content coverage to deeper conceptual understanding (Bruner, 1960)

- **Timing and Context:** leveraging the Cold War's political context to advocate for educational reform (Bruner, 1960)

- **Broad Coalitions:** bridging the divide between cognitive science and progressive educators to build support (Schunk, 2008)

- **Practical Implementation:** offering curriculum examples, such as the *Man: A Course of Study* program, that demonstrated the viability of his ideas in classrooms (Bruner, 1966)

Bruner's work redefined educational challenges and provided a concrete roadmap for reform.

James Comer and the School Development Program

James Comer's School Development Program (SDP) emphasizes a holistic approach to child development. His policy influence extended from local to national levels:

- **Core Principles:** emphasizing child development across cognitive, social, emotional, and physical domains (Comer, 1980)

- **Engagement Across Multiple Levels:** engaging with various educational systems to affect broad policy change (Comer, 1980)

- **Implementation Capacity:** focusing on professional development and support for successful program implementation (Comer, 1980)

- **Broad Coalition:** garnering support from educators, parents, and policymakers across political divides (Comer, 1980)

Comer's work highlights the power of consistency in principles and multi-level engagement in driving reform.

Linda Darling-Hammond and Teacher Policy Reform

Linda Darling-Hammond's influence on teacher preparation and certification is a key example of research translating into policy:

- **Evidence for Policy:** aligning her research with policymakers' priorities, such as economic competitiveness and achievement gaps (Darling-Hammond, 2000)

- **Multi-Level Engagement:** working at federal, state, and district levels to shape teacher policy (Darling-Hammond, 2000)

- **Solution Scaling:** advocating for core principles while allowing for context-specific implementation (Darling-Hammond, 2000)

- **Building Coalitions:** uniting various stakeholders, including teacher unions and reform advocates, to support her proposals (Darling-Hammond, 2000)

Darling-Hammond's work has deeply impacted teacher policy through evidence-based practice and practical application.

Howard Gardner and Multiple Intelligences

Howard Gardner's theory of multiple intelligences transformed educational practice globally. His policy engagement focused on the following:

- **Commitment to Core Principles:** emphasizing the idea of plural intelligences while adapting his theory to different educational contexts (Gardner, 1983)

- **Building Coalitions:** garnering support from diverse stakeholders, including cognitive scientists and arts educators (Gardner, 1983)

- **Framing Evidence for Education:** translating his theory into practical educational strategies, such as differentiated instruction (Gardner, 1983)

- **Addressing Implementation Challenges:** providing concrete examples of how multiple intelligences could be applied within school limitations (Gardner, 1983)

Gardner's ability to maintain the integrity of his theory while adapting it to practical educational needs has made his ideas influential in global policy.

Common Themes in Historical Policy Engagement

Despite their different contexts and focuses, these leaders shared several strategies in their policy work:

- **Reframing Problems:** shifting the way educational issues are understood (Bruner, 1960; Comer, 1980)

- **Principle-Driven Flexibility:** maintaining core values while adapting to various contexts (Gardner, 1983; Darling-Hammond, 2000)

- **Coalition Building:** uniting diverse groups to gain widespread support (Comer, 1980; Gardner, 1983)

- **Focus on Practical Implementation:** offering tangible solutions that could be applied in real classrooms (Bruner, 1966; Darling-Hammond, 2000)

- **Multi-Level Engagement:** engaging at all levels of government to ensure broad influence (Darling-Hammond, 2000)

These strategies not only helped them achieve policy influence but also allowed them to refine and adapt their ideas through feedback from the policy and practice realms. The examples of Bruner, Comer, Darling-Hammond, and Gardner show how thoughtful policy engagement can amplify educational ideas and extend their impact across systems.

As we move forward, we'll explore other dimensions of educational thought leadership, from ethics to future trends, and look at how policy engagement interacts with these other factors to shape the future of education.

Chapter 9:
Ethical Dimensions of Educational Thought Leadership

The ethical foundations of educational thought leadership are crucial yet often overlooked. While much of the conversation around educational ideas focuses on methodological rigor, clarity, and practical application, the ethical principles that underpin these ideas often remain unstated.

However, these ethical considerations are what ultimately determine whether educational thought leadership promotes true betterment or simply upholds existing power structures. Do these ideas expand human potential, or do they merely improve system efficiency? Do they honor human dignity, or do they reduce people to mere tools for institutional ends?

This chapter delves into the ethical dimensions of educational thought leadership. It explores how educational thought leaders confront fundamental ethical questions about the purpose of education, how they navigate the tensions between conflicting values, and how they develop approaches that align their methods with their goals, without sacrificing ethical principles for convenience.

Understanding Ethical Frameworks in Educational Contexts

Educational thought leaders bring a nuanced understanding of how ethical frameworks apply to educational issues. They understand that education is inherently about value-based decisions that can't be resolved by empirical research alone.

The following questions require ethical reasoning, not just technical analysis:

- What is the purpose of education?

- What values should guide educational priorities?

Educational decisions involve value judgments:

- What knowledge is worth teaching?

- Which human capacities should we nurture?

- What kinds of relationships should be formed between generations, and what social structures should be upheld or changed?

Understanding these ethical dimensions is key to engaging thoughtfully with the ethics of education.

Virtue Ethics

One important ethical framework is virtue ethics, which provides tools for examining education's role in shaping character. Originally developed by Aristotle and expanded by contemporary philosophers like Alasdair MacIntyre (1981) and Martha Nussbaum (2011), virtue ethics emphasizes the cultivation of virtuous traits—such as curiosity, honesty, and compassion—through practice and habituation, rather than simply following rules or calculating consequences. This perspective focuses on education's role in developing dispositions that enable human betterment, especially within communities of practice.

Through the lens of virtue ethics, we see education as more than just the transmission of knowledge or the development of skills. It becomes a process of character formation. Thought leaders who adopt this perspective recognize that education shapes who people become, not just what they know or can do. This framework also sheds light on questions about educational aims and teacher-student relationships. It suggests that educational environments should not only focus on intellectual growth but also on fostering moral virtues. Teachers who model virtues in their behavior influence students profoundly, often more so than the formal curriculum.

Deontological Ethics: Rights and Duties in Education

Another essential framework is deontological ethics, which provides a way to examine rights and duties in educational contexts. Developed by Immanuel Kant and later refined by philosophers like John Rawls (1993) and Onora O'Neill (2002), deontological ethics emphasizes the need to respect individuals as ends in themselves rather than means to other ends. It highlights universal principles that protect human dignity, regardless of the consequences.

Deontological ethics emphasizes the importance of respecting student autonomy alongside education's developmental function. By balancing guidance with respect for students' growing agency, education can navigate the tension between authority and self-determination, something other frameworks may oversimplify. Thought leaders who embrace this approach recognize that education must respect individuals as people while helping them grow. This framework also highlights the limits of educational authority, helping define essential student rights and protections, regardless of their background or abilities.

Consequentialist Ethics: Examining Educational Outcomes

Consequentialist ethics focuses on the broader social consequences of educational practices. Developed by John Stuart Mill (1863) and expanded by philosophers like Peter Singer and Amartya Sen (1999), consequentialism prioritizes the need to promote overall welfare rather than strictly adhering to rules or developing virtues. This framework encourages an analysis of how educational practices impact different groups, particularly marginalized or vulnerable communities.

Consequentialist ethics highlight the social justice dimensions of education. It asks how education can address inequalities and foster greater societal welfare. Thought leaders who adopt this framework recognize that education produces outcomes that extend beyond the individual, affecting society as a whole. This approach is particularly useful when examining issues such as resource allocation and opportunity distribution within educational systems.

Care Ethics: The Relational Nature of Education

Another critical framework is care ethics, which was pioneered by Carol Gilligan (1982) and Nel Noddings (1984) and further developed by philosophers like Virginia Held and Eva Feder Kittay. Care ethics emphasizes the importance of relational dynamics in education, focusing on the attentiveness to specific needs in caring relationships. Rather than adhering to impersonal rules or abstract principles, this framework stresses the importance of responding to the unique needs of students within the context of teacher-student relationships.

Care ethics deepens our understanding of education as fundamentally relational. It reminds us that the quality of relationships within educational settings—emotional safety, trust, and mutual respect—plays a central role in fostering student development. Thought leaders who draw on care ethics understand that education is not just about knowledge transfer but about nurturing students through responsive, caring relationships.

Social Justice Frameworks: Education and Structural Inequality

Social justice frameworks are essential for understanding education's broader structural dimensions. Drawing from theorists like John Rawls (1971), Iris Marion Young (2000), and Charles Mills (1997), social justice frameworks focus on how educational institutions distribute advantages and disadvantages and how they either perpetuate or challenge existing social inequalities. These frameworks highlight the political dimensions of education, urging educators and policymakers to consider how their decisions impact social structures.

Through a social justice lens, education is seen not just as a tool for individual development but as a mechanism for addressing broader issues of inequality and power. Thought leaders who apply this perspective recognize that educational systems are embedded in political and social contexts, and any discussion of educational reform must include an analysis of how resources and opportunities are distributed among different groups.

Capabilities Approaches: Expanding Human Freedom Through Education

Finally, capabilities approaches provide a framework for understanding education's role in expanding human freedom. Developed by Amartya Sen (1999) and Martha Nussbaum (2011), capabilities approaches focus on enabling individuals to achieve lives they can value, rather than simply providing resources or material satisfaction (Sen, 1999; Nussbaum, 2011). This framework emphasizes the development of substantive freedoms—real opportunities to achieve various functions, rather than just formal rights or material goods.

Capacities frameworks encourage us to think about education as a means to expand genuine freedom and human potential. Instead of reducing education to economic preparation or credentialing, they advocate for an approach that enhances individuals' ability to choose and pursue meaningful lives. Thought leaders who use capabilities approaches aim to ensure that education promotes substantive freedom, addressing not only academic achievement but also human betterment.

Synthesizing Ethical Frameworks in Education

These six frameworks offer educational thought leaders essential tools for understanding and engaging with the ethical dimensions of educational issues. Rather than relying on a single framework, the most influential thought leaders often draw on multiple perspectives. They understand that education involves many dimensions, character development, human dignity, social welfare, relationships, justice, and freedom, each of which requires attention. By synthesizing these ethical frameworks, thought leaders can create more comprehensive and thoughtful approaches to education that reflect the complex moral questions at their core.

Navigating Tensions Between Competing Educational Values

Educational thought leaders face the challenge of navigating complex tensions between competing values in education. These tensions are an inherent part of the educational landscape, and they cannot be easily resolved. For example, values like excellence versus equity, freedom versus guidance, individual development versus social cohesion, and tradition versus innovation often pull in different directions, creating dilemmas for educators and policymakers. Thought leaders approach these value conflicts with strategies that allow for nuanced and thoughtful resolutions. Instead of simplifying these tensions or choosing one value over another, they develop frameworks that respect the complexity of educational goals.

Integration Strategies

One effective strategy for navigating competing values is integration, seeking deeper purposes that underlie seemingly conflicting values. Rather than framing educational tensions as zero-sum conflicts that require either/or choices, thought leaders look for ways that opposing values can serve a shared underlying goal. By identifying these common purposes, they create frameworks that integrate important educational aims. This approach leads to more sophisticated and productive resolutions as opposed to false dichotomies or oversimplified compromises.

John Dewey's (1916) educational philosophy provides a clear example of this integration approach. Dewey understood that individual development and social participation are not opposing values but are both driven by a common purpose: growth. By connecting growth with both personal and community development, Dewey's framework integrates these values, allowing education to foster individuals who grow through their participation in society.

Martha Nussbaum's (2011) capabilities approach also exemplifies integration, particularly in balancing universal principles with the uniqueness of language and culture. Nussbaum emphasizes that, while cultures may differ, all people deserve access to capabilities that enable them to lead dignified lives. This allows educational systems to respect cultural differences while ensuring that all individuals have access to the fundamental freedoms needed for betterment.

Contextual Balancing

Another key strategy is contextual balancing, which adjusts the priority of competing values based on specific situations. Rather than applying a universal hierarchy of values, thought leaders recognize that different contexts, student needs, and educational goals may require different emphases. This approach allows for more responsive and flexible strategies in addressing educational challenges.

Howard Gardner's (1983) theory of multiple intelligences provides a practical example of contextual balancing. Gardner argued that people possess different kinds of intelligences, and educational strategies should vary depending on the strengths and needs of individual students. This approach moves beyond rigid value hierarchies, allowing educators to respond to the unique characteristics of their students and adjust their teaching methods accordingly.

Similarly, Lisa Delpit's (2006) work on cultural responsiveness highlights how effective teaching strategies depend on understanding the cultural backgrounds of students. By balancing the value of explicit instruction with the importance of student-centered approaches, Delpit emphasizes that effective teaching requires flexibility based on context.

Means-Ends Alignment

A third strategy is means-ends alignment, which ensures that educational practices are consistent with the values they are intended to promote. Thought leaders critically examine whether the methods used in education align with the ends they claim to achieve, addressing any contradictions between rhetoric and reality. This strategy ensures that educational systems remain consistent and coherent in their practices.

Paulo Freire's (1970) critical pedagogy is a prime example of means-end alignment. Freire critiqued traditional "banking" methods of education, where students are passive recipients of information. He argued that such methods contradicted the liberatory aims of education, as they stifled students' critical thinking and autonomy. Freire's dialogical approach instead created a more consistent alignment between educational methods and the goal of fostering emancipatory learning.

Similarly, Nel Noddings' (1984) ethics of care challenges educators to examine whether the relationships they claim to value are truly reflected in their day-to-day practice. Her work highlights the disconnect that can exist between caring language and uncaring methods, arguing that genuine care must be embedded in how we teach and lead. When there's a gap between what educators say they believe and what they do, it's often because either they don't fully believe it, or they believe it, but lack the capacity, support, or tools to act on it meaningfully.

Developmental Sequencing

Developmental sequencing addresses value tensions by recognizing that the emphasis placed on certain values should shift over time, in line with developmental stages. Rather than aiming for a static resolution between competing values, thought leaders develop frameworks that evolve as individuals grow and change.

Lawrence Kohlberg's (1981) theory of moral development illustrates this approach. He identified stages of moral reasoning, suggesting that moral education should emphasize different values depending on the learner's stage. For instance, young children may respond best to concrete rules and consequences, while older students are better positioned to grapple with abstract ethical reasoning.

William Perry's (1970) model of intellectual development further reinforces this view. Perry observed that students' beliefs about certainty, authority, and relativism evolve through predictable stages. Effective education, therefore, must be responsive to where students are in this developmental arc, rather than imposing a fixed epistemological stance.

Importantly, developmental sequencing involves both values and beliefs. Values tend to be more fluid, context-dependent, and shaped by experience, new knowledge, or social roles. Beliefs, however, are often more stable and rooted in deeply held life principles and, therefore, slower to change (Bove et al., 2024; Skitka et al., 2005). Recognizing this distinction is crucial. While values may adapt over time, effective educational leadership must also consider the enduring role of beliefs in shaping how individuals make meaning and engage with change.

Pluralistic Constraint

Another strategy for managing educational tensions is pluralistic constraint, which establishes minimum standards while allowing for diverse approaches to achieving those standards. Thought leaders using this strategy avoid imposing uniform solutions and instead identify essential constraints that all legitimate educational methods must meet, while still permitting flexibility and diversity in how those constraints are met.

Amartya Sen's (1999) capabilities approach is a prime example of pluralistic constraint. Sen emphasizes that while all educational systems must ensure basic capabilities that enable people to lead dignified lives, how those capabilities are developed can vary widely. This flexibility allows for different cultural and contextual adaptations while maintaining a commitment to basic human development requirements.

Similarly, John Rawls' (1971) theory of justice establishes minimum fairness principles that educational systems must satisfy, such as ensuring equal opportunities for all. However, Rawls allows for diverse systems and methods beyond these minimum requirements, enabling educational systems to adapt to local contexts while adhering to fundamental principles of justice.

Practical Wisdom

Finally, educational thought leaders often emphasize practical wisdom (phronesis) over rigid rules or algorithms. This strategy focuses on developing educators' judgment to navigate complex educational situations, allowing for flexibility in responding to value tensions in specific contexts.

Aristotle's (ca. 350 B.C.E./1985) virtue ethics underscores the importance of practical wisdom in ethical decision-making. According to Aristotle, virtue is not about following prescribed rules but about developing the judgment to act appropriately in varied circumstances. Educational systems should aim to cultivate this wisdom in teachers, enabling them to respond to the complexities of student needs and educational goals.

Joseph Dunne's (1993) work on practical knowledge emphasizes the importance of teachers' judgment in responding to the unique challenges of the classroom. Rather than applying uniform rules, Dunne argues that effective teaching requires the development of wisdom to make decisions based on the specific context.

A Multifaceted Approach to Educational Value Tensions

These strategies represent the thoughtful approaches that educational thought leaders use to navigate tensions between competing educational values. Rather than simply denying these tensions or choosing sides, they embrace the complexity of education and develop more sophisticated, flexible frameworks that address the variety of issues at play.

Most influential educational thought leaders employ multiple strategies, recognizing that no single approach can fully resolve the multifaceted tensions within education. Their ability to address the underlying purposes, developmental stages, and contextual factors while ensuring that educational practices align with stated values enables them to create more responsive and thoughtful educational frameworks.

Aligning Educational Means With Ethical Ends

Educational thought leaders often face the challenge of aligning the methods they use with the ethical values they aim to promote. In many educational settings, there is a noticeable gap between the values that educators espouse and the practices they employ. This disconnection undermines the effectiveness of education, making it essential for thought leaders to create more consistent and ethical frameworks. By developing strategies that bridge this gap, educational leaders ensure that their methods genuinely reflect the values they seek to instill.

Identifying Contradictions Between Rhetoric and Reality

The first strategy for aligning educational means with ethical ends is to identify contradictions between what is promised and what is practiced. Thought leaders do not accept surface-level claims that educational methods align with their ethical values; instead, they critically examine whether these practices reflect the values they claim to promote.

Paulo Freire's (1970) critique of traditional education exemplifies this contradiction-identification strategy. As referenced earlier, he analyzed the "banking model" of education, where teachers deposit knowledge into passive students, exposing a fundamental contradiction between the stated goal of education as a liberatory process and the authoritarian methods used to deliver it. Similarly, John Dewey (1916) raised comparable concerns decades earlier, noting that the democratic ideals often cited as central to education were frequently undercut by rigid structures and practices that limited student agency and inquiry. Together, these critiques illustrate how uncovering contradictions within dominant educational paradigms can drive the development of more equitable, authentic practices.

This strategy encourages educational leaders to scrutinize the gap between what is promised in rhetoric and what is practiced, enabling a more honest and critical assessment of educational systems.

Embodying Values Through Methods

The second strategy is to ensure that the methods used in education inherently reflect the values being promoted. Instead of viewing educational methods as mere tools to achieve separate ends, this approach integrates the process itself with the values it seeks to instill.

Maria Montessori's (1964) educational method, for instance, embodies the values of autonomy and self-directed learning. Her classroom design and teacher roles foster an environment where students take charge of their learning, manifesting the very values of independence and agency that the curriculum promotes.

Matthew Lipman's (2003) *Philosophy for Children* also exemplifies this approach. In Lipman's model, the act of engaging in philosophical inquiry is not separate from the teaching of philosophy itself—students actively engage in thinking, not just learning about thinking. This method allows the values of critical thinking and inquiry to be embodied in the learning process itself.

By focusing on methods that inherently embody the desired values, educational thought leaders can ensure greater consistency between educational practices and ethical goals.

Analyzing the Hidden Curriculum

The third strategy involves analyzing the hidden curriculum—implicit lessons taught through the structure, relationships, and dynamics within educational institutions. These messages often convey values and norms that may contradict the overt goals of education, making it crucial to assess both the explicit and implicit content of education.

Philip Jackson's (1968) work on the hidden curriculum underscores how the physical arrangement of schools and classroom behaviors subtly teach compliance, competition, and conformity, which may contradict educational goals of fostering critical thinking or cooperation. Similarly, Michael Apple's (2004) analysis of curriculum materials highlights how they may promote certain ideological and economic values, even when the stated intent is to remain neutral.

The hidden curriculum enables educators to address the full spectrum of influences on students, ensuring alignment between formal curriculum goals and the broader messages embedded in the educational environment.

Examining Power Dynamics in Education

Educational thought leaders also examine the power structures within schools and classrooms, as these authority arrangements often shape educational outcomes in ways that affect ethical goals. Authoritarian relationships themselves constitute a powerful means of education, whether or not they are acknowledged.

Michel Foucault's (1977) analysis of educational institutions focuses on how power dynamics, particularly surveillance and normalization, shape students' behaviors and perceptions. Foucault argued that the very structure of educational institutions—how students are monitored and controlled—contributes significantly to the educational experience, often undermining emancipatory goals.

Bell Hooks (1994) also critiqued traditional classroom authority dynamics, asserting that they could reinforce societal hierarchies and limit students' ability to critically engage with ideas.

By focusing on power arrangements, educational leaders can better understand how authority structures influence ethical outcomes, ensuring that educational practices support the desired ethical goals.

Aligning Assessment Practices With Educational Values

Another key strategy is ensuring that assessment practices align with the ethical values educators seek to promote. Traditional assessment methods often prioritize rote memorization and standardized testing, which can be at odds with educational goals that emphasize creativity, critical thinking, and social responsibility.

Grant Wiggins' (1998) work on authentic assessment focuses on evaluating students based on their ability to apply knowledge meaningfully, rather than just recalling facts. This approach better aligns with the educational goals of deep understanding and practical application. Similarly, Howard Gardner's (1983) theory of multiple intelligences encourages assessment methods that recognize the diverse ways in which students learn, ensuring that evaluations reflect a more holistic understanding of student abilities.

By designing assessments that align with broader educational goals, thought leaders can ensure that evaluation methods contribute to, rather than undermine, the ethical purposes of education.

Incorporating Diverse Stakeholder Voices in Evaluation

The final strategy involves incorporating diverse stakeholder perspectives in the evaluation of educational practices. Instead of relying solely on expert opinions or top-down assessments, this approach seeks to include the voices of those most affected by educational practices, particularly students and their families.

Michael Quinn Patton's (2008) utilization-focused evaluation emphasizes the importance of including diverse stakeholders in the evaluation process, ensuring that the educational system serves the needs of all involved. This approach not only makes evaluations more comprehensive but also ensures that the methods used in education truly serve the diverse populations they are meant to support.

Including diverse perspectives in the alignment process allows for a more inclusive and accurate assessment of whether educational practices are truly achieving their intended ethical goals.

Multidimensional Alignment

These strategies—contradiction identification, method embodiment, hidden curriculum analysis, power analysis, assessment alignment, and stakeholder voice—represent how educational thought leaders address the complex issue of aligning educational means with ethical ends. By employing multiple strategies, thought leaders recognize that alignment is not a one-dimensional task. It requires contradictions, power dynamics, assessment practices, and the implicit messages conveyed by educational structures to be addressed. This multifaceted approach ensures that educational methods truly reflect the ethical values they aim to promote.

Case Studies in Ethical Educational Thought Leadership

Examining real-world examples of ethical thought leadership in education helps to illustrate how the strategies discussed previously manifest in practice. These cases highlight common patterns while showcasing distinctive applications across different educational contexts.

Paulo Freire and Critical Pedagogy

Paulo Freire's development of critical pedagogy represents a pivotal moment in educational thought leadership. From his early literacy work in Brazil to the global impact of his seminal work *Pedagogy of the Oppressed*, Freire's ethical approach transformed educational practices around the world. His work exemplifies how ethical education leadership can challenge and redefine traditional educational methods.

Identifying Contradictions in Educational Practices

One of the core elements of Freire's ethical approach was his ability to identify contradictions within educational practices. Freire's critique of the traditional "banking model" of education revealed significant inconsistencies between liberatory rhetoric and actual practices. He pointed out that many educational systems that treated students as passive recipients of knowledge contradicted their stated goals of promoting emancipation and critical thinking.

Freire's analysis of the banking method demonstrates his sophisticated understanding of how educational methods can often undermine the very ends they claim to serve. By revealing the gap between the rhetoric of liberation and the reality of passive learning, Freire opened the door to more honest assessments of educational practices.

Embodying Values through Educational Methods

Freire's pedagogical approach was not just a critique but also a solution. His dialogical method—a form of teaching centered around mutual dialogue and inquiry—embodied the very values he sought to promote. In contrast to traditional methods that treated education as a one-way transmission of knowledge, Freire's method actively engaged students in the process of learning, fostering critical consciousness through shared dialogue.

By developing a process that embodied critical thinking and problem-solving, Freire ensured that the educational means themselves aligned with the liberatory ends he sought. This method-embodiment strategy helped create a more consistent and authentic educational experience.

Power Analysis

Freire's power-analysis strategy is another key aspect of his ethical thought leadership. He understood that educational authority structures were not neutral; they shaped and influenced the learning process. Instead of focusing solely on curriculum content, Freire examined how teacher-student relationships and classroom authority impacted students' educational experiences.

Through this lens, Freire revealed how power dynamics—whether authoritarian or egalitarian—were crucial in determining the ethical outcomes of education. His analysis of these authority structures allowed for a more comprehensive understanding of how educational means could either reinforce or challenge existing social hierarchies.

Integrating Competing Educational Values

In his work, Freire also demonstrated an ability to integrate seemingly competing educational values. Many debates in education center around the tension between teacher authority and student autonomy. Traditional education often portrays these as opposing forces; either the teacher must dominate, or the students must be entirely self-directed. Freire, however, introduced the concept of a teacher-student partnership, where both parties contribute to the learning process.

This approach allowed Freire to transcend the false dichotomy between authoritarianism and complete student freedom. Instead, he proposed a collaborative model where both the teacher and the student shared responsibility for the learning process, thus integrating these two values in a way that supported the overarching goal of critical consciousness development.

Adapting to Contexts While Maintaining Ethical Integrity

Freire's ability to adapt his pedagogical approach to different cultural and political contexts further demonstrates his ethical leadership. Rather than applying a rigid, one-size-fits-all method, Freire emphasized the importance of adapting critical pedagogy to local conditions. This contextual-balancing strategy ensured that the core ethical commitment to critical consciousness was maintained while respecting the unique circumstances of each educational setting.

This adaptability allowed Freire's approach to be applied across diverse contexts without sacrificing its ethical foundations, proving that educational methods can be both flexible and principled.

Empowering Marginalized Voices

Empowering marginalized voices represents the culminating step in the metaphorical process of liberation. Paulo Freire's work offers a compelling example of this stakeholder-voice strategy. He was deeply committed to incorporating the perspectives of marginalized communities in both the development and evaluation of educational practices. For Freire, education was never a top-down transmission of knowledge from experts to passive recipients. Instead, he envisioned it as a collaborative process rooted in dialogue, where those most impacted by educational systems, particularly oppressed groups, played an essential role in shaping their own learning experiences.

By focusing on these voices, Freire developed more responsive and inclusive educational methods, ones grounded in the realities of learners' lives. This approach not only made education more effective but also aligned it with a broader vision of social justice. In doing so, Freire demonstrated that true liberation in education is not achieved until those historically excluded are empowered to lead and co-create the systems meant to serve them.

Nel Noddings and Care Ethics in Education

Nel Noddings' development of care ethics in education represents a groundbreaking approach to ethical thought leadership in the field. Her work, beginning with the theoretical framework presented in *Caring* and extending through its practical applications in schools, has reshaped how we think about relationships in education. Noddings' contributions highlight the importance of fostering caring, human-centered environments that prioritize student well-being and personal growth (Noddings, 1984).

Uncovering Contradictions Between Rhetoric and Practice

One of the defining features of Noddings' ethical approach is her ability to identify contradictions between the rhetoric of care and the actual practices in educational settings. She didn't take the claim that education is inherently nurturing at face value; instead, she critically examined how many educational structures—such as competitive grading, impersonal student-teacher relationships, standardized testing, and coercive discipline—contradicted the caring values they purported to uphold (Noddings, 1984).

Noddings' analysis of these contradictions provides a more honest and nuanced understanding of education. She highlighted how institutional practices, which often prioritize efficiency over the relational aspects of teaching and learning, frequently undermine the goals of care and student welfare. This critical perspective urges educators to reevaluate how their methods align (or fail to align) with their stated values (Held, 2006).

Embodying Care Through Educational Relationships

Instead of treating care as an abstract or separate subject to be taught, Noddings' relational approach embeds care directly into the educational process. In her framework, caring isn't just an ideal to aspire to; it is something actively demonstrated through the relationships between teachers and students. The process of teaching itself, through attentiveness, engagement, and mutual respect, becomes the method of communicating care (Noddings, 1984).

By focusing on relational dynamics, Noddings emphasizes that genuine care is communicated not just through instructional content but through the quality of the relationships that form the foundation of the educational experience. This method-embodiment strategy creates a more authentic and consistent alignment between the educational process and its ethical goals (Held, 2006).

Integrating Academic and Personal Development

A significant part of Noddings' ethical leadership is her ability to integrate seemingly competing educational values. Traditional educational models often treat academic achievement and personal development as separate, sometimes opposing, goals. Noddings (1984), however, demonstrated that when properly understood, both academic and personal development contribute to a broader goal: human betterment.

This integration transcends the false dichotomy that splits intellectual growth from emotional or social well-being. By framing both academic success and personal development as interrelated aspects of a well-rounded education, Noddings (2005) presents a more holistic approach that better serves the needs of students as whole individuals.

Aligning Means With Caring Ends

In her work, Noddings constantly returns to the idea that educational practices must align with the values they seek to promote. She did not merely question whether the outcomes of education served the right ends; she also examined how the means, such as teaching methods, classroom structures, and student-teacher interactions, could either support or undermine the values of care (Noddings, 1984).

For Noddings, it was essential that educational practices themselves were aligned with the nurturing and supportive relationships that care ethics requires. This means that educators must not only teach academic content but also ensure that their methods, classroom management, and interactions reflect a commitment to care and respect for students (Held, 2006).

Uncovering the Hidden Curriculum

Another crucial aspect of Noddings' approach is her focus on the hidden curriculum, the implicit values and messages conveyed through the structure of the educational system, beyond what is explicitly taught. While traditional educational models focus primarily on the formal curriculum, Noddings (1984) also emphasized how institutional practices, such as grading systems, competition, and hierarchical teacher-student dynamics, implicitly teach values that may conflict with the stated goals of education.

By examining the hidden curriculum, Noddings expanded the scope of ethical analysis in education. She showed that it is not enough to simply look at what is taught in the classroom; educators must also critically assess how school structures and social dynamics convey values that may inadvertently shape students' attitudes and behaviors (Held, 2006).

Adapting Care to Contexts

Noddings was also keenly aware of the importance of context in applying care ethics. She argued that care should not be a one-size-fits-all approach; rather, it must be adapted to the specific needs and circumstances of individual students and relationships. While maintaining a core commitment to responsiveness and attentiveness, educators should adjust their approach based on the unique challenges and opportunities each situation presents (Noddings, 2013).

This contextual-balancing strategy allows educators to respond flexibly to the needs of their students while ensuring that the ethical commitment to care remains consistent. Noddings' focus on adaptability in education shows how ethical principles can be applied in diverse contexts without compromising their core values (Held, 2006).

Her ethical thought leadership challenges educators to consider not just what they teach, but how they teach—and, crucially, the relationships they foster along the way. Noddings' work (1984, 2013) serves as a powerful reminder that education is not just about transmitting knowledge but about nurturing individuals in ways that support their growth as whole, flourishing human beings.

John Dewey and Democratic Education

John Dewey's contributions to democratic education have left a profound mark on both ethical thought leadership and educational theory. Through his foundational work in *Democracy and Education* and the implementation of laboratory schools, Dewey demonstrated a commitment to creating educational systems that support democratic values. His approach focuses on the relationship between education and democracy, suggesting that education is not just about preparing students for citizenship but actively embodying democratic principles throughout the learning process (Dewey, 1916).

Integrating Individual Development and Social Participation

One of Dewey's most influential contributions was his ability to merge individual development with social participation. Rather than treating these as separate or competing aims, Dewey argued that both serve a larger purpose: growth through experience. This integration challenged the polarized debates in education that often saw individual and social aims as contradictory (Dewey, 1916).

For Dewey, the goal of education was not simply to develop individual skills or prepare students for societal roles but to cultivate growth through shared experiences in a democratic context. His view transcended simplistic dichotomies and offered a holistic framework in which both individual and collective growth could be pursued together, demonstrating the value of social participation in personal development (Dewey, 1916).

Revealing Contradictions Between Democratic Rhetoric and Autocratic Practices

Dewey's ethical approach also involved identifying contradictions between the democratic rhetoric that many educational systems espoused and the autocratic practices they often employed. He pointed out the inconsistency between claims of fostering democratic values and the reality of authoritarian teaching, passive learning, artificial tasks, and competitive evaluation systems (Dewey, 1916).

Through this critical lens, Dewey urged educators to reflect on the practices that shaped their institutions. He examined how traditional educational structures, which were often rigid and impersonal, undermined the very democratic ideals they claimed to promote. By revealing these contradictions, Dewey (1916) encouraged a more honest assessment of educational practices, calling for a greater alignment between democratic ideals and teaching methods.

Embodying Democratic Values in Educational Processes

Rather than seeing democratic education as a mere preparation for future citizenship, Dewey argued that democratic values should be embodied in the educational process itself. In his view, classrooms should be places where students actively engage in collaborative inquiry, shared decision-making, and meaningful problem-solving. These processes were not just theoretical lessons; they were the mechanisms by which democratic dispositions could be developed (Dewey, 1916).

Dewey's method-embodiment strategy focused on creating an educational environment where democratic values were not only taught but practiced daily. This approach emphasized that democracy is best learned through democratic experience, not just abstract instruction. By actively involving students in democratic processes, Dewey's (1916) educational model sought to align the means with the ends of education, ensuring that the processes themselves contributed to the values being cultivated.

Aligning Educational Practices With Growth Through Experience

A key feature of Dewey's ethical leadership was his focus on aligning educational practices with the broader goal of growth through experience. Dewey emphasized that education should be about more than just acquiring knowledge; it should be a process of personal and social growth that is facilitated by the learning environment. He examined how classroom structures, teacher-student interactions, and learning activities could either foster or hinder this growth (Dewey, 1916).

Rather than focusing solely on academic outcomes, Dewey's approach called for an educational system that constantly aligned its methods with the goal of fostering experience-driven growth. His emphasis on experiential learning highlighted the importance of consistent, purposeful practices that promote both intellectual and personal development (Dewey, 1916).

Adapting Education to Contexts While Maintaining Ethical Commitments

Dewey's approach also emphasized the importance of adapting educational methods to the specific needs of students and their communities. Rather than applying a uniform set of methods across all situations, Dewey (1916) encouraged educators to consider the unique context of each learning environment while maintaining a core commitment to growth through meaningful activity.

This contextual-balancing strategy allowed Dewey's educational framework to remain flexible and responsive to different circumstances without compromising its ethical foundations. By focusing on situation-specific problem-solving, Dewey's (1916) approach demonstrated how educators could maintain consistent ethical commitments while adapting to the diverse needs of students and communities.

Developing Practical Wisdom in Educators

Dewey's final key strategy was the development of practical wisdom in educators. Rather than relying on rigid rules or formulas to determine the right approach in every situation, Dewey advocated for fostering teachers' ability to exercise thoughtful judgment. This emphasis on practical wisdom reflected his understanding of the complexity of educational environments and the need for educators to respond flexibly to the unique challenges they encounter (Dewey, 1916).

Dewey's approach highlighted that education is not about applying rules mechanically but about making informed decisions based on the specific context. This focus on reflective teaching and judgment development allowed educators to adapt their methods while maintaining a strong ethical grounding (Dewey, 1916).

Dewey's Transformative Ethical Thought Leadership

John Dewey's approach to democratic education offers a powerful model for aligning educational practices with democratic ideals. Through his integration of individual and social aims, identification of contradictions between democratic rhetoric and autocratic practices, embodiment of democratic values in educational processes, and commitment to context-specific adaptation, Dewey provided a comprehensive framework for ethical educational leadership. His focus on practical wisdom and growth through experience challenged traditional educational paradigms and laid the groundwork for a more thoughtful, human-centered approach to teaching and learning (Dewey, 1916).

Dewey's work shows that education is not merely about imparting knowledge; it is about fostering the democratic dispositions that support both personal growth and collective well-being. His ethical thought leadership continues to inspire educators to rethink how they teach and the ends they seek to achieve in a democratic society.

Martha Nussbaum and the Capabilities Approach in Education

Martha Nussbaum's application of the capabilities approach to education has become a crucial example of ethical thought leadership in the field. Through her theoretical work in *Creating Capabilities* and its educational applications, Nussbaum has reshaped our understanding of how education connects to human development. Her approach emphasizes the importance of providing students with the tools to live a life of dignity and freedom, offering a framework that goes beyond traditional economic measures of success (Nussbaum, 2011).

Integrating Universal Principles With Cultural Diversity

One of Nussbaum's major contributions to educational thought is her ability to integrate seemingly conflicting values. Rather than treating universal human principles as contradictory to cultural diversity, she showed how both could be aligned to support the broader goal of enabling substantive freedom within different cultural contexts (Nussbaum, 2011). This perspective moves beyond the false dichotomy between universalism and relativism, which has often polarized debates in educational philosophy.

Nussbaum's integration strategy reflects a nuanced understanding of educational aims. By showing how both universal capabilities and cultural expression can work together to promote human dignity, she offered a framework that recognizes diversity while maintaining a universal commitment to human betterment (Nussbaum, 2011).

Allowing Pluralism While Ensuring Minimum Capabilities

Another key element of Nussbaum's ethical approach is her commitment to minimum capability requirements while allowing diverse educational practices to flourish. She identified essential capabilities that education must promote, such as critical thinking, imaginative understanding, and scientific literacy, while leaving room for flexibility in how these are implemented across different cultural contexts (Nussbaum, 2011).

This concept of "bounded pluralism" reflects Nussbaum's sophisticated understanding of educational diversity. She recognized that while educational approaches may vary across cultures, there are certain fundamental capabilities that all people need to lead lives of dignity. Her framework allows for context-specific adaptations without compromising the basic human development requirements that are universal (Nussbaum, 2011).

Identifying Contradictions in Education's Developmental Rhetoric

Nussbaum also employed a strategy of identifying contradictions between education's stated developmental goals and its narrower economic focus. Many educational systems, especially those emphasizing standardized testing and workforce preparation, often claim to promote human development. However, Nussbaum (2011) critiqued how these systems frequently prioritized economic metrics over the broader goal of fostering human betterment.

This critical analysis allowed Nussbaum to expose how the emphasis on economic utility in education sometimes undermines the very development it claims to support. By examining the tension between rhetoric and practice, she pushed for a more honest and comprehensive view of what education should achieve, one that includes fostering a wide range of human capabilities, not just skills for economic success (Nussbaum, 2011).

Aligning Educational Assessments With Capabilities

One of Nussbaum's most important contributions to educational thought leadership is her examination of educational assessments. She questioned whether conventional evaluation methods truly measured the broad range of capabilities that education is supposed to develop. Instead of accepting standardized tests or narrow metrics, Nussbaum (2011) advocated for assessments that align to foster human betterment.

Her approach emphasizes that educational assessments should be designed to evaluate the diverse capabilities essential for a dignified life, not just the limited skills valued by the economy. By aligning assessments with the comprehensive goals of education, Nussbaum's (2011) framework addresses the gaps that often exist between educational rhetoric and actual outcomes.

Including Diverse Voices in Defining Essential Capabilities

Nussbaum also championed the inclusion of diverse voices, particularly those from marginalized groups, in determining the essential capabilities that education should develop. Rather than relying solely on expert judgments or Western philosophical traditions, she advocated for a more inclusive process that took into account different cultural and social perspectives.

This stakeholder-inclusive strategy expanded the scope of what is considered essential for a dignified life, acknowledging that different communities may have different needs and aspirations. Nussbaum's (2011) work underscores the importance of incorporating a range of voices when defining the goals of education, ensuring that these goals reflect a variety of human experiences.

Aligning Educational Practices With Human Capabilities

Nussbaum's approach also examines how educational practices can either develop or hinder essential human capabilities. She focused on evaluating pedagogical methods, such as Socratic questioning, narrative imagination, and scientific literacy, to determine whether they truly foster the capabilities they claim to promote (Nussbaum, 2011).

For Nussbaum, education is not just about transmitting knowledge; it's about developing the capabilities necessary for a flourishing life. Her analysis shows how educational practices must align with ethical ends, ensuring that the methods used in classrooms promote the broader goal of human development, rather than undermining it with narrow or inconsistent approaches (Nussbaum, 2011).

Nussbaum's Impact on Educational Thought Leadership

Martha Nussbaum's capabilities approach provides a transformative framework for thinking about education in ethical terms. By integrating universal principles with cultural diversity, establishing minimum capability requirements, identifying contradictions between rhetoric and practice, aligning assessments with comprehensive goals, incorporating diverse voices, and ensuring that educational practices foster essential human capabilities, Nussbaum (2011) has reshaped the way we think about education's role in human development.

Her work is a powerful example of how ethical thought leadership can influence educational practice, offering a comprehensive vision that moves beyond the technical aspects of education and addresses the fundamental question of what education is for: the development of human beings in all their complexity.

Common Patterns in Ethical Thought Leadership

Across the case studies discussed in this chapter, several common patterns emerge:

- **Contradiction Identification:** This strategy uncovers inconsistencies between educational rhetoric and the reality of how education is practiced. By highlighting these gaps, ethical thought leaders can challenge superficial claims and push for more genuine educational reforms.

- **Method Embodiment:** This approach ensures that the educational processes themselves embody the very values they aim to promote. In other words, the way education is delivered must reflect the ideals it seeks to instill in students.

- **Integration Strategies:** Rather than treating seemingly conflicting values as incompatible, ethical thought leaders look for deeper connections that unify these values. This approach moves beyond dichotomies, offering a more nuanced understanding of how different educational aims can coexist.

- **Alignment Approaches:** These strategies focus on ensuring that educational practices genuinely serve their stated purposes. Instead of merely offering theoretical solutions, these approaches prioritize the consistency between what is promised by educational goals and what is achieved in practice.

- **Contextual Wisdom:** This involves adapting ethical principles to fit specific situations. By acknowledging the importance of context, educational leaders can make more informed, flexible decisions that remain aligned with ethical commitments while addressing local needs.

- **Inclusive Perspectives:** Ethical thought leaders actively incorporate diverse voices when determining educational purposes. This ensures that educational goals are shaped by a wide range of experiences and needs, fostering more inclusive and equitable outcomes.

These patterns reflect strategies that are foundational to effective educational thought leadership. They demonstrate how thoughtful ethical engagement can reshape educational practices, ensuring that they are not just technically effective but aligned with broader humanistic and democratic values.

The case studies reveal how ethical engagement goes beyond simply articulating values. In each instance, the ethical analysis deeply influenced the evolution of educational approaches. By addressing core questions about the purposes and methods of education, educational thought leaders have contributed not just to the development of educational practices but also to the very framework through which education is understood.

Thought leadership is not merely about advocating for specific practices but about questioning and refining the fundamental purposes and values that guide education. Ethical educational thought leaders provide the intellectual and moral direction that shapes educational systems, ensuring they remain relevant and effective in an ever-changing world.

In the next chapter, we will explore the future of educational thought leadership. This will involve examining emerging challenges and opportunities that will shape how influential educational ideas develop and spread over the coming decades. The rapid pace of technological, social, and institutional changes means that educational thought leaders will need to adapt their ethical frameworks to maintain relevance and impact.

We will look at how the ethical dimensions discussed in this chapter interact with these evolving challenges. As education continues to evolve in response to global shifts, educational thought leaders will need to remain agile and thoughtful in addressing the complex issues of educational systems.

The ethical dimension of educational thought leadership provides a crucial foundation for meaningful influence. Understanding ethical frameworks, managing conflicting values, aligning educational methods with goals, and drawing lessons from past examples are all essential for shaping a more inclusive and equitable future for education.

By focusing on these ethical dimensions, educational thought leaders can ensure that their ideas address the fundamental human questions that education seeks to answer. In doing so, they contribute not only to intellectual discourse but also to practical improvements in how education impacts the lives of individuals and communities. Thoughtful ethical engagement in education is not just about theory—it's about creating positive, lasting change.

Chapter 10:
Future Directions in Educational Thought Leadership

Educational thought leadership is evolving in response to rapid technological, social, and institutional changes. As education systems face new challenges and opportunities, thought leaders must adapt while staying true to the core values of education. This chapter explores how influential ideas in education are changing to meet contemporary needs, how diverse voices are reshaping traditional conversations, and how leaders can maintain ethical commitments amidst these changes.

Technological advancements, demographic shifts, and social justice movements are driving significant transformations in education. AI, personalized learning, and online platforms present both opportunities for democratization and risks of deepening inequality. At the same time, growing diversity calls for more inclusive educational frameworks that reflect the varied needs of students. Yet, this effort unfolds within a broader context of growing polarization across our politics, our educational systems, and our communities.

Thought leaders must navigate these complex intersections with a commitment to equity and inclusion, ensuring that education remains a force for empowerment and cohesion, even as societal divides deepen. By holding space for diverse perspectives and fostering dialogue across differences, educational leadership can help bridge divides while adapting to a rapidly changing world.

Responding to Technological Transformation in Education

Educational thought leaders are increasingly grappling with the profound technological shifts reshaping the landscape of learning. Technologies like AI, machine learning, virtual reality, and neurotechnology offer unprecedented possibilities while challenging foundational ideas about learning, knowledge, and human development. Rather than responding with mere technical solutions, effective thought leaders are creating conceptual frameworks that address technology's deeper implications, guiding education systems through transformation thoughtfully and purposefully.

Rethinking AI in Education

AI is increasingly reshaping education, not merely as a tool for efficiency but as a catalyst challenging foundational assumptions about knowledge, learning, and the role of educators. While earlier critiques by scholars like Mimi Ito (2013 and Audrey Watters (2015) highlighted the sociopolitical dimensions of educational technology, recent developments underscore AI's transformative potential in practical applications.

Contemporary research identifies four primary applications of AI in education: intelligent assessment systems, personalized tutoring, adaptive learning platforms, and predictive analytics. Among these, intelligent assessment systems and personalized tutoring are the most extensively studied, demonstrating significant promise in enhancing learning outcomes (Wu et al., 2024).

For instance, AI-powered tools like QANDA utilize optical character recognition and large language models to provide step-by-step solutions, catering to diverse learner needs across various countries. Moreover, AI's role extends to supporting students with disabilities. AI-driven applications are aiding students with dyslexia and other learning challenges by offering personalized assistance, thereby promoting inclusivity and equal access to education (Anderson, 2024).

However, the integration of AI in education is not without challenges. Concerns about data privacy, algorithmic bias, and the potential for over-reliance on technology necessitate a cautious and ethical approach. Educational leaders are called upon to critically assess AI tools, ensuring they complement rather than replace human educators and align with pedagogical goals that prioritize student well-being and holistic development.

In this evolving landscape, AI's impact on education is profound, offering opportunities for personalized learning and greater accessibility. Yet, its implementation must be guided by thoughtful consideration of ethical implications and a commitment to enhancing the human elements of teaching and learning.

Integrating Digital Literacy and Critical Thinking

As technology transforms education, it's crucial to redefine digital literacy. Thought leaders are advocating for a more integrated approach that combines technical skills with critical analysis. Rather than focusing solely on competence in using digital tools, the goal is to foster an understanding of how technology shapes knowledge, influences decisions, and impacts societal values.

Renee Hobbs' (2010) digital and media literacy framework, which blends technical proficiency with critical thinking, offers a comprehensive view of digital literacy. Similarly, Henry Jenkins' (2006) work on participatory culture stresses the importance of ethical engagement in digital spaces, encouraging students to both create content and understand the implications of their digital actions.

Understanding Technology's Impact on Human Development

Educational thought leaders are also developing a more contextual understanding of how technology affects human development at different stages. Instead of taking a one-size-fits-all approach, they are exploring how digital tools impact cognitive and emotional growth in diverse age groups and contexts.

Hirsh-Pasek et al.'s (2015) research on technology and child development illustrates the need for a tailored approach, showing how digital experiences vary in their developmental impact depending on design and context. Similarly, Mizuko Ito's (2008) studies on youth digital practices emphasize how the social environment and cultural context influence how young people engage with technology.

Epistemological Shifts: What Is Knowledge in the Digital Age?

The advent of digital technologies has profoundly transformed traditional conceptions of knowledge. Rather than viewing technology merely as a conduit for information delivery, contemporary thought leaders are examining how it fundamentally alters the nature of knowledge itself. Digital tools are reshaping the creation, validation, and dissemination of knowledge, prompting critical questions about authority and ownership in our interconnected world.

Building upon earlier analyses by scholars like David Weinberger (2007), who explored the transition from fixed, bounded knowledge models to more fluid, networked understandings, recent research continues to delve into these transformations. For instance, Burkle and Cobo (2018) discuss how digitalization leads to decentralization and disintermediation, enabling more democratized and collaborative knowledge production processes. They emphasize the importance of flexible learning environments and interdisciplinary approaches to accommodate the evolving landscape of knowledge in the digital era.

Similarly, Etienne Wenger's (1998) concept of communities of practice remains relevant, highlighting how digital environments foster collaborative learning and shared expertise. These communities exemplify the shift toward collective knowledge construction, where learning is a social and participatory process.

In summary, the digital age necessitates a reevaluation of epistemological frameworks, recognizing that knowledge is no longer a static entity but a dynamic, collaborative, and context-dependent construct. Educational systems must adapt to these changes by promoting flexible, inclusive, and interdisciplinary learning models that reflect the complexities of knowledge in our digital society.

Balancing Technology's Cognitive Effects

Educational thought leaders are also developing more balanced views on technology's impact on attention and cognitive development. Rather than either blindly celebrating the multitasking abilities of digital tools or idealizing pre-digital attention patterns, they are examining how different technological environments affect cognitive processes.

Maryanne Wolf's (2007) research on reading brain development highlights how digital reading can affect deep reading processes differently than print-based reading, potentially altering attention, empathy, and critical thinking. Similarly, James Paul Gee's (2003) earlier studies on video games and learning emphasized the potential of well-designed game environments to support problem-solving and systems thinking. More recent research has expanded on this, showing that action video games, in particular, may enhance aspects of cognitive function such as visual attention, spatial skills, and working memory, depending on design and duration of play (Bediou et al., 2018).

Addressing Educational Equity Through Technology

Another critical area of focus is technology's role in educational equity. Thought leaders are examining how different approaches to technology implementation can either bridge or widen existing educational gaps. Technology has the potential to democratize education, but it also risks perpetuating or exacerbating inequalities.

Justin Reich's (2018) work on the failure to disrupt highlights how educational technologies often reproduce existing inequities despite their promise of democratization. Similarly, S. Craig Watkins' (2013) research on digital access shows that technology alone is not enough to create meaningful inclusion; access must be accompanied by opportunities for real engagement.

Evolving Educational Thought Leadership

These emerging directions, ranging from AI analysis to digital literacy, cognitive development, epistemological shifts, and equity, characterize the evolving landscape of educational thought leadership. Thought leaders who address these dimensions with sophistication and nuance will be better equipped to guide education systems through technological transformation. By considering technology's broader implications, educational thought leaders can help shape a future where technology enhances learning without compromising the human values at the core of education.

Incorporating Diverse Perspectives and Decolonizing Knowledge in Education

Educational thought leadership today increasingly emphasizes the inclusion of voices historically excluded from dominant academic paradigms. These include Indigenous knowledge systems, non-Western philosophical traditions, and cultural perspectives shaped by historical and social realities. Rather than relying solely on Eurocentric frameworks, contemporary thought leaders are drawing from multiple epistemologies to address complex educational challenges more effectively.

Integrating Indigenous Knowledge

Newer approaches to Indigenous knowledge integration go far beyond token inclusion. Educators now view Indigenous knowledge systems as fully developed epistemologies that offer rich insights into environmental stewardship, intergenerational learning, and relational worldviews. For example, early childhood programs are being redesigned to explicitly incorporate Indigenous languages, cultural practices, and ways of knowing, efforts which are not merely additive but structural (Derman-Sparks et al., 2024). This aligns with the call for Indigenous education to be a required, rather than optional, component of early childhood curriculum (Maluleka et al., 2024).

Navigating Cross-Cultural Boundaries in Knowledge Traditions

Knowledge does not emerge in a vacuum—it is culturally embedded. Leading scholars argue that education should foster spaces where diverse knowledge traditions can interact rather than be ranked or isolated. Gloria Ladson-Billings (2022) continues to assert the importance of culturally relevant pedagogy, where students' lived experiences are central to the learning process. Her work, alongside cross-cultural theorists like Edward Said, supports the idea that meaningful learning comes from engaging across epistemic boundaries.

Understanding the Power Dynamics in Knowledge Validation

Another essential theme is the relationship between knowledge and power. Educators are rethinking what counts as "valid" knowledge and who decides that. As Dwyer (2023) notes, educational development practices must be scrutinized for how they reproduce racial hierarchies and colonial assumptions. This reflection extends to curriculum design, assessment methods, and even faculty training, calling into question taken-for-granted norms about neutrality and objectivity in education.

Embracing Linguistic Diversity in Education

Linguistic diversity is increasingly being recognized as a strength, not a barrier. Educational leaders are advocating for approaches that support multilingual learners through practices like translanguaging—drawing on students' full linguistic repertoires to aid understanding and expression. Recent work highlights how Black English and other marginalized language practices deserve space in the classroom, particularly in early childhood education settings where language identity is being formed (Hickman & NAEYC Faculty, 2024). This represents a shift from assimilationist models toward linguistic equity.

Understanding Educational Purposes Across Cultural Traditions

Different cultures bring distinct purposes and goals to education. Western models often emphasize autonomy and competition, whereas other traditions value collective well-being, moral development, or ecological balance. With these variations in mind, educators are encouraged to design systems that reflect diverse visions of what it means to live well. For example, Indigenous and African educational philosophies often center the community and relationality as core aims of learning (Maluleka et al., 2024).

Adapting Traditional Knowledge to Contemporary Challenges

Traditional knowledge need not be frozen in time. Educators and activists like Wangari Maathai (2006) and Vandana Shiva (2000) have shown how traditional ecological practices can be adapted to tackle modern problems like deforestation and food insecurity. Today, this principle is being applied across educational contexts, where Indigenous and local wisdom is being brought into dialogue with contemporary science, not in opposition but as complementary frameworks (Derman-Sparks et al., 2024).

A Multidimensional Approach to Educational Thought Leadership

Contemporary educational thought leadership is increasingly characterized by its multidimensionality: It integrates Indigenous epistemologies, crosses cultural boundaries, challenges power structures, embraces linguistic diversity, respects differing educational purposes, and updates traditional knowledge. This broader, more inclusive approach offers a richer and more relevant educational vision—one that moves beyond both Eurocentric universalism and superficial multiculturalism.

Addressing Global Challenges Through Educational Innovation

Educational thought leadership is increasingly being called upon to confront a range of global challenges—climate change, technological disruption, rising nationalism, pandemics, and deepening societal polarization. These challenges demand innovative educational responses that go beyond traditional pedagogy. Today's thought leaders are reimagining education as preparation for the world as it is and as a transformative force for shaping the world as it could be.

Climate Change Education

Climate change is no longer a future issue—it is a lived reality. Educational thought leaders are crafting climate literacy frameworks that blend science education with civic engagement and systems thinking. David Orr (2004) argued that ecological literacy requires more than an understanding of carbon cycles or weather patterns; it demands ethical responsibility and the development of sustainability mindsets. This approach educates for action, not just awareness.

Greta Thunberg's School Strike for Climate movement illustrates this shift in real time—youth acting as public educators and political actors. It's a living example of how education can catalyze social engagement (Orr, 2004; World Economic Forum, 2024). Schools are increasingly seen as spaces for cultivating environmental agency, helping students connect global crises with local action.

Economic Transformation and Education

Automation and economic disruption are reshaping the workforce. Rather than training students for specific careers, educators are now focusing on adaptability, creativity, and critical thinking. Yong Zhao (2012) advocates for an entrepreneurial education model that prioritizes autonomy and innovation, skills necessary for thriving in an unpredictable economy. This complements Martha Nussbaum's (2011) capabilities approach, which emphasizes education's role in expanding individual agency and human dignity, not just economic productivity.

By combining Zhao's forward-looking model with Nussbaum's ethical lens, educational thought leaders are developing approaches that respond to economic shifts while maintaining a commitment to human betterment (Hart, 2019).

Civic Education in Divided Societies

In an era of political polarization and rising nationalism, civic education must do more than teach government structures; it must prepare students for respectful dialogue, moral reasoning, and participation in diverse democratic societies (Allen, 2023). Diana Hess (2009) champions the deliberate teaching of controversial issues, fostering classrooms in which disagreement becomes an opportunity for democratic learning rather than conflict avoidance.

Danielle Allen's (2004) work further underscores the need for "participatory readiness," developing citizens who not only understand democratic systems but also feel empowered to step into them meaningfully. Her recent work continues to stress the role of education in building civic responsibility in increasingly divided societies (Harvard Gazette, 2023).

Global Citizenship Education

As global interconnections grow alongside emerging nationalism and societal polarization, so does the need for education systems that prepare students for life as global citizens. Thought leaders in education are working on frameworks that develop students' commitment to universal human rights while respecting cultural diversity.

Kwame Anthony Appiah's (2006) concept of "rooted cosmopolitanism" illustrates this approach, advocating for a global citizenship education that balances universal ethical values with an appreciation for cultural diversity. This integrated model ensures that students learn to navigate both the commonalities and differences of a globalized world, fostering both ethical universalism and cultural respect.

Martha Nussbaum's (1997) cosmopolitan education framework further complements this by emphasizing the role of narrative imagination in cultivating global citizenship. These frameworks challenge the extremes of either imposing a singular global perspective or adopting rigid relativism, aiming instead for a balanced approach that prepares students for a more interconnected world.

Complementing Technology

Rather than training students to compete with machines, educators are shifting toward cultivating skills that complement technology: creativity, collaboration, ethics, and empathy. Cathy Davidson (2017) calls for educational systems that prioritize human skills in an age of AI. Similarly, Brynjolfsson and McAfee (2014) argue for a symbiotic relationship between human and machine capabilities, emphasizing roles where technology amplifies human potential.

This approach doesn't ignore automation; it reframes it. Students need more than coding skills—they need the judgment and flexibility that machines lack.

Education in the Post-Pandemic World

COVID-19 forced a rapid shift to online learning, revealing both the flexibility and the inequities within educational systems. Now, educational thought leaders are designing hybrid models that integrate the strengths of in-person and virtual education. Pasi Sahlberg (2021) argues for a balanced education model that maintains human connection while embracing the benefits of digital tools.

Justin Reich (2020) builds on this by emphasizing the need to address long-standing disparities exposed during the pandemic. His research calls for schools to move from crisis management to intentional redesign, centering equity, resilience, and meaningful learning.

Multidimensional Responses to Global Challenges

Today, educational thought leadership is inherently multidimensional. Whether the issue is climate action, economic upheaval, social fragmentation, or digital transformation, the most compelling frameworks are those that integrate ethical reasoning, systems thinking, and a commitment to justice. The goal is not simply to react to crises but to reshape education so that students are prepared to meet complexity with clarity and change with purpose.

Maintaining Ethical Commitment in Changing Contexts

Educational thought leaders today must navigate rapid technological and societal shifts while staying rooted in ethical principles. As new dilemmas emerge, many of which traditional frameworks weren't designed to address, the challenge is to adapt responsibly, without abandoning foundational commitments or clinging to outdated models. The work is less about choosing between values and innovation and more about finding practical ways to align them.

Addressing Privacy and Surveillance in Digital Learning

The rise of data-driven platforms in education has intensified ethical questions around privacy, consent, and surveillance. Instead of simply embracing digital tools for their efficiency or rejecting them wholesale due to privacy concerns, leading voices are exploring how to harness technology while safeguarding student agency.

Allen (2023) outlines how predictive analytics and surveillance technologies are reshaping K–12 and higher education, often in ways that disempower students and educators. She argues for a "consent-based data ethic" that prioritizes transparency and student participation in decisions about their data. Similarly, the World Economic Forum's *Education 4.0* framework (WEF, 2024) emphasizes the importance of ethical AI design in education, calling for robust data governance that centers the learner.

These perspectives suggest that privacy and innovation must be co-developed, not seen as trade-offs.

Navigating Market Forces in Education

As education systems intersect more directly with market dynamics, through ed-tech companies, charter systems, and performance-based funding, ethical concerns arise about commodification, equity, and purpose.

Labaree (2023) critiques the growing emphasis on credentialism and education as private investment, noting how market logic distorts public education's civic mission. Meanwhile, Shah and Hoadley (2022) advocate for "equity-conscious design" in educational technology markets, arguing that product development must reflect broader social values, not just commercial viability.

This work reflects a shift toward frameworks that acknowledge economic realities but push back against the erosion of educational integrity by market pressures.

Ethical Implications of AI in Education

AI is quickly becoming a fixture in classrooms, from chatbots and grading tools to curriculum design systems. But this surge raises urgent ethical questions: Who designs the algorithms? Whose knowledge is prioritized? How does AI reshape learning relationships?

UNESCO's 2023 *Guidelines for AI in Education* emphasize the need for a human-centered design, calling on policymakers and educators to ensure that AI supports inclusive, equitable, and socially grounded learning experiences. In parallel, Bali and Caines (2023) have argued that AI integration must preserve human agency and relational pedagogy, warning against its potential to de-skill teachers or reproduce bias at scale.

The consensus among current thought leaders is that AI in education must be critically examined, not just adopted.

Balancing Inclusion and Excellence in Education

The debate over whether to prioritize excellence or inclusion is giving way to a more productive conversation: How can diverse learners contribute to—and redefine—what excellence looks like?

Recent studies from the National Academies (2022) support this direction, showing that diverse teams enhance problem-solving and innovation in educational and professional settings. Meanwhile, Harper and Simmons (2023) emphasize "structural inclusion" in high-achieving academic spaces, showing that when systems are designed to support diverse learners, outcomes improve for everyone.

This shift reframes inclusion not as a concession but as a foundation for excellence.

Rethinking Accountability in Education

Standardized testing still dominates many accountability systems, but its limitations have come into sharper focus. Contemporary educational leaders are advocating for broader, more nuanced metrics.

The Learning Policy Institute (2023) recommends multiple measures frameworks that incorporate academic growth, school climate, and social-emotional learning, not just test scores. Likewise, recent work by Darling-Hammond and Cook-Harvey (2022) explores how accountability systems can better reflect the complexity of learning and the context in which it happens.

These updates suggest a shift toward systems that support growth, equity, and deeper learning, not just quantifiable outcomes.

Personalized Learning vs. Social Cohesion

Personalized learning has gained traction as a way of supporting individual needs, but it also raises questions about collective experiences and civic identities. If everyone follows their path, what holds the system—and society—together?

Mehta and Fine (2022) stress the importance of "civic coherence" in personalized education models, arguing that deep learning must still include shared public values. Meanwhile, Hess and McAvoy's updated research (2021) on democratic education in polarized times warns against personalization that leads to ideological isolation or echo chambers.

The takeaway: Personalized learning must be designed with both the individual and the collective in mind.

Evolving Ethical Thought Leadership

The most effective educational thought leaders today are not sidestepping complexity—they're embracing it. Rather than focusing on single issues in isolation, they're developing integrated frameworks that respond to the ethical tensions across privacy, markets, AI, inclusion, accountability, and personalization.

Their leadership is grounded in an ongoing process: adapting thoughtfully to new contexts while remaining anchored in enduring educational values. In doing so, they offer models of leadership that are both ethically committed and future-ready.

Conclusion

As we look to the future of educational thought leadership, several key trends emerge, suggesting both continuity with longstanding traditions and a response to the unprecedented challenges of our time. While specific issues will continue to evolve, certain enduring characteristics are likely to shape influential educational thinking in the coming decades. These patterns offer valuable guidance for aspiring thought leaders and insight for those seeking to understand the trajectory of educational ideas.

Educational thought leadership will increasingly move beyond traditional academic, professional, and cultural boundaries. Instead of maintaining rigid separations between theory and practice, or between different educational traditions, the future of educational thinking will blend insights from diverse sources. This integrative approach will enable a more comprehensive understanding of the complex challenges of education today, addressing questions that no single perspective can fully answer.

Future thought leaders will act as intellectual bridge-builders, connecting disciplines like cognitive science with sociocultural perspectives or Western educational traditions with those from the global South. This cross-boundary integration will foster richer and more innovative solutions to educational issues, pushing the boundaries of conventional educational thought.

Rather than presenting value commitments as objective facts or treating empirical findings as entirely neutral, future educational thinkers will engage with both empirical evidence and the values that shape it. They will openly acknowledge how normative commitments influence which questions are asked, which evidence is considered relevant, and what conclusions are drawn. This transparent approach will ensure more honest, intellectually rigorous educational discourse.

Influential thought leaders will combine empirical rigor with an explicit engagement with values, recognizing that all educational research is inherently shaped by these values. This approach will create educational frameworks that are both evidence-based and reflective of the values driving educational decisions.

While global educational frameworks are essential, the future of educational thought leadership will be marked by a more nuanced understanding of context. Thought leaders will identify core educational principles while recognizing that their application varies across different cultural, institutional, and developmental contexts.

The most influential thought leaders will demonstrate both a commitment to these fundamental principles and the flexibility to adapt them to varying circumstances. By embracing principled contextualism, educational leaders will provide more relevant and adaptable guidance, helping to navigate the balance between universal ideas and local realities.

Future educational thought leadership will be more attuned to the influence of power on knowledge creation. Educational thought leaders will increasingly examine how existing power structures shape which voices are heard, which ideas are prioritized, and how educational agendas are set. They will demonstrate an awareness of these power dynamics while maintaining intellectual integrity. Rather than sacrificing rigorous academic standards for political expediency or ignoring power structures altogether, they will develop frameworks that critique and question the status quo. This power-conscious integrity will foster a more open and honest educational dialogue.

As technology continues to shape every aspect of education, future educational thought leaders will navigate the ethical and practical challenges it presents. Rather than uncritically embracing technology or rejecting it outright, influential thinkers will develop frameworks that leverage technological tools to enhance human learning and connection, while ensuring that technology serves, rather than replaces, human values.

Educational thought leaders will carefully integrate technology into the learning process, using its potential to amplify creativity, collaboration, and critical thinking while setting clear boundaries to preserve core human values. This balanced approach will help prevent over-reliance on technology and ensure that educational innovation remains rooted in human development.

Future educational thought leadership will be increasingly global in scope while remaining sensitive to local contexts. They will develop frameworks that connect global challenges, such as climate change and technological disruption, with local educational practices, adapting global insights to meet the specific needs of diverse communities.

Furthermore, they will bridge the global and the local, developing solutions that address global issues while honoring the unique cultural, social, and economic conditions of individual regions. This "glocal" approach will ensure that educational solutions are both globally informed and locally relevant.

Emerging patterns such as boundary-crossing integration, values-transparent empiricism, principled contextualism, power-conscious integrity, humanistic technology integration, and glocal perspective offer a promising vision for the future of educational thought leadership. The most influential educational thought leaders will balance multiple dimensions of educational practice, rather than emphasizing one aspect at the expense of others.

As education systems around the world face both unprecedented challenges and opportunities, educational thought leadership that embodies these balanced qualities will prove crucial in guiding the evolution of education. By integrating diverse perspectives, acknowledging values, respecting context, addressing power dynamics, and thoughtfully engaging with technology, educational thought leaders can help navigate complex transformations while preserving education's core human purposes.

Ultimately, the future of educational thought leadership lies in the ability to adapt. Educational thought leaders must address both the timeless questions of human development and the new challenges created by technological, social, and environmental shifts. By holding steadfast to education's enduring human purposes while engaging with emerging challenges, they will shape educational systems that are both responsive to the present and grounded in lasting principles. This thoughtful, adaptive approach will ensure that educational thought leadership remains relevant, effective, and true to its core values.

The future calls for a balanced evolution of educational thought leadership, one that neither clings to outdated paradigms nor abandons past wisdom. It will be about reinterpreting and applying foundational principles to address the challenges of a rapidly changing world, ensuring that education evolves thoughtfully, with integrity, and in ways that serve all learners.

References

Allen, D. (2004). Talking to strangers: Anxieties of citizenship since Brown v. Board of Education. University of Chicago Press.

Allen, D. (2023). Danielle Allen's prescription for democracy: Citizens who step up. Harvard Gazette. https://news.harvard.edu/gazette/story/2023/11/danielle-allens-prescription-for-democracy-citizens-who-step-up/

Anderson, A. (2016). Expanding the reach of education research with research-practice partnerships: Building collaborative capacity for systemic improvement. William T. Grant Foundation. https://wtgrantfoundation.org/library/uploads/2016/06/Research-Practice-Partnerships-at-the-William-T.-Grant-Foundation.pdf

Anderson, E. (1993). Value pluralism and the role of the state. Philosophy & Public Affairs, 22(2), 99–132. https://www.jstor.org/stable/2265306

Anderson, M. (2024, April 11). AI is helping kids learn better, especially those with learning differences. AP News. https://apnews.com/article/ff1f51379b3861978efb0c1334a2a953

Appiah, K. A. (2006). Cosmopolitanism: Ethics in a world of strangers. W. W. Norton & Company. https://wwnorton.com/books/9780393329339

Apple, M. (2004). Ideology and curriculum (3rd ed.). Routledge. https://openlibrary.org/books/OL9331232M/Ideology_and_Curriculum

Argyris, C., & Schön, D. A. (1978). Organizational learning. Addison-Wesley Publishing Company. https://books.google.co.za/books/about/Organizational_learning.html?id=2aYOAQAAMAAJ&redir_esc=y

Aristotle. (1985). Nicomachean Ethics (W. D. Ross, Trans.). The Revised Oxford Translation. (Original work published ca. 350 B.C.E).

Bali, M. (2020). Critical AI pedagogy: Towards an ethics of education. Journal of Educational Technology Systems, 48(1), 9–22. https://doi.org/10.1177/0047239519877162

Bali, M., & Caines, A. (2023). From human-centered to humanizing pedagogy: Toward critical digital education. Hybrid Pedagogy. https://hybridpedagogy.org/from-human-centered-to-humanizing-pedagogy/

Ball, D. L. (2003). Mathematical knowledge for teaching: What does research say? In The knowledge base for teaching (pp. 271-296). Springer. https://doi.org/10.1007/978-1-4020-2706-0_14

Ball, D. L., Thames, M. H., & Phelps, G. (2008). Content knowledge for teaching: What makes it special? Journal of Teacher Education, 59(5), 389–407. https://doi.org/10.1177/0022487108324554

Bambrick-Santoyo, P. (2010). Driven by data: A practical guide to improve instruction. Jossey-Bass. https://www.amazon.com/Driven-Data-Practical-Guide-Instruction/dp/047058507X

Banks, J. A. (2004). The canon debate, knowledge construction, and multicultural education. Educational Researcher, 33(5), 3–14. https://doi.org/10.3102/0013189X033005003

Bediou, B., Adams, D. M., Mayer, R. E., Tipton, E., Green, C. S., & Bavelier, D. (2018). Meta-analysis of action video game impact on perceptual, attentional, and cognitive skills. Frontiers in Psychology, 9, 902. https://doi.org/10.3389/fpsyg.2018.00902

Beetham, H., & Sharpe, R. (2013). Rethinking pedagogy for a digital age: Designing for 21st century learning (2nd ed.). Routledge. https://doi.org/10.4324/9780203078952

Berger, R. (2003). An ethic of excellence: Building a culture of craftsmanship with students. Heinemann. https://www.heinemann.com/products/e03316

Berger, R. (2003). Expeditionary learning: The power of learning through experience. Expeditionary Learning Outward Bound. https://www.expeditionarylearning.org

Berger, R. (2014). Leaders of learning: How district, school, and classroom leaders improve student achievement. Harvard Education Press. https://www.amazon.com/Leaders-Learning-Classroom-Achievement-Professional/dp/1935542664

Berliner, D. C. (2006). Our impoverished view of educational reform. Teachers College Record, 108(6), 949–995. https://doi.org/10.1111/j.1467-9620.2006.00682.x

Berliner, D. C. (2011). Rational responses to high-stakes testing: The case of curriculum narrowing and the harm that follows. Cambridge Journal of Education, 41(3), 287–302. https://doi.org/10.1080/0305764X.2011.607151

Black, P., & Wiliam, D. (1998). Assessment and classroom learning. Assessment in Education: Principles, Policy & Practice, 5(1), 7–74. https://doi.org/10.1080/0969595980050102

Bloom, B. S. (1956). Taxonomy of educational objectives: The classification of educational goals. Longmans, Green. https://en.wikipedia.org/wiki/Bloom%27s_taxonomy

Boaler, J. (2016). Mathematical mindsets: Unleashing students' potential through creative math, inspiring messages, and innovative teaching. Jossey-Bass. https://psycnet.apa.org/record/2016-07883-000

Bove, A. et al. (2024). Why values are plastic but beliefs are not: Sociological perspectives on moral development. Nature Humanities and Social Sciences Communications. https://www.nature.com/articles/s41599-024-02749-4

Brookfield, S. D. (2017). Becoming a critically reflective teacher (2nd ed.). Jossey-Bass. https://journals.sfu.ca/jalt/index.php/jalt/article/view/165

Brown, A. L. (1992). Design experiments: An exploration of more functional methods for the design and study of learning. Educational Researcher, 21(1), 5–14. https://doi.org/10.3102/0013189X021001005

Bruner, J. (1960). The process of education. Harvard University Press. https://www.hup.harvard.edu/catalog.php?isbn=9780674710016

Bruner, J. (1966). Man: A course of study (MACOS). Prentice-Hall. https://open-education-repository.ucl.ac.uk/235/

Bryk, A. S. (2010). Relational trust and its role in educational reform. In A. Hargreaves, A. Lieberman, M. Fullan, & D. Hopkins (Eds.), Second international handbook of educational change (pp. 749–760). Springer. https://doi.org/10.1007/978-90-481-2660-6_43

Bryk, A. S. (2015). Improvement science: A framework for transforming public education. Education Policy Analysis Archives, 23(74), 1–12. https://doi.org/10.14507/epaa.v23.1998

Bryk, A. S., & LeMahieu, P. (2015, February 27). Learning to improve: How America's schools can get better at getting better. Carnegie Foundation for the Advancement of Teaching.

https://www.carnegiefoundation.org/resources/publications/learning-to-improve/

Bryk, A. S., & Schneider, B. (2002). Trust in schools: A core resource for improvement. Russell Sage Foundation. https://www.russellsage.org/publications/trust-schools

Bryk, A. S., & Schneider, B. (2004). Trust in schools: A core resource for improvement. American Journal of Education, 111(1), 132–134. https://doi.org/10.1086/424724

Bryk, A. S., Gomez, L. M., & Grunow, A. (2015). Learning to improve: How America's schools can get better at getting better. Harvard Education Press. https://www.hepg.org/hep-home/books/learning-to-improve

Bryk, A. S., Gomez, L. M., Grunow, A., & LeMahieu, P. G. (2015). Learning to improve: How America's schools can get better at getting better. Harvard Educational Review, 85(4), 675–679. https://doi.org/10.17763/1943-5045-85.4.675a

Bryk, A. S., Sebring, P. B., Allensworth, E., Luppescu, S., & Easton, J. Q. (2010). Organizing schools for improvement: Lessons from Chicago. University of Chicago Press. https://press.uchicago.edu/ucp/books/book/chicago/O/bo6226325.html

Bryk, A., & Schneider, B. (2010). Trust in schools. Russell Sage Foundation. https://www.russellsage.org/publications/trust-schools-0

Brynjolfsson, E., & McAfee, A. (2014). The second machine age: Work, progress, and prosperity in a time of brilliant technologies. W.W. Norton & Company. https://wwnorton.com/books/9780393239355

Buck Institute for Education. (2014). Project-based learning: A short guide to PBL. Buck Institute for Education. https://www.pblworks.org/what-is-pbl

Burkle, M., & Cobo, C. (2018). Redefining knowledge in the digital age. Journal of New Approaches in Educational Research, 7(2), 79–80. https://doi.org/10.7821/naer.2018.7.294

Burns, J. M. (1978). Leadership. Harper & Row. https://www.harpercollins.com/products/leadership-james-m-burns

Burt, R. S. (2004). Structural holes and good ideas. American Journal of Sociology, 110(2), 349–399. https://doi.org/10.1086/421787

Cajete, G. (2000). Native science: Natural laws of interdependence. Clear Light Publishers. https://www.clearlightpublishers.com/native-science

Caldwell, R. (2012). Systems thinking, organizational change and agency: A practice theory critique of Senge's learning organization. Journal of Change Management, 12(2), 145–164. https://doi.org/10.1080/14697017.2011.647923

Calkins, L. (n.d.). Units, tools, and methods for teaching reading and writing. https://www.discoverydayacademy.com/wp-content/uploads/2020/01/Comprehensive-Overview-Lucy-Calkins-1.pdf

Calkins, L. M. (2001). The art of teaching writing. Heinemann. https://www.heinemann.com/products/e00170.aspx

Canagarajah, S. (2013). Translingual practice: Global Englishes and cosmopolitan relations. Routledge. https://www.routledge.com/Translingual-Practice-Global-Englishes-and-Cosmopolitan-Relations/Canagarajah/p/book/9780415896480

Carr, N. (2010). The shallows: What the Internet is doing to our brains. W. W. Norton & Company. https://wwnorton.com/books/9780393339758

Center on School Turnaround at WestEd. (2017). Four domains for rapid school improvement: A systems framework. WestEd. https://centeronschoolturnaround.org/wp-content/uploads/2020/05/CST_Four-Domains-Framework-Final.pdf

Chaiklin, S. (2003). The zone of proximal development in Vygotsky's analysis of learning and instruction. Vygotsky's Educational Theory in Cultural Context, 39–64. https://doi.org/10.1017/cbo9780511840975.004

Charney, R. (2002). Teaching the responsive classroom approach: The impact on student achievement. Education Week, 22(1), 12-15. https://www.edweek.org

Chenoweth, K. (2007). How high-performing districts can close the achievement gap: Lessons from the country's best-run districts. Harvard Education Press. https://www.hepg.org/hep-home/books/how-high-performing-districts-can-close-the-achievement-gap

Chenoweth, K., & Theokas, C. (2011, October 1). Getting it done. Harvard Education Press. https://books.google.co.za/books/about/Getting_It_Done.html?id=oaVhDwAAQBAJ&redir_esc=y

Cherry, K. (2023). Piaget's stages of cognitive development. Verywell Mind. https://www.verywellmind.com/piagets-stages-of-cognitive-development-2795457

City, E. A., Elmore, R. F., Fiarman, S. E., & Teitel, L. (2009). Instructional rounds in education: A network approach to improving teaching and learning. Harvard Education Press.

https://www.hepg.org/hep-home/books/instructional-rounds-in-education

Coalition of Essential Schools. (n.d.). Common principles. essentialschools.org. https://essentialschools.org/common-principles

Coburn, C. E. (2003). Rethinking scale: Moving beyond numbers to deep and lasting change. Educational Researcher, 32(6), 3–12. https://doi.org/10.3102/0013189X032006003

Coburn, C. E., & Penuel, W. R. (2016). Research-Practice partnerships in education: Outcomes, dynamics, and open questions. Educational Researcher, 45(1), 48–54. https://eric.ed.gov/?id=EJ1091883

Cochran-Smith, M., & Lytle, S. L. (1990). Research on teaching and teacher research: The issues that divide. Educational Researcher, 19(2), 2–11. https://doi.org/10.3102/0013189X019002002

Cochran-Smith, M., & Lytle, S. L. (2009). Inquiry as stance: Practitioner research for the next generation. Teachers College Press. https://www.tcpress.com/inquiry-as-stance-9780807749954

Cohen, D. K., & Moffitt, S. L. (2009). Accountability in an intergovernmental context: Federal education policy as a cautionary tale. Journal of Public Administration Research and Theory, 21(2), 387–391. https://doi.org/10.1093/jopart/mur002

Cohen, D. K., & Moffitt, S. L. (2009). The ordeal of equality: Did federal regulation fix the schools? Harvard University Press. https://www.hup.harvard.edu/catalog.php?isbn=9780674030723

Cohen, J. E. (2013). What privacy is for. Harvard Law Review, 126(7), 1904–1933. https://harvardlawreview.org/2013/06/what-privacy-is-for/

Cohen, W. M., & Levinthal, D. A. (1990). Absorptive capacity: A new perspective on learning and innovation. Administrative Science Quarterly, 35(1), 128-152. https://doi.org/10.2307/2393553

Collins, A., Joseph, D., & Bielaczyc, K. (2004). Design research: Theoretical and methodological issues. The Journal of the Learning Sciences, 13(1), 15–42. https://doi.org/10.1207/s15327809jls1301_2

Collins, P. H. (2000). Black feminist thought: Knowledge, consciousness, and the politics of empowerment. Routledge. https://www.routledge.com/Black-Feminist-Thought-Knowledge-Consciousness-and-the-Politics-of-Empowerment/Collins/p/book/9780415922245

Comer, J. (1980). School power: Implications of an intervention program. Free Press. https://openlibrary.org/books/OL4092690M/School_power

Comer, J. P. (2004). Helping children succeed: A developmental approach to school reform. Yale University Press. https://yalebooks.yale.edu/book/9780300104597/helping-children-succeed

Csikszentmihalyi, M. (1999). Implications of a systems perspective for the study of creativity. In R. J. Sternberg (Ed.), Handbook of creativity (pp. 313–335). Cambridge University Press. https://www.cambridge.org/core/books/handbook-of-creativity/9B30327A2B7EBC2E9C39224F2C88E35F

Cuban, L. (1988). The managerial imperative and the practice of leadership in schools. SUNY Press. https://sunypress.edu/p-439-the-managerial-imperative-and-the-p.aspx

Cuban, L. (2016). Technology integration in districts and schools: Next project (Part 1).

https://larrycuban.wordpress.com/2016/01/19/technology-integration-in-districts-and-schools-next-project-part-1/

Cubberley, E. P. (1916). Public school administration: A statement of the fundamental principles underlying the organization and administration of public education. Houghton Mifflin Company. https://archive.org/details/publicschooladmi00cubbrich

Danielson, C. (2007). Framework for teaching evaluation instrument. The Danielson Group. https://www.danielsongroup.org/framework/

Darling-Hammond, L. (2000). Teacher quality and student achievement: A review of state policy evidence. Education Policy Analysis Archives, 8(1), 1–44. https://doi.org/10.14507/epaa.v8n1.2000

Darling-Hammond, L. (2006). Powerful teacher education: Lessons from exemplary programs. Jossey-Bass. https://www.wiley.com/en-us/Powerful+Teacher+Education%3A+Lessons+from+Exemplary+Programs-p-9780787982849

Darling-Hammond, L. (2010). The flat world and education: How America's commitment to equity will determine our future. Teachers College Press. https://www.tcpress.com/the-flat-world-and-education-9780807748919

Darling-Hammond, L. (2010). The flat world and education: How America's commitment to equity will determine our future. Internet Archive; New York Teachers College Press. https://archive.org/details/flatworldeducati0000darl

Darling-Hammond, L. (2014). Multiple measures accountability: Moving beyond standardized testing. Educational Policy, 22(3), 1–30. https://www.jstor.org/stable/42728876

Darling-Hammond, L. (2017). Teacher education around the world: What can we learn from international practice? European Journal of Teacher Education, 40(3), 291–309. https://doi.org/10.1080/02619768.2017.1315399

Darling-Hammond, L. (2021). Preparing educators for the time of COVID... and beyond. Journal of Teacher Education, 72(2), 131–135. https://journals.sagepub.com/doi/abs/10.1177/00224871211004865

Darling-Hammond, L., & Bransford, J. (2005). Preparing teachers for a changing world: What teachers should learn and be able to do. Jossey-Bass. https://www.wiley.com/en-us/Preparing+Teachers+for+a+Changing+World%3A+What+Teachers+Should+Learn+and+Be+Able+to+Do-p-9780787986977

Darling-Hammond, L., & Cook-Harvey, C. M. (2022). Educating the whole child: Improving school climate to support student success. Learning Policy Institute.

Darling-Hammond, L., Cook-Harvey, C. M., Podolsky, A., Lam, L., Mercer, C., & Stosich, E. L. (2023). Redesigning high schools for equity and empowerment: Lessons from deeper learning. Learning Policy Institute. https://files.eric.ed.gov/fulltext/ED658860.pdf

Darling-Hammond, L., Hyler, M. E., & Gardner, M. (2017). Effective teacher professional development. Learning Policy Institute. https://learningpolicyinstitute.org/product/effective-teacher-professional-development-report

Davidson, C. (2017). The new education: How to revolutionize the university to prepare students for a world in flux. Basic Books.

Delpit, L. (2006). Other people's children: Cultural conflict in the classroom. The New Press. https://www.thenewpress.com/books/other-peoples-children

Derman-Sparks, L., Edwards, J. O., & the NAEYC Faculty. (2024). Decolonization in early childhood education. National Association for the Education of Young Children. https://www.naeyc.org/resources/pubs/yc/summer2024/decolon ization-in-ece

Deunk, M. I., Smale-Jacobse, A. E., Boer, H. de, Doolaard, S., & Bosker, R. J. (2018). Effective differentiation practices: A systematic review and meta-analysis of studies on the cognitive effects of differentiation practices in primary education. Educational Research Review, 24, 31–54. https://doi.org/10.1016/j.edurev.2018.02.002

Dewey, J. (1916). Democracy and education. Macmillan. https://archive.org/details/democracy-education

Douglas, M. (1982). In the active voice. Routledge & Kegan Paul. https://www.amazon.com/Active-Voice-Mary-Douglas/dp/0710006983

Drago-Severson, E. (2009). Supporting adult development in schools: A practical guide for fostering professional growth. Teachers College Press. https://www.tcpress.com/supporting-adult-development-in-schools-9780807750486

Drago-Severson, E. (2009, November 23). Leading adult learning. Corwin Press. https://books.google.co.za/books/about/Leading_Adult_Learnin g.html?id=O4lyAwAAQBAJ&redir_esc=y

DuFour, R. (2004). Learning by doing: A handbook for professional learning communities at work. Solution Tree. https://www.solutiontree.com/learning-by-doing.html

DuFour, R. (2004). What is a "Professional Learning Community"? AllThingsPLC. https://allthingsplc.info/wp-

content/uploads/2023/10/DuFourWhatIsAProfessionalLearning
Community.pdf

DuFour, R. (2004, May). What is a professional learning community.
https://mlc-wels.edu/wp-content/uploads/2019/05/PLC-dufour-
1.pdf

DuFour, R., & Eaker, R. (1998). Professional learning communities at
work: Best practices for enhancing student achievement. Solution
Tree. https://www.solutiontree.com/professional-learning-
communities-at-work.html

DuFour, R., DuFour, R., Eaker, R., & Many, T. (2010). Learning by
doing: A handbook for professional learning communities at work.
Solution Tree Press. https://www.solutiontree.com/learning-by-
doing-handbook.html

Duke, N. K., & Cartwright, K. B. (2021). The science of reading
progresses: Communicating advances beyond the simple view of
reading. Reading Research Quarterly, 56(S1).
https://doi.org/10.1002/rrq.411

Duke, N. K., Cervetti, G. N., Wise, C. N., & Halvorsen, A.-L. (2021).
Literacy in the disciplines: A research-based approach to teaching
reading, writing, speaking, and listening in content areas. Teachers
College Press. https://www.tcpress.com/literacy-in-the-
disciplines-9780807766173

Dweck, C. (2006). Mindset: The new psychology of success. Random
House. https://www.amazon.com/Mindset-Psychology-Carol-S-
Dweck/dp/0345472322

Dweck, C. S. (2015). Growth mindset, revisited. Education Week,
35(5), 20–24.

Dwyer, H. (2023). A call to interrogate educational development for
racism and colonization. Faculty Focus.

https://www.facultyfocus.com/articles/equality-inclusion-and-diversity/a-call-to-interrogate-educational-development-for-racism-and-colonization/

Dylan, W. (2011). Embedded formative assessment. Bloomington, IN: Solution Tree Press. https://archive.org/details/embeddedformativ0000wili

Edmondson, A. (1999). Psychological safety and learning behavior in work teams. Administrative Science Quarterly, 44(2), 350–383. https://doi.org/10.2307/2666999

Edmondson, A. C. (1999). Psychological safety and learning behavior in work teams. Administrative Science Quarterly, 44(2), 350–383. https://doi.org/10.2307/2666999

Elmore, R. F. (2004). School reform from the inside out: Policy, practice, and performance. Internet Archive; Cambridge Mass: Harvard Education Press. https://archive.org/details/schoolreformfrom0000elmo_b8b7

Elmore, R. F. (2006). School reform from the inside out: Policy, practice, and performance. Harvard Education Press.

Elmore, R. F., & City, E. A. (2007). Instructional rounds in education: A network approach to improving teaching and learning. Harvard Education Press.

Ernst, C., & Chrobot-Mason, D. (2011). Boundary spanning leadership: Six practices for solving problems, driving innovation, and transforming organizations. McGraw Hill.

Farnsworth, V., Kleanthous, I., & Wenger-Trayner, E. (2016). Communities of practice as a social theory of learning. British Journal of Educational Studies, 64(2), 139–160. https://doi.org/10.1080/00071005.2015.1133799

Fischer, F. (2003). Reframing public policy: Discursive politics and deliberative practices. Oxford University Press. https://global.oup.com/academic/product/reframing-public-policy-9780198294051

5 Obstacles (and solutions) to transforming school systems for the 21st century. (2025). Getting Smart. https://www.gettingsmart.com/2025/01/5-obstacles-and-solutions-to-transforming-school-systems/

Foucault, M. (1977). Discipline and punish: The birth of the prison. Pantheon Books.

Freire, P. (1970). Pedagogy of the oppressed. Herder and Herder.

Freire, P. (2019). Education as a Practice of Freedom. In J. Green, V. Langland, & L. Moritz Schwarcz (Eds.), The Brazil Reader: History, Culture, Politics (pp. 396-398). Duke University Press. https://www.degruyterbrill.com/document/doi/10.1515/978082 2371793-103/html

Fullan, M. (2001). Leading in a culture of change. Jossey-Bass.

Fullan, M. (2001). The new meaning of educational change (3rd ed.). Teachers College Press.

Fullan, M. (2006). Change theory: A force for school improvement. Michael Fullan. https://michaelfullan.ca/wp-content/uploads/2016/06/06_change_theory.pdf

Fullan, M. (2007). The new meaning of educational change (4th ed.). Teachers College Press.

Fullan, M. (2007). The new meaning of educational change. Michael Fullan; Teachers College Press. https://michaelfullan.ca/books/new-meaning-educational-change/

Fullan, M. (2010). All systems go: The change imperative for whole system reform. Corwin Press.

Fullan, M. (2010). Motion leadership: The skinny on becoming change savvy. Corwin Press.

Fullan, M. (2011). Change leader: Learning to do what matters most. Jossey-Bass.

Fullan, M. (2011). Choosing the wrong drivers for whole system reform. Voprosy Obrazovaniya/ Educational Studies. Moscow, 204(4), 79–105. https://doi.org/10.17323/1814-9545-2011-4-79-105

Fullan, M. (2016). The new meaning of educational change (5th ed.). Teachers College Press.

Fullan, M., & Quinn, J. (2016). Coherence: The right drivers in action for schools, districts, and systems. Corwin Press.

Fullan, M., & Quinn, J. (2016). Coherence: The right drivers in action for schools, districts, and systems. Michael Fullan. https://michaelfullan.ca/books/coherence-right-drivers-action-schools-districts-systems/

Fullan, M., Mackay, T., Redman, K., Cropley, M., & Miller, A. (2021). The right drivers for whole system success. https://michaelfullan.ca/wp-content/uploads/2021/03/Fullan-CSE-Leading-Education-Series-01-2021R2-compressed.pdf

Fullen, M. (2007). The new meaning of educational change. New York Teachers College Press. https://www.scirp.org/reference/ReferencesPapers?ReferenceID=1214431

Fundación Proacceso. (2023). Red de innovación y aprendizaje (RIA). https://fundacionproacceso.org

García, O. (2009). Bilingual education in the 21st Century: A global perspective. Wiley-Blackwell.

Gardner, H. (1983). Frames of mind: The theory of multiple intelligences. Basic Books.

Gardner, H. (2008). Five minds for the future. Harvard Business Press.

Gay, G. (2010). Culturally responsive teaching: Theory, research, and practice (2nd ed.). Teachers College Press.

Gee, J. P. (2003). What video games have to teach us about learning and literacy. Computers in Entertainment, 1(1), 20–20.

Geekie. (2023). Geekie: Educação personalizada e equitativa. https://geekie.com.br

Gilligan, C. (1982). In a different voice: Psychological theory and women's development. Harvard University Press.

Granovetter, M. (1973). The strength of weak ties. American Journal of Sociology, 78(6), 1360–1380.

Great pedagogical thinkers: John Dewey. (2019, October 30). Pedagogy4Change. https://www.pedagogy4change.org/john-dewey/

Great pedagogical thinkers: John Dewey. (2019, October 30). Pedagogy4Change. https://www.pedagogy4change.org/john-dewey/

Greene, J. (n.d.). Employing mixed methods in evaluation. https://inquirylearningcenter.org/wp-content/uploads/2015/08/Greene-mixed-methods-justification-2007-1.pdf

Greene, J. C. (2007). Mixed methods in social inquiry. Jossey-Bass.

Greene, M. (1995). Releasing the imagination: Essays on education, the arts, and social change. Jossey-Bass.

Guinier, L. (2015). Democratic merit: Rethinking educational excellence in diverse contexts. Harvard Educational Review, 85(1), 1-20.

Guskey, T. (2002). Does it make a difference? Evaluating professional development. Educational Leadership, 59(6), 45–51. https://tguskey.com/wp-content/uploads/Professional-Learning-4-Evaluating-Professional-Development.pdf

Guskey, T. R. (2000). Evaluating professional development. Internet Archive; Thousand Oaks, Calif.: Corwin Press. https://archive.org/details/evaluatingprofes0000gusk

Guskey, T. R. (2014). Planning professional learning. https://tguskey.com/wp-content/uploads/Professional-Learning-2-Planning-Professional-Learning.pdf

Guskey, T. R. (2020). What works in professional development: New analysis from the field. Learning Forward. https://learningforward.org

Halpin, A. W. (1955). The leader behavior and leadership ideology of educational administrators and aircraft commanders. Harvard Educational Review, 25(1), 45–52. https://www.jstor.org/stable/42738374

Hargreaves, A. (2005). Teaching in the knowledge society: Education in the age of insecurity. Teachers College Press. https://www.amazon.com/Teaching-Knowledge-Society-Education-Insecurity/dp/0807745726

Hargreaves, A. (2005). The emotions of teaching and educational change. Amsterdam Springer. https://www.scirp.org/reference/referencespapers?referenceid=2269472

Hargreaves, A. (2014). Collaborative professionalism: When teaching together means learning for all. Corwin. https://www.amazon.com/Collaborative-Professionalism-Teaching-Together-Learning/dp/145229133X

Hargreaves, A., & Fink, D. (2006). Sustainable leadership. Jossey-Bass. https://www.amazon.com/Sustainable-Leadership-Andy-Hargreaves/dp/0787974287

Hargreaves, A., & Fullan, M. (2012). Professional capital: Transforming teaching in every school. Teachers College Press. https://www.amazon.com/Professional-Capital-Transforming-Teaching-School/dp/0807753373

Hargreaves, A., & O'Connor, M. T. (2014). Leading collaborative professionalism. https://www.andyhargreaves.com/uploads/5/2/9/2/5292616/seminar_series_274-april2018.pdf

Hargreaves, A., & Shirley, D. (2009). The fourth way: The inspiring future for educational change. Corwin. https://www.amazon.com/Fourth-Way-Inspiring-Future-Educational/dp/1412967228

Harper, S. R., & Simmons, I. (2023). Structurally inclusive excellence: Advancing equity in selective postsecondary institutions. Journal of Diversity in Higher Education, 16(1), 1–14. https://doi.org/10.1037/dhe0000478

Harris, A. (2013). Distributed leadership: Friend or foe? Educational Management Administration & Leadership, 41(5), 545-551. https://doi.org/10.1177/1741143213490701

Hart, C. S. (2019). Capability Approach and Human Development: A Critical Introduction. ResearchGate. https://www.researchgate.net/publication/336602042_Capability_Approach_and_Human_Development

Hattie, J. (2009). Visible learning: A synthesis of over 800 meta-analyses relating to achievement. Routledge. https://www.amazon.com/Visible-Learning-synthesis-meta-analyses-achievement/dp/0415476186

Heck, R., & Hallinger, P. (2010). Collaborative leadership effects on school improvement: Integrating unidirectional- and reciprocal-effects models. The Elementary School Journal, 111(2), 226–252. https://doi.org/10.1086/656299

Heifetz, R. A. (1994). Leadership without easy answers. Belknap Press. https://www.hup.harvard.edu/catalog.php?isbn=9780674215172)

Heifetz, R. A., Grashow, A., & Linsky, M. (2009). The practice of adaptive leadership: Tools and tactics for changing your organization and the world. Harvard Business Press.

Heifetz, R. A., Linsky, M., & Grashow, A. (1994). The practice of adaptive leadership: Tools and tactics for changing your organization and the world. Harvard Business Press. https://www.hks.harvard.edu/publications/practice-adaptive-leadership-tools-and-tactics-changing-your-organization-and-world#citation

Held, V. (2006). The ethics of care: Personal, political, and global. Oxford University Press.

Hess, D. (2009). Controversy in the classroom: The democratic power of discussion. Routledge.

Hess, D. E., & McAvoy, P. (2021). The political classroom: Evidence and ethics in democratic education (2nd ed.). Routledge.

Hickman, J., & the NAEYC Faculty. (2024). Including Black language in early childhood Education. NAEYC.

https://www.naeyc.org/resources/pubs/yc/winter2024/including
-black-language-ece

Hirsh-Pasek, K., et al. (2015). The contribution of early learning to the development of cognitive and social skills: A review of the evidence. Child Development Perspectives, 9(2), 74-79. https://doi.org/10.1111/cdep.12109

Hobbs, R. (2010). Digital and Media Literacy: A Plan of Action. The Aspen Institute. https://www.aspeninstitute.org

Hooks, B. (1994). Teaching to transgress: Education as the practice of freedom. Routledge. https://www.amazon.com/Teaching-Transgress-Education-Practice-Freedom/dp/0415900410

House, E. R. (2004). The politics of evaluation: Participation and policy. Sage. https://www.amazon.com/Politics-Evaluation-Participation-Policy/dp/0761913412

How to Create a Thought Leadership Strategy (+14 Tips). (2023, September 26). Intelligent Relations. https://intelligentrelations.com/insights/thought-leadership-strategy/

Ito, M. (2008). Living and learning with new media: Summary of findings from the digital youth project. MacArthur Foundation. https://www.macfound.org

Ito, M., Gutiérrez, K., Livingstone, S., Penuel, B., Rhodes, J., Salen, K., Schor, J., Sefton-Green, J., & Watkins, S. C. (2013). Connected learning: An agenda for research and design. Digital Media and Learning Research Hub. https://dmlhub.net

Ito, M., Gutiérrez, K., Livingstone, S., Penuel, B., Rhodes, J., Salen, K., Schor, J., Sefton-Green, J., Watkins, C., Ito, J., Watkins, J., & Craig, S. (2014). Connected learning: An agenda for research and design. Digital Media and Learning Research Hub.

https://eprints.lse.ac.uk/48114/1/__lse.ac.uk_storage_LIBRARY
_Secondary_libfile_shared_repository_Content_Livingstone%2C
%20S_Livingstone_Connected_learning_agenda_2010_Livingsto
ne_Connected_learning_agenda_2013.pdf

Jackson, P. (1968). Life in classrooms. Holt, Rinehart & Winston.
(https://www.amazon.com/Life-Classrooms-Philip-
Jackson/dp/0912750601)

Jakopovic, P., & Johnson, K. G. (2023). Communities of practice as
levers for instructional change. The Scholarly Teacher.
https://scholarlyteacher.com

Jenkins, H. (2006). Confronting the challenges of participatory
culture: Media education for the 21st century. The John D. and
Catherine T. MacArthur Foundation. https://www.macfound.org

Jonassen, D. H. (2006). Meaningful learning with technology (3rd
ed.). Pearson. https://www.amazon.com/Meaningful-Learning-
Technology-3rd-Edition/dp/0131182500

Khan Academy. (2023). About Khan Academy.
https://www.khanacademy.org

King, J. A. (2004). Participatory evaluation in education: A framework
for successful collaboration. Educational Policy Analysis Archives,
12(20), 1-24. https://doi.org/10.14507/epaa.v12n20.2004

King, J. A., Bradley, C. J., & Whitmore, E. (2007). Making sense of
participatory evaluation: Framing participatory evaluation. New
Directions for Evaluation; Jossey Bass.
https://eric.ed.gov/?id=EJ792376

Kingdon, J. W. (2011). Agendas, alternatives, and public policies
(Updated 2nd ed.). Longman.
https://www.amazon.com/Agendas-Alternatives-Public-Policies-
Updated/dp/0321442029

Ki-Zerbo, J. (1990). African philosophy: The essential texts. Harcourt Brace. https://www.amazon.com/African-Philosophy-Essential-Texts-Ki-Zerbo/dp/0155803741

Kohlberg, L. (1981). The philosophy of moral development: Moral stages and the idea of justice. Harper & Row. https://archive.org/details/philosophyofmora0000kohl

Kotter, J. P. (1996). Leading change. Harvard Business School Press. https://www.amazon.com/Leading-Change-John-Kotter/dp/0875847471

Krathwohl, D. R. (2002). A revision of Bloom's taxonomy. Jstor.org. https://doi.org/10.2307/1477405

Kurt, S. (2023, September 20). SAMR model: Substitution, augmentation, modification, and redefinition. Educational Technology. https://educationaltechnology.net/samr-model-substitution-augmentation-modification-and-redefinition/

Kurtzman, J. (1994). A brief history of thought leadership. Strategy+Business. https://petercook.com/blog/a-brief-history-of-thought-leadership

Labaree, D. F. (2023). A perfect mess: The unlikely ascendancy of American higher education. University of Chicago Press.

Ladson-Billings, G. (1992). Culturally relevant teaching: The key to making multicultural education work. In C. A. Grant (Ed.), Research and multicultural education (pp. 106–121). London: Falmer Press. https://econedlink.org/wp-content/uploads/2020/06/LadsonBillings_Culturally-Relevant-Pedagogy.pdf

Ladson-Billings, G. (1994). The dreamkeepers: Successful teachers of African American children. Jossey-Bass.

https://www.amazon.com/Dreamkeepers-Successful-Teachers-African-American/dp/0787903608

Ladson-Billings, G. (1995). Toward a theory of culturally relevant pedagogy. American Educational Research Journal, 32(3), 465–491. https://doi.org/10.3102/00028312032003465

Ladson-Billings, G. (1995a). Toward a critical race theory of education. Teachers College Record, 97(1), 47–68. https://eric.ed.gov/?id=EJ519126

Ladson-Billings, G. (2022). What should culturally relevant teaching look like today? Education Week. https://www.edweek.org/leadership/what-should-culturally-relevant-teaching-look-like-today-gloria-ladson-billings-explains/2022/04

Lankshear, C., & Knobel, M. (2006). New literacies: Everyday practices and classroom learning (2nd ed.). Open University Press. https://www.amazon.com/New-Literacies-Everyday-Practices-Classroom/dp/0335213490

Lave, J., & Wenger, E. (1991). Situated learning: Legitimate peripheral participation. Cambridge University Press. https://www.amazon.com/Situated-Learning-Legitimate-Peripheral-Participation/dp/0521423740

Learning Policy Institute. (2023). The promise of performance assessments: Innovations in measuring student learning. https://learningpolicyinstitute.org

Leithwood, K. A. (1992). The move toward transformational leadership. Educational Leadership, 49(5), 8–12. https://files.ascd.org/staticfiles/ascd/pdf/journals/ed_lead/el_199202_leithwood.pdf

Leithwood, K., Day, C., Sammons, P., Harris, A., & Hopkins, D. (2004). Seven strong claims about successful school leadership. National College for School Leadership. https://www.education.gov.uk

Lemov, D. (2010). Teach like a champion: 49 techniques that put students on the path to college. Jossey-Bass. https://www.amazon.com/Teach-Like-Champion-Techniques-Students/dp/0470550477

Levin, H. M. (2001). Cost-effectiveness analysis in education: A practical approach. Sage Publications. (https://www.amazon.com/Cost-Effectiveness-Analysis-Education-Practical-Approach/dp/0761945821)

Lieberman, A. (1990). Schools as collaborative cultures: Creating the future now. Falmer Press. https://www.amazon.com/Schools-Collaborative-Cultures-Creating-Future/dp/1850005044

Lieberman, A. (2000). Networks as learning communities: Shaping the future of teacher development. Journal of Teacher Education, 51(3), 221–227. https://doi.org/10.1177/0022487100051003010

Lieberman, A., & Miller, L. (2001). Teachers caught in the action: Professional development that matters. Teachers College Press. https://www.amazon.com/Teachers-Caught-Action-Professional-Development/dp/0807740688

Lieberman, A., & Miller, L. (2004, July 26). Teacher leadership. Amazon.com. https://www.amazon.com/Teacher-Leadership-Ann-Lieberman/dp/0787962457

Lieberman, A., & Miller, L. (2008). Teachers in professional communities: Improving teaching and learning. Teachers College Press. https://www.amazon.com/Teachers-Professional-Communities-Improving-Learning/dp/0807748553

Lieberman, A., & Miller, L. (2011, March 31). Teacher leadership. John Wiley & Sons. https://books.google.co.za/books/about/Teacher_Leadership.html?id=5xwQe2CDQYMC&redir_esc=y

Lieberman, A., & Wood, D. (2003). Inside the national writing project: Connecting network learning and classroom teaching. Teachers College Press. https://www.amazon.com/National-Writing-Project-Connecting-Classroom/dp/0807744010)

Lipman, M. (2003). Philosophy for children. Teachers College Press. https://www.amazon.com/Philosophy-Children-Matthew-Lipman/dp/0807737960

Lipsky, M. (1980). Street-level bureaucracy: Dilemmas of the individual in public services. Russell Sage Foundation. https://www.amazon.com/Street-Level-Bureaucracy-Dilemmas-Individual/dp/0871545205

Little, J. W. (1990). The influence of work conditions on teachers' instructional choices. Educational Evaluation and Policy Analysis, 12(3), 213-226. https://doi.org/10.3102/01623737012003213

Little, J. W. (1990a). The mentor phenomenon and the social organization of teaching. https://doi.org/16,297-351

Little, J. W. (1990b). The persistence of privacy: Autonomy and initiative in teachers' professional relations. Teachers College Record. https://doi.org/91%20(4),509-536

Looney, L., Minkoff, A. C., & Wilson, G. (2023). Creating clarity through understanding complexity: Building a case for development as a critical component of educator preparation. Issues in Teacher Education, 32(1), 93–108. https://files.eric.ed.gov/fulltext/EJ1380073.pdf

Louis, K. S. (2006). Changing the culture of schools: Professional community, organizational learning, and trust. Journal of School Leadership, 16(5), 477–489. https://doi.org/10.1177/105268460601600502

Louis, K. S. (2006). Creating and sustaining professional communities. ResearchGate. https://www.researchgate.net/publication/265747858_Creating_and_Sustaining_Professional_Communities_1

Louis, K. S., Kruse, S. D., & Marks, H. M. (1996). Schoolwide professional community. In F. M. Newmann & Associates (Eds.), Authentic achievement: Restructuring schools for intellectual quality (pp. 179–203). Jossey-Bass. https://www.amazon.com/Authentic-Achievement-Restructuring-Schools-Intellectual/dp/0787902246

Maathai, W. (2006). The green belt movement: Sharing the approach and the experience. Lantern Books. https://www.amazon.com/Green-Belt-Movement-Sharing-Approach/dp/1590561044

MacIntyre, A. (1981). After virtue. University of Notre Dame Press. https://www.amazon.com/After-Virtue-Normative-Theory-Modern/dp/0268005964

Maluleka, M., Bisschoff, T., & van Wyk, M. (2024). Integrating Indigenous education in early childhood settings. Africa Education Review. https://www.tandfonline.com/doi/full/10.1080/18117295.2024.2374133

Manna, P. (2006). Schools in: Federalism and the national education agenda. Georgetown University Press. https://www.amazon.com/Schools-Federalism-National-Education-Agenda/dp/1589011499

Manna, P. (2009). Schools in: Federalism and the national education agenda. Georgetown University Press. https://books.google.co.za/books/about/School_s_in.html?id=X PNKDAAAQBAJ&redir_esc=y

Marion, S., Els, J., & Leather, P. (2004). Reciprocal accountability for transformative change: New Hampshire's performance assessment of competency education. https://files.eric.ed.gov/fulltext/EJ1148461.pdf

Marzano Research Laboratory. (2011). Meta-Analytic synthesis of studies conducted at Marzano research on instructional strategies. https://eric.ed.gov/?id=ED538088

Marzano, R. (2007). The art and science of teaching: A comprehensive framework for effective instruction. ASCD. https://www.amazon.com/Art-Science-Teaching-Comprehensive-Instruction/dp/141660572X

Marzano, R. J., Pickering, D. J., & Pollock, J. E. (2001). Classroom instruction that works: Research-based strategies for increasing student achievement. ASCD. https://www.amazon.com/Classroom-Instruction-Works-Research-Strategies/dp/0871205127

Maxwell, J. A. (2013). Qualitative research design: An interactive approach (3rd ed.). SAGE Publications. https://www.amazon.com/Qualitative-Research-Design-Interactive-Approach/dp/145225757X

Mayne, J. (2001). Contribution analysis: An approach to exploring cause and effect. IDRC Evaluation Unit. https://www.idrc.ca/en/book/contribution-analysis-approach-exploring-cause-and-effect

Mayne, J. (2011). Contribution analysis: Addressing cause and effect. ResearchGate, 53–96.

https://www.researchgate.net/publication/303836616_Contribut
ion_analysis_Addressing_cause_and_effect

McLaughlin, M. W. (1987). Learning from experience: Lessons from policy implementation. Educational Evaluation and Policy Analysis, 9(2), 171–178. https://doi.org/10.3102/01623737009002171

McLaughlin, M. W. (2006). Implementation as a political process. The Yearbook of Education Policy, 5, 15-29. https://journals.sagepub.com/doi/10.3102/003465430490021

McLaughlin, M. W., & Talbert, J. E. (2010). Professional learning communities: Building blocks for school culture and student learning. ResearchGate. https://www.researchgate.net/publication/265655002_Profession al_Learning_Communities_Building_Blocks_for_School_Cultur e_and_Student_Learning

McMillan Cottom, T. (2012). Digitized institutions and inequalities. https://tressiemc.com/wp-content/uploads/2012/10/McMillanCotttomDigitizedInstitution sandInequalities.pdf

Meadows, D. (2012, April 5). Leverage points: Places to intervene in a system. The Academy for Systems Change. https://donellameadows.org/archives/leverage-points-places-to-intervene-in-a-system/

Meadows, D. H. (1999). Leverage points: Places to intervene in a system. The Sustainability Institute. https://donellameadows.org/archives/leverage-points-places-to-intervene-in-a-system/

Means, B. (n.d.). Barbara Means, Ph.D. AAAS | IUSE. https://aaas-iuse.org/team/barbara-means-ph-d/

Mehta, J. (2013). Deeper learning: Re-thinking the future of education. The Journal of Educational Change, 24(2), 120-141.

Mehta, J., & Fine, S. (2019). In search of deeper learning: The quest to remake the American high school. Harvard University Press. https://www.hup.harvard.edu/catalog.php?isbn=9780674184312

Meier, D. (1995). The power of their ideas: Lessons for America from a small school in Harlem. Beacon Press. https://openlibrary.org/works/OL8321642W/The_Power_of_T heir_Ideas

Middle-range theorising supporting and supported by action research. (2024). Production Planning & Control, 35(2), 123-134. Taylor & Francis Online. https://www.tandfonline.com/doi/full/10.1080/09537287.2024. 2327347

Mill, J. S. (1863). Utilitarianism. Parker, Son, and Bourn. https://www.amazon.com/Utilitarianism-John-Stuart-Mill/dp/1503280466

Mills, C. W. (1997). The racial contract. Cornell University Press. https://www.amazon.com/Racial-Contract-Cornell-Studies-Political/dp/0801484999

Mishra, P., & Koehler, M. J. (2006). Technological pedagogical content knowledge: A framework for teacher knowledge. Teachers College Record, 108(6), 1017–1054. (SAGE Journals) https://www.punyamishra.com/wp-content/uploads/2008/01/mishra-koehler-tcr2006.pdf

Mitra, S. (2016). Sugata Mitra – the professor with his head in the cloud. The Guardian. https://www.theguardian.com/education/2016/jun/07/sugata-mitra-professor-school-in-cloud

Montessori, M. (2023). Montessori education. Wikipedia. https://en.wikipedia.org/wiki/Montessori_education

Nation | Student Guilds, Charters & Scholars. (n.d.). Encyclopedia Britannica. Retrieved June 2, 2025, from https://www.britannica.com/topic/nation-medieval-university-group

Nation | Student Guilds, Charters & Scholars. (n.d.). Encyclopedia Britannica. Retrieved June 2, 2025, from https://www.britannica.com/topic/nation-medieval-university-group

National Academies of Sciences, Engineering, and Medicine. (2022). Advancing antiracism, diversity, equity, and inclusion in STEMM organizations: Beyond broadening participation. The National Academies Press. https://doi.org/10.17226/26345

National Commission on Excellence in Education. (1983). A nation at risk: The imperative for educational reform. U.S. Department of Education. https://eric.ed.gov/?id=ED226006

National Reading Panel. (2000). Teaching children to read: An evidence-based assessment of the scientific research literature on reading and its implications for reading instruction (NIH Publication No. 00-4769). U.S. Department of Health and Human Services, National Institute of Child Health and Human Development. https://www.nichd.nih.gov/sites/default/files/publications/pubs/nrp/documents/report.pdf

National Writing Project. (2020). Teacher inquiry communities: Collaborative problem-solving in writing instruction. National Writing Project. https://www.nwp.org/

National Writing Project. (n.d.). The NWP archives project. https://www.nwp.org/stories/the-nwp-archives-project

Netolicky, D. M. (2020). Future alternatives for educational leadership: Diversity, inclusion, equity, and complexity. In F. W. English (Ed.), The Palgrave handbook of educational leadership and management discourse (pp. 1–18). Palgrave Macmillan. https://www.taylorfrancis.com/books/edit/10.4324/9781003131 496/future-alternatives-educational-leadership-deborah-netolicky

Netolicky, D. M., & Golledge, C. (2021). Wayfinding: Navigating complexity for sustainable school leadership. Future Alternatives for Educational Leadership, 38–53. https://doi.org/10.4324/9781003131496-5

Nieto, S. (2004). Affirming diversity: The sociopolitical context of multicultural education (4th ed.). Pearson. https://www.pearsonhighered.com/assets/preface/0/1/3/4/01340 47230.pdf

Noddings, N. (1984). Caring: A feminine approach to ethics and moral education. University of California Press. https://www.amazon.com/Caring-Feminine-Ethics-Moral-Education/dp/0520050765

Noddings, N. (2005). The ethics of care and education. Infed.org. https://infed.org/mobi/nel-noddings-the-ethics-of-care-and-education/

Noguera, P. (2003). Excellence through equity: Creating conditions for great teaching and learning. https://www.cosa.k12.or.us/sites/default/files/images/03_pedro_noguera_2.pdf

Noguera, P. A. (2003). The trouble with Black boys: The role and influence of environmental and cultural factors on the academic performance of African American males. Urban Education, 38(4), 431–459. https://nyuscholars.nyu.edu/en/publications/the-trouble-with-black-boys-the-role-and-influence-of-environment

Nonaka, I., & Takeuchi, H. (1995). The knowledge-creating company: How Japanese companies create the dynamics of innovation. Oxford University Press. https://academic.oup.com/book/52097

Northern Illinois University. (n.d.). Howard Gardner's theory of multiple intelligences. Center for Innovative Teaching and Learning. https://www.niu.edu/citl/resources/guides/instructional-guide/gardners-theory-of-multiple-intelligences.shtml

Nussbaum, M. (1997). Cultivating humanity: A classical defense of reform in liberal education. Harvard University Press. https://www.hup.harvard.edu/books/9780674179493

Nussbaum, M. (2011). Creating capabilities: The human development approach. Belknap Press. https://www.hup.harvard.edu/catalog.php?isbn=9780674072350

Oakes, J. (1985). Keeping track: How schools structure inequality. Yale University Press. https://www.amazon.com/Keeping-Track-Schools-Structure-Inequality/dp/0300030186

Odden, A. (2009). Aligning resources to sustain school reform. Educational Leadership, 66(6), 22-27.

O'Neil, C. (2016). Weapons of math destruction: How big data increases inequality and threatens democracy. Crown Publishing Group. https://www.amazon.com/Weapons-Math-Destruction-Increases-Inequality/dp/0553418815

O'Neill, O. (2002). Autonomy and trust in bioethics. Cambridge University Press. https://www.amazon.com/Autonomy-Trust-Bioethics-Olivia-ONeill/dp/0521795264

Page, S. E. (2007). The diversity bonus: How diversity improves performance and innovation. Harvard University Press.

https://www.perlego.com/book/3284075/earth-in-mind-on-education-environment-and-the-human-prospect-pdf

Paley, V. G. (1990). The boy who would be a helicopter: The use of storytelling in the classroom. Harvard University Press. https://www.hup.harvard.edu/books/9780674080317

Palmer, P. J. (1998). The courage to teach: Exploring the inner landscape of a teacher's life. Jossey-Bass. https://www.couragerenewal.org/

Palus, C. J., & Horth, D. M. (2002). The leader's edge: Six creative competencies for navigating complex challenges. Jossey-Bass. https://archive.org/details/leadersedgesixcr0000palu

Pape, S. J., Bryant, C. L., JohnBull, R. M., & Karp, K. S. (2022). Improvement science as a frame for the dissertation in practice: The Johns Hopkins experience. Impacting Education: Journal on Transforming Professional Practice, 7(1), 59–66. https://doi.org/10.5195/ie.2022.241

Patton, M. Q. (2008). Utilization-focused evaluation: The new century text (4th ed.). Sage Publications. https://openlibrary.org/books/OL16365737M/Utilization-focused_evaluation

Patton, M. Q. (2008, June 18). Utilization-focused evaluation. SAGE Publications. https://books.google.co.za/books/about/Utilization_Focused_Evaluation.html?id=DFYXBAAAQBAJ&redir_esc=y

Patton, M. Q. (2011). Developmental evaluation: Applying complexity concepts to enhance innovation and use. The Canadian Journal of Program Evaluation, 26(2), 108–110. https://doi.org/10.3138/cjpe.26.009

Pawson, R., & Tilley, N. (1997, April). Realistic evaluation. SAGE Publications Ltd. https://uk.sagepub.com/en-gb/eur/realistic-evaluation/book205276

PBLWorks. (2014). Project-based learning: A short guide to PBL. Buck Institute for Education. https://www.pblworks.org/what-is-pbl

Pellegrino, J. W. (2022). A learning sciences perspective on the design and use of assessment in education. Cambridge University Press EBooks, 238–258. https://doi.org/10.1017/9781108888295.015

Perkins, D. (1992). Smart schools: From training memories to educating minds. Free Press. https://www.amazon.com/Making-Learning-Whole-Principles-Transform/dp/0470633719

Perkins, D. (2009). Making learning whole: How seven principles of teaching can transform education. Jossey-Bass. https://uk.sagepub.com/en-gb/eur/the-intelligent-school/book224901

Perkins, D. N. (2000). The intelligent school. Longman. https://archive.org/details/formsofintellect0000perr

Perry, W. G. (1970). Forms of intellectual and ethical development in the college years: A scheme. Holt, Rinehart & Winston. https://archive.org/details/formsofintellect00will

Piaget, J. (1952). The origins of intelligence in children (M. Cook, Trans.). International Universities Press. https://psycnet.apa.org/record/2007-10742-000

Pink, D. H. (2009). Drive: The surprising truth about what motivates us. Riverhead Books. https://www.danpink.com/books/drive/

Pinnell, G. S., & Fountas, I. C. (2009). Teaching for comprehension and fluency: A research-based guide. Heinemann.

https://www.fountasandpinnell.com/teachingforcomprehending andfluency/

Pozas, M., Letzel, V., Lindner, K.-T., & Schwab, S. (2021). DI (differentiated instruction) does matter! The effects of DI on secondary school students' well-being, social inclusion and academic self-concept. Frontiers in Education, 6. https://doi.org/10.3389/feduc.2021.729027

Project Zero. (n.d.). Thinking routines toolbox. Harvard Graduate School of Education. https://pz.harvard.edu/thinking-routines

Project Zero. (n.d.). Visible thinking. Harvard Graduate School of Education. https://pz.harvard.edu/projects/visible-thinking

QUBES. (2023). Quantitative undergraduate biology education. https://www.qubeshub.org

Ravitch, D. (2013). Reign of error: The hoax of the privatization movement and the danger to America's public schools. Alfred A. Knopf. https://archive.org/details/reignoferrorhoax0000ravi

Rawls, J. (1971). A theory of justice. Harvard University Press. https://www.hup.harvard.edu/catalog.php?isbn=9780674000780

Rawls, J. (1993). Political liberalism. Columbia University Press. https://www.amazon.com/Political-Liberalism-John-Rawls/dp/0231130897

Reich, J. (2019). The first and second digital divides. Kappan Online. https://kappanonline.org/justin-reich-recommends-comment-the-first-and-second-digital-divides/

Reich, J. (2020). Failure to disrupt: Why technology alone can't transform education. Harvard University Press. https://www.hup.harvard.edu/books/9780674278684

Resnick, L. B. (2010). Learning in school and out. Educational Researcher, 39(1), 1-12. https://www.academia.edu/34488533/Learning_in_school_and_out

Richardson, W., & Mancabelli, R. (2011). Personal learning networks: Using the power of connections to transform education. Solution Tree Press. https://www.perlego.com/book/4141885/personal-learning-networks-using-the-power-of-connections-to-transform-education-pdf

Ritchhart, R., & Perkins, D. (2008). Making thinking visible when learners speak, write, or draw their ideas, they deepen their cognition. Project Zero's visible thinking approach shows how. Educational Leadership, 65(5), 57–61. https://pz.harvard.edu/sites/default/files/makingthinkingvisibleEL.pdf

Ritchhart, R., Church, M., & Morrison, K. (2011). Making thinking visible: How to promote engagement, understanding, and independence for all learners. Jossey-Bass. https://pz.harvard.edu/sites/default/files/Chapter%201%20MTV%20Ritchhart%20Sample.pdf

Robinson, K. (2006). Do schools kill creativity? [TED Talk]. TED. https://www.ted.com/talks/sir_ken_robinson_do_schools_kill_creativity

Robinson, K. (2009). The element: How finding your passion changes everything. Viking. https://www.amazon.com/Element-Finding-Passion-Changes-Everything/dp/0143116738

Robinson, K. (2011). Out of our minds: Learning to be creative (2nd ed.). Capstone. https://archive.org/download/ChaosAndFractalsNewFrontiersOfScience/out%20of%20our%20minds.pdf

Robinson, K. (2015). Creative schools: The grassroots revolution that's transforming education. Penguin. https://penguinrandomhousehighereducation.com/book/?isbn=9780670016716

Robinson, V. M. J. (2011). Student-centered leadership. Jossey-Bass. https://eric.ed.gov/?id=ED529294

Robison, V. (2011, June 24). Student-Centered leadership. John Wiley & Sons. https://books.google.co.za/books/about/Student_Centered_Leadership.html?id=6Xy1dtzoZjQC&redir_esc=y

Rogers, E. M. (2003). Diffusion of innovations (5th ed.). Free Press. https://openlibrary.org/books/OL3511214M/Diffusion_of_innovations

Rogers, Y. (2013). How are new technological interfaces shaping the future of learning? [Video]. YouTube. https://www.youtube.com/watch?v=D4uufYEpPIQ

Rogoff, B. (1990). Apprenticeship in thinking: Cognitive development in social context. Oxford University Press. https://academic.oup.com/book/53473

Rogoff, B. (2003, February 13). The cultural nature of human development. Oxford University Press. https://books.google.co.za/books/about/The_Cultural_Nature_of_Human_Development.html?id=HSkaQ3FTsLIC&redir_esc=y

Rose, M. (2009). Lives on the boundary: A moving account of the struggles and achievements of America's underprepared students. Penguin Books. https://archive.org/details/livesonboundarym00rose

Rose, M. (2009). Why school? Reclaiming education for all of us. The New Press. https://archive.org/details/whyschoolreclaim0000rose

Rosenstock, L. (2007). Building high tech high: Transforming education with project-based learning. Educational Leadership, 64(2), 20-24.

Ryan, R. M., & Deci, E. L. (2000). Self-determination theory and the facilitation of intrinsic motivation, social development, and well-being. American Psychologist, 55(1), 68-78. https://psycnet.apa.org/record/2000-13324-007

Sabatier, P. A., & Jenkins-Smith, H. C. (1993). Policy change and learning: An advocacy coalition approach. Westview Press. https://searchworks.stanford.edu/view/2756921

Sahlberg, P. (2021). Let the children play: How more play will save our schools and help children thrive. Oxford University Press. https://eric.ed.gov/?id=ED599671

Said, E. (1993). Culture and imperialism. Knopf. https://www.monoskop.org/images/f/f9/Said_Edward_Culture_and_Imperialism.pdf

Sandel, M. J. (2012). What money can't buy: The moral limits of markets. Farrar, Straus and Giroux. https://psycnet.apa.org/record/2012-13135-000

Santos, B. de S. (2014). Epistemologies of the South: Justice against epistemicide. Paradigm Publishers. https://www.taylorfrancis.com/books/mono/10.4324/97813156 34876/epistemologies-south-boaventura-de-sousa-santos

Sarason, S. B. (1996). Reforming schools: The quest for equity. Teachers College Press.

Sarason, S. B. (1996). The culture of the school and the problem of change. Internet Archive. https://archive.org/details/cultureofschoolp0000sara_q0r6

Scardamalia, M., & Bereiter, C. (2012). Knowledge building. In R. K. Sawyer (Ed.), The Cambridge handbook of the learning sciences (2nd ed., pp. 97–115). https://www.cambridge.org/core/books/cambridge-handbook-of-the-learning-sciences/knowledge-building-and-knowledge-creation/630B1A3A704CED8B93322E5E11B5789D

Schleicher, A. (n.d.). Organisation for economic co-operation and development (OECD). https://www.oecd.org/en/about/directorates/directorate-for-education-and-skills/andreas-schleicher.html

Schmoker, M. (2006). Results now: How we can achieve unprecedented improvements in teaching and learning. ASCD. https://eric.ed.gov/?id=ED494304

Schön, D. A. (1983). The reflective practitioner: How professionals think in action. Basic Books. https://www.taylorfrancis.com/books/mono/10.4324/97813152 37473/reflective-practitioner-donald-sch%C3%B6n

Schunk, D. H. (2008). Learning theories: An educational perspective (5th ed.). Pearson. https://www.pearson.com/store/p/learning-theories-an-educational-perspective/P100000672906

Sen, A. (1999). Development as freedom. Alfred A. Knopf. https://www.penguinrandomhouse.com/books/159718/development-as-freedom-by-amartya-sen/

Senge, P. (1990). Learning organization. Infed.org. https://infed.org/mobi/peter-senge-and-the-learning-organization/

Senge, P. M. (1990). The fifth discipline: The art and practice of the learning organization. Doubleday. https://www.penguinrandomhouse.com/books/153070/the-fifth-discipline-by-peter-m-senge/

Senge, P. M., Cambron-McCabe, N., Lucas, T., Smith, B., Dutton, J., & Kleiner, A. (2012). Schools that learn (updated and revised): A fifth discipline fieldbook for educators, parents, and everyone who cares about education. Crown Business. https://www.amazon.com/Schools-That-Learn-Updated-Revised/dp/0385518226

Shah, M., & Hoadley, C. (2022). Ethics in educational technology: Toward equity-conscious design. Educational Researcher, 51(7), 490–499. https://doi.org/10.3102/0013189X221114153

Shapiro, J. P., & Gross, S. J. (2013). Ethical educational leadership in turbulent times: (Re)solving moral dilemmas. Routledge. https://www.taylorfrancis.com/books/edit/10.4324/9780203809310/ethical-educational-leadership-turbulent-times-joan-poliner-shapiro-steven-jay-gross

Shiva, V. (2000). Stolen harvest: The hijacking of the global food supply. South End Press. https://link.springer.com/article/10.1007/s10460-012-9388-4

Shulman, L. S. (1986). Those who understand: Knowledge growth in teaching. Educational Researcher, 15(2), 4–14. https://doi.org/10.3102/0013189X015002004

Shulman, L. S. (1987). Knowledge and teaching: Foundations of the new reform. Harvard Educational Review, 57(1), 1–22. https://doi.org/10.17763/haer.57.1.j463w79r56455411

Sinek, S. (2009). Start with why: How great leaders inspire everyone to take action. Portfolio. https://simonsinek.com/books/start-with-why/

Sizer, T. (1992). Encyclopedia of educational reform and dissent. Google Books. https://books.google.co.za/books?id=JSh1AwAAQBAJ&pg=PA 170&redir_esc=y#v=onepage&q&f=false

Sizer, T. R. (1984). Horace's compromise: The dilemma of the American high school. Houghton Mifflin. https://eric.ed.gov/?id=ED264171

Skitka, L. J., Washburn, A. N., & Carsel, T. S. (2005). The psychological foundations of moral conviction: Implications for politics, attitudes, and behavior. PMC. https://www.ncbi.nlm.nih.gov/pmc/articles/PMC6504687

Slavin, R. E. (2002). Evidence-based education policies: Transforming educational practice and research. Educational Researcher, 31(7), 15–21. https://doi.org/10.3102/0013189X031007015

Slavin, R. E. (2008). Educational psychology: Theory and practice (8th ed.). Boston: Allyn & Bacon. https://archive.org/details/educationalpsych0008slav

Smith, L. T. (2012). Decolonizing methodologies: Research and Indigenous peoples. Zed Books. https://www.msd.govt.nz/about-msd-and-our-work/publications-resources/journals-and-magazines/social-policy-journal/spj17/decolonizing-methodologies-research-and-indigenous-peoples.html

Snowden, D. J., & Boone, M. E. (2007). A leader's framework for decision making. Harvard Business Review, 85(11), 68-76. https://hbr.org/2007/11/a-leaders-framework-for-decision-making

Solution Tree. (n.d.). History of PLC at work. AllThingsPLC. https://allthingsplc.info/about/history-of-plc/

Spillane, J. P. (2005). Distributed leadership. The Educational Forum, 69(2), 143–150. https://doi.org/10.1080/00131720508984678

Spillane, J. P. (2006). Distributed leadership. Educational Researcher, 35(6), 23-28. https://doi.org/10.3102/0013189X035006023

Spillane, J. P. (2006a). Distributed leadership. Jossey-Bass/Wiley. https://psycnet.apa.org/record/2006-10111-000

Spillane, J. P., Halverson, R., & Diamond, J. B. (2004). Towards a theory of leadership practice: A distributed perspective. Journal of Curriculum Studies, 36(1), 3–34. https://www.scholars.northwestern.edu/en/publications/towards-a-theory-of-leadership-practice-a-distributed-perspective-2

Spring, J. (2012). Education networks: Power, wealth, cyberspace, and the digital mind. Routledge. https://www.taylorfrancis.com/books/mono/10.4324/97802031 56803/education-networks-joel-spring

Steele, C. M. (2010). Whistling Vivaldi: And other clues to how stereotypes affect us. W.W. Norton & Company. https://psycnet.apa.org/record/2011-06361-000

Stone, D. (2012). Policy paradox: The art of political decision making (3rd ed.). W.W. Norton & Company. https://archive.org/details/policyparadoxart0000ston

Thought leadership in education strategies. (2025, February 9). University HUB. https://universityhub.com/blog/thought-leadership-in-education-the-key-to-driving-industry-innovation-and-influence/

Timperley, H. (2008). Teacher professional learning and development. UNESCO. https://unesdoc.unesco.org/ark:/48223/pf0000179161

Tomlinson, C. A. (2014). The Differentiated classroom: Responding to the needs of all learners. ASCD. https://www.scirp.org/reference/referencespapers?referenceid=24 64900

Toyama, K. (2011). Technology as amplifier in international development. In Proceedings of the 2011 iConference (pp. 75–82). ACM. https://www.kentarotoyama.org/papers/Toyama%202011%20iC onference%20-%20Technology%20as%20Amplifier.pdf

Trust, T. (2012). Professional learning networks designed for teacher learning. Journal of Digital Learning in Teacher Education, 28(4), 133–138. https://files.eric.ed.gov/fulltext/EJ972454.pdf

Tu, W. (1998). Confucianism and modernization: The intellectual dilemmas of contemporary Confucianism. Cambridge University Press. http://tuweiming.net/publications/books/

TuSmith, B. (2010). The educational thought of W.E.B. Du Bois. International Journal of Multicultural Education, 12(1), 1–15. https://ijme-journal.org/index.php/ijme/article/view/213/309

Tyack, D., & Cuban, L. (1995). Tinkering toward utopia: A century of public school reform. Harvard University Press. https://www.gse.harvard.edu/ideas/ed-magazine/04/03/tinkering-toward-utopia-century-public-school-reform

Tyack, D., & Tobin, W. (1994). The "grammar" of schooling: Why has it been so hard to change?. American Educational Research Journal, 31(3), 453–453. https://doi.org/10.2307/1163222

Uhl-Bien, M., Marion, R., & McKelvey, B. (2007). Complexity leadership theory: Shifting leadership from the industrial age to the knowledge era. The Leadership Quarterly, 18(4), 298–318. https://doi.org/10.1016/j.leaqua.2007.04.002

UNESCO. (2023). Guidance for generative AI in education and research. https://unesdoc.unesco.org/ark:/48223/pf0000386138

Vygotsky, L. S. (1978). Mind in society: The development of higher psychological processes (M. Cole, V. John-Steiner, S. Scribner, & E. Souberman, Eds. & Trans.). Harvard University Press. https://home.fau.edu/musgrove/web/vygotsky1978.pdf

Vygotsky, L. S. (1990). Vygotsky and education: Instructional implications and applications of sociohistorical psychology (L. C. Moll, Ed.). Cambridge University Press. https://archive.org/details/vygotskyeducatio0000unse

Warren, M. R. (2005). Communities and schools: A new view of urban education reform. Harvard Educational Review, 75(2), 133–173. https://doi.org/10.17763/haer.75.2.m7185767x16n2411

Warschauer, M. (2004). Technology and equity in schooling: Deconstructing the digital divide. https://education.uci.edu/uploads/7/2/7/6/72769947/tes.pdf

Watkins, S. C. (2013). The digital edge: How Black and Latino youth navigate the internet. MIT Press. https://www.academia.edu/110440541/The_digital_edge_how_Black_and_Latino_youth_navigate_digital_inequality

Watkins, S. C. (n.d.). Connected learning alliance. https://clalliance.org/person/s-craig-watkins/

Watters, A. (2015a). The hidden curriculum of ed-tech. Hack Education. https://hackeducation.com/2015/03/13/hidden-curriculum

Watters, A. (2015b). The problem with personalized learning. https://edtechhub.org/2022/04/21/personalised-learning/

Watters, A. (2015c). The shadow side of ed-tech: Privacy and surveillance in digital education. EdTech Magazine, 10(3), 18-25.

Weick, K. E. (1976). Educational organizations as loosely coupled systems. Administrative Science Quarterly, 21(1), 1–1. https://doi.org/10.2307/2391875

Weiss, C. H. (1979). The many meanings of research utilization. Public Administration Review, 39(5), 426–431. https://www.amazon.com/Everything-Miscellaneous-Power-Digital-Disorder/dp/0805088113

Weiss, C. H. (1991). Policy research: Data, ideas, or arguments? In P. Wagner et al. (Eds.), Social sciences and modern states: National experiences and theoretical crossroads (pp. 307–332). Cambridge University Press. https://www.cambridge.org/core/books/social-sciences-and-modern-states/8086B9ECA5A4FB1D544275C8253C96A7

Wenger, E. (1998). Communities of practice: Learning, meaning, and identity. Cambridge University Press. https://psycnet.apa.org/record/1998-06054-000

Wenger, E., McDermott, R., & Snyder, W. M. (2002). Cultivating communities of practice: A guide to managing knowledge. Harvard Business Press. https://archive.org/details/cultivatingcommu0000weng

Wenger-Trayner, E., & Wenger-Trayner, B. (2015). Learning in landscapes of practice: Boundaries, identity, and knowledgeability in practice-based learning. Routledge.

Weritz, P., Braojos, J., Matute, J., & Benitez, J. (2024). Impact of strategic capabilities on digital transformation success and firm performance: theory and empirical evidence. European Journal of Information Systems, 1–21. https://doi.org/10.1080/0960085x.2024.2311137

Wertsch, J. V. (1991). Voices of the mind: A sociocultural approach to mediated action. Apa.org; Harvard University Press. https://psycnet.apa.org/record/1991-97611-000

Westley, F., Zimmerman, B., & Patton, M. Q. (2007). Getting to maybe: How the world is changed. Vintage Canada. https://www.academia.edu/47845983/Getting_to_maybe_How_the_world_is_changed_F_Westley_B_Zimmerman_M_Q

Wheatley, M. J. (2006). Leadership and the new science: Discovering order in a chaotic world (3rd ed.). Berrett-Koehler. https://margaretwheatley.com/books/leadership-and-the-new-science/

Whitney, A. E. (2008). Teacher transformation in the National Writing Project. Research in the Teaching of English, 43(2), 144–187. https://www.jstor.org/stable/40171725

Wiggins, G., & McTighe, J. (2011). Understanding by design framework. ASCD. https://files.ascd.org/staticfiles/ascd/pdf/siteASCD/publications/UbD_WhitePaper0312.pdf

Wikipedia contributors. (2024). QANDA. In Wikipedia, The Free Encyclopedia. https://en.wikipedia.org/wiki/QANDA

Wiliam, D. (2011). What is assessment for learning studies in educational evaluation, 37, 3-14. - References - Scientific Research Publishing. (2021). Scirp.org. https://www.scirp.org/reference/referencespapers?referenceid=3023541

Wiliam, D. (2014). Formative assessment and self-regulated learning. https://www.dylanwiliam.org/Dylan_Wiliams_website/Papers_files/Formative%20assessment%20and%20contingency%20in%20the%20regulation%20of%20learning%20processes%20%28AERA%202014%29.docx

Williams, J. (2018). Stand out of our light: Freedom and resistance in the attention economy. Cambridge University Press. https://www.cambridge.org/core/books/stand-out-of-our-light/3F8D7BA2C0FE3A7126A4D9B73A89415D

Wing, J. M. (2006). Computational thinking. https://www.cs.cmu.edu/~15110-s13/Wing06-ct.pdf

Wolf, M. (2007). Proust and the squid: The story and science of the reading brain. HarperCollins. https://www.maryannewolf.com/proust-and-the-squid

Wolf, M. (2018). Reader, come home: The reading brain in a digital world. Harper. https://www.maryannewolf.com/reader-come-home-1

World Economic Forum. (2024). Education 4.0: Creating a future-ready education system. https://www.weforum.org

World Economic Forum. (2024). Shaping the future of learning. https://www3.weforum.org/docs/WEF_Shaping_the_Future_of_Learning_2024.pdf

Wu, J., He, Y., Wen, Q., Zhang, X., & Jiang, L. (2024). The application and development trend of artificial intelligence in education: A systematic review. Expert Systems with Applications, 244, 120603. https://doi.org/10.1016/j.eswa.2024.120603

Yeager, D. S., & Dweck, C. S. (2020). What can be learned from growth mindset controversies? American Psychologist, 75(9), 1269–1284. https://doi.org/10.1037/amp0000794

Young, I. M. (2000). Inclusion and democracy. Oxford University Press. https://www.amazon.com/Inclusion-Democracy-Iris-Young/dp/0198297565

Zeide, E. (2015). Student privacy principles for the age of big data: Moving beyond FERPA and FIPPs. Drexel Law Review, 8(2),

339–394.
https://drexel.edu/~/media/Files/law/law%20review/v8-2/V8-2%20-%20Zeide.ashx

Zhao, Y. (2009). Catching up or leading the way: American education in the age of globalization. ASCD.
https://www.academia.edu/42770550/Catching_Up_or_Leading_the_Way_American_Education_in_the_Age_of_Global

Zhao, Y. (2012). World class learners: Educating creative and entrepreneurial students. Corwin Press.
http://zhaolearning.com/wp-content/uploads/2012/05/Zhao_World-Class-Learners_eflyer-3.pdf

Zuboff, S. (2019). The age of surveillance capitalism: The fight for a human future at the new frontier of power. PublicAffairs.
https://academic.oup.com/sf/article-abstract/98/2/1/5489222

www.ingramcontent.com/pod-product-compliance
Lightning Source LLC
Chambersburg PA
CBHW062044080426
42734CB00012B/2559